LENIN'S MISTRESS

MICHAEL PEARSON

RANDOM HOUSE
NEW YORK

L

ENIN'S

ISTRESS

THE LIFE OF

INESSA ARMAND

All rights reserved under International and Pan-American
Copyright Conventions. Published in the United States by
Random House, Inc., New York, and simultaneously in Canada
by Random House of Canada Limited, Toronto.

RANDOM HOUSE and colophon are registered trademarks of
Random House, Inc.

This work was originally published in the United Kingdom by
Gerald Duckworth & Co. Ltd. in 2001, in slightly different
form, as *Inessa: Lenin's Mistress*.

Credits for photographs appear on pp. 277–78.

Library of Congress Cataloging-in-Publication Data

Pearson, Michael.
    Lenin's mistress : the life of Inessa Armand / Michael Pearson.
        p.   cm.
    Originally published: London : Duckworth, 2001.
    Includes bibliographical references and index.
    ISBN 0-375-50589-X (alk. paper)
        1. Armand, I. F. (Inessa Fedorovna), 1874–1920. 2. Women
    communists—Europe—Biography. 3. Women communists—
    Russia—Biography. 4. Lenin, Vladimir Ilyich, 1870–1924—
    Relations with women. 5. Russia—Politics and
    government—1894–1917. I. Title.

    HX313.8.A75 P4   2002
    947.084'1'092—dc21
    [B]   2001048464

Printed in the United States of America on acid-free paper
Random House website address: www.atrandom.com

9 8 7 6 5 4 3 2

FIRST U.S. EDITION

Title page photo: The Russian Center for the Conservation and
Study of Documents of Contemporary History (RTsKhIDNI)

Book design by Barbara M. Bachman

FOR ROBERT, MY SON

ACKNOWLEDGMENTS

First, I must thank Professor Robert Service, who, learning of my interest in Inessa, suggested I write about her for the general reader and guided me on Moscow sources; second, I am grateful to Patrick Walsh, my new agent, for his enthusiasm and active promotion of the project.

I am also especially indebted to two previous biographers of Inessa: Dr. R. C. Elwood, professor of history at Carleton University and author of the scholarly *Inessa Armand: Revolutionary and Feminist,* who has corresponded with me at length and given me most useful help on sources; and Georges Bardawil, author of the fine *Inès Armand,* published in French, which explored newly available sources. He most generously loaned me his extensive notes for my use and discussed Inessa's character with me at length.

I have been extremely fortunate to receive cooperation, and indeed hospitality, from many members of the Armand family, in particular from Blona Yakovlevna Romas, Inessa's granddaughter (Varvara's daughter) and Vsevolod Markovich Fedoseyev-Yegorov (grandson of Inessa's sister-in-law Vera), as well as from Vladimir Andreyevich Armand (Inessa's grandson, Andre's son); Rene Pavlovna Armand (granddaughter of Inessa's sister Renee); Klavdia Ivanovna Armand (wife of Vladimir, son of Alexander Evgenevich Armand by his second marriage); and Yevgeny Alexandrovich Armand and Sergei Alexandrovich (grandsons of Inessa by her son Alexander) and Natalya Sergeyevna Yevseyeva-Armand (Sergei's daughter), who kindly came with us to Pushkino with her friend and distant cousin, Maria Vladimirovna Armand. I am also indebted to Maria's uncle

Alexei Davidovich Armand, who made available to me the unpublished autobiography of his father; and finally Galina, wife of Alexander Evgenevich (Inessa's great-grandson).

I would like to thank Larissa Nikolayevna Malashenka, who led us so efficiently through Inessa's fond in the central archives, and appreciate, too, the aid of her colleague Yelena Yefimovna Kirillova.

I must record my deep gratitude to Lena Yakovleva, an Inessa admirer herself, who made all arrangements for me in Moscow, organized introductions, and interpreted, translated, and exchanged what must have been a hundred e-mails on my return to my desk; and also to my son, Robert, an Oxford University history graduate, to whom this book is dedicated. He traveled with me to Russia, provided stalwart and organized support with the research, and, because of his prodigious memory and perception, shared with me many conversations after our return.

I am also grateful to my editors, Sarah Such and Lee Boudreaux, for their patient assistance and creative enthusiasm from an early stage; and to Dr. Harold Shukman, late of St. Anthony's College, Oxford, who himself has written much on Lenin and kindly read the manuscript and answered many questions. I have appreciated, too, the help with translation in my home country by Olga Haigh and Frédéric Constant; with the transcription of my notes by Jean Rayment; and with the staffs of the British Library, whose Russian holdings are wonderfully extensive, the London Library as always, the University of London's School of Slavonic and East European Studies, and the London School of Economics and Political Science. All have made my task much easier.

Finally, I thank Susan, my wife, and our family for their tireless support and endless discussions that accompany the writing of a book of this nature.

CONTENTS

I first discovered Inessa Armand many years ago, when I was researching *The Sealed Train,* Lenin's eight-month rise from poverty to power.

No one knew much about her then because the base sources were restricted. And as a result—although she became the most powerful woman in postrevolutionary Moscow—even today hardly anyone outside the small, academic world of Russian historians has heard of her.

I found Inessa fascinating partly because she was a devoted mother of five children. Further, she had an extraordinary relationship with her wealthy husband, Alexander Armand, who accepted her revolutionary lifestyle as well as her decision to live openly with his brother. Finally, she intrigued me because she was the rumored mistress of Lenin, with suggestions of a ménage à trois with his wife, Nadya.

Inessa was long depicted as an attractive, vivacious woman, fluent in four languages and a brilliant pianist. Before meeting Lenin, as was reported, she had been jailed several times and had escaped from exile in Archangel Province.

However, much of the information then available under Communist rule was wrong. Sometimes the errors were marginal: Her father was an opera singer, not a vaudeville comic. Sometimes the errors were more imaginative: Inessa was said to be a fatherless child brought up within the Armand family by an aunt employed as a tutor. This, too, was fiction.

What was clear, however, from the letters, then published, from Lenin, was that she had been very important to him, acting as a troubleshooter, a confidante, and an organizer, even speaking in his place at conferences. They were friendly letters, often laced with jokes, but the censors allowed little that would suggest the amorous realities.

Inessa died dramatically in 1920 at the age of forty-six, succumbing to cholera after a lengthy, broken journey in the Caucasus, where her train often came under fire.

For long, she has stayed vividly in my mind. I felt her life would lend itself to operatic treatment, toyed myself with a novel, but once the Central Party Archives (now the RTsKhIDNI) were opened, offering access to her files—and Lenin's—I realized Inessa was an ideal subject for biography.

A few months of her story—her journey back to Russia with Lenin in April 1917 in the sealed train and the events leading to the Bolshevik strike for power in November—were told in detail in *The Sealed Train,* and I have leaned heavily on that book and its sources for this short period of the twenty-seven years that I describe.

There is no doubt now that Inessa Armand was Lenin's mistress. Over the years, however, especially during the frustration of exile, the relationship went through various phases. At first, she worshipped Lenin, but in time, though loving him, she came to challenge him. At one stage, she was barely talking to him; at another, she went into tsarist Russia for him, knowing she would be jailed.

At times, she played with him, refusing to answer his letters or replying only to his wife or declining to translate for him passages in his articles with which she disagreed.

The attempt on his life in 1918 that so nearly killed him sparked a new, closer stage in their relationship. Days before Inessa died, she admitted in writing that, together with her children, Lenin—and the cause they shared—had been her life.

The Julian calendar, which was thirteen days behind the Gregorian calendar in general use elsewhere, was used in Russia until February 1, 1918. I have employed local dates in the country where the action takes us, giving both dates when confusion is likely.

I quote many letters written by Lenin or Inessa Armand. All originals are held in the RTsKhIDNI Archives (Russian Center for the Conservation and Study of Documents of Contemporary History), previously the Central Party Archives, in Moscow.

However, most of Lenin's letters can be found more easily in his *Collected Works*. The fifth edition of these has been published only in Russian. The fourth edition was translated into English and volume 43 of it contains letters between 1893 and 1917, published for the first time in the Russian fifth edition—some sixty of them to Inessa. My notes refer mainly, until 1917, to the English edition. Some of the letters quoted do appear in the Russian fifth edition, especially among those written after 1917, and in various Russian journals, as well as in the forty-volume *Leninskii sbornik* and the twelve-volume *Vladimir Ilyich Lenin biograficheskaia khronika*.

Since Inessa's relations with Lenin were a delicate topic for the Soviet leadership, Lenin's collected works have been subject to censorship and omission. Now, however, all previously censored letters are available in the archives. There are also three published sources—Richard Pipes, *The Unknown Lenin* (New Haven, 1996); the *Neizvestnye Dokumenty*, 1891–1922 (Rosspian, Moscow, 1999); and A. G. Latyshev, *Rassekrechennyi Lenin* (Moscow, 1996)—that are purely about this material.

Inessa's letters to her husband, Alexander; his brother and her lover, Vladimir; and her children and friends are cataloged in date order by addressee, in Fond 127 of the RTsKhIDNI, though some have been published in edited form in I. F. Armand, *Stat'i, rechi, pis'ma* (Moscow, 1975) and in "Pis'ma Inessy Armand" in *Novyi Mir* 6 (1970): 196–218, and also in other journals. Both Inessa and Lenin often neglected to date their letters, and archivists have had to rely on the contents to indicate, roughly, especially with Inessa's, when they were written.

LENIN'S MISTRESS

CHAPTER 1

PUSHKINO 1893

I t was before the early snows in October 1893, and already dark by mid-afternoon, when Inessa Stephane married Alexander Armand in the Church of St. Nikolai in the little town of Pushkino—and transformed a future that would take her eventually into the highest levels of power in Russia.

Until this day, as an educated, unmarried girl, the only occupation open to her in Russia was to be a tutor, and even that was under question, since technically Inessa was illegitimate.

Now, in that beautiful church ablaze with candles, she walked behind the ikon boy in his scarlet shirt and shared with Alexander the rituals—such as the kissing of the rings and the circling of the praying desk beneath the crowns of silver—and became a young wife of status and wealth. Her husband was the eldest son in a large family that owned local textile plants as well as estates in the region and property in Moscow.

A slight, pretty girl with auburn hair and green eyes, she was immature even for her nineteen years. The letters she had written to Alexander before the marriage suggest an emotional muddle.

There was no doubt, though, about her artistic potential. She was well-read, fluent in four languages, and a talented pianist, able to play classics from memory for two hours at a stretch. But none of those present in the church that day could have guessed that she also had the qualities to survive the intellectual rough-and-tumble of Lenin's years in exile, nor that she could ever stay stubbornly cool in debate against such formidable heavyweights as Trotsky or Plekhanov or Axelrod, while Lenin himself would usually lose his temper.

Inessa Armand was to become Lenin's lover, in a relationship that was volatile but bound them, even when she was barely speaking to him, by deep emotional roots. She was his troubleshooting lieutenant, his "front" when he wished to stay in the background, and his friend who could discuss tactics with him, console him after setbacks, and also share his victories. At meetings and conferences, some of which she organized, she helped to execute his torturous strategies, which were ultimately to yield him greater authority than even the tsar could command.

Lenin had, for twelve years, been married, but Nadya—Nadezhda Konstantinovna, whose cover name was Krupskaya—looked after the back office, the running of his faction of the Social Democratic Party, and the coded correspondence with its members.[1] Inessa, though, would be in the field, directing the hand-to-hand combat in the large exile community that, riddled with frustrations and conflicts, was preparing for the day they all dreamed of, even if they disagreed about its form.

All that, of course, lay years ahead. At nineteen, Inessa was politically innocent, even disinterested. But without this marriage and possibly this husband, she might never have been drawn to meet Lenin—nor, for that matter, gained the power that enabled her to write in 1918 to the commissar of a military district, requesting the "Respected Comrade" to "receive my acquaintance," a childhood friend. She was then confident that her wish would be enough to achieve the object, since anyone in authority would know how close she was to the ruler of all the Russias.

. . .

The Church of St. Nikolai, with its twin bell towers and blue-and-gold cupola, was on a hill that overlooked Pushkino. In the 1890s, the forest town, with its lake, two rivers, and a thriving summer theater, was a favored place for holiday dachas, being only an hour by train from Moscow—especially by the families of the city's French community, in which the Armands were prominent.

It was also a company town. Two tall brick chimneys, which still exist today, reached high above the Armand textile plant. Workers' cottages, built in timber, with carved wooden friezes, lined the roads.

The Armand family home was extraordinary. Originally four separate houses, it was a strange, sprawling complex of carved and decorated timber, linked by galleries on the ground floor and flanked by verandas. It had elaborate gardens featuring gazebos and an avenue bordered on both sides by poplars. At its center was a large covered area, containing an eighteen-foot table, used for parties, children's games, name-day celebrations, and impressive theatrical productions, with elaborate programs designed by Alexander's sister Maria.

It was here that Alexander's father, Eugene—Evgenii Evgenevich—lived with his two brothers, Emil and Adolf, each family occupying separate houses within the complex.

Like many French Muscovite families, the Armands had settled in Russia early in the nineteenth century, in the wake of Napoleon's retreat from the city, in which Alexander's ancestor Paul was killed. Legend has it that Paul's son, Ivan, was captured by peasants and, on being released, started a wine-import business—only to be threatened with failure by the sinking of a delivery ship. It was Ivan's son, the first Eugene, Alexander's grandfather, who founded the Armand fortunes on a more stable basis with a factory in Pushkino, making army uniforms, and the purchase of property with the profits.

Foreign families were required by law to take Russian nationality, but only as "honorary citizens," not as full-fledged Russians. Second-class, in other words, and ignored by the local nobility. Alexander's father, also named Eugene, had made some concession to his country of residence by converting from the Roman Catholic faith to Russian Orthodoxy, and Alexander, like most of his brothers and sisters, had followed him.

Inessa's mother, Natalie Wild, also came from a French family that had settled in Moscow, although her roots lay in Franche-Comte, then a Protestant area of France. Her father was a language teacher, and the Wilds naturally came to know the Armands.

Natalie, though, had run away from Moscow to live with a French opera singer, Theodore Stephane, and Inessa had been born in Paris. Ines, as she was called by then, was the eldest of three girls, born four months before her parents were married—a future problem in Russia that Natalie tried to address by having the date of her wedding to Theodore forged on her daughter's birth certificate. Confusingly, on this her name was Elise—or Elisabeth or Elisaveta in transliterated Russian.

Inessa was five when her father's contract with the Grand-Théâtre in Lyons ended. He was a man of buoyant spirits and great optimism, a quality which had come to infuriate Natalie, who feared it had little base in reality, though quite why is not clear. The notices of his performances in such operas as *The Thief of Baghdad*, *Rigoletto*, and even *Faust* were often good, enough to later earn him an obituary in *Le Figaro*.[2]

The break with the Lyons opera house, however, seemed to confirm Natalie's suspicions. They returned to Paris, where he rejoined the Théâtre de la Gaieté, but the marriage had become troubled, and they parted, leaving Natalie, pregnant, facing the prospect of raising three children under five on her own.

Natalie's mother and her sister, Sophie, visited Paris in 1879, probably to help while Natalie bore her third child. To ease Natalie's burden, they took Inessa back with them to Moscow. Sophie was herself a tutor to various Moscow families, possibly at times to the Armands, and she and her mother educated Inessa at home.[3]

The details of Inessa's childhood in Russia remain obscure. According to early accounts, including that of Lenin's wife, Nadya, Inessa was taken to the Armand home on the death of her father by her aunt Sophie, to be brought up with the family's children. This story, though attractive, is wrong, probably fabricated by Soviet propagandists, for whom a tutor, being an employee, and a poor fatherless little girl fit the picture they liked to draw of the proletarian revolution (though in fact virtually all its prominent figures were bourgeois).

Inessa's father, as testified to by his death certificate, lived on, in fact, for six years after she had left Paris.

Her daughter Inna has confirmed that Inessa was brought up by her aunt and grandmother. Her letters to Alexander before the marriage confirm much of this picture. The education the two women gave her—especially in music, languages, and literature—was very sound and ideal for a good marriage, but, as she was to be sensitively aware for much of her life, it was not intellectual.

In 1891, when Inessa was seventeen, her grandmother died, and Natalie brought her other two daughters to Russia to live in the Moscow apartment, probably near Kouznietsky-Most, the French business area of old Moscow.

A few months later, Alexander Armand, who had been away from Pushkino for some years, training to take his place in the Armand business, returned home. He knew Inessa quite well. In the summertimes, she had often been to Pushkino, where the Wilds had friends, and she had mixed with the Armand children in the huge, rambling home where there were nannies and forty-five servants, some of the older ones having been Armand serfs.

But Inessa had matured since he'd last seen her, blossoming into a young woman he found totally compelling, and he fast fell in love with her.

Inessa encouraged him, writing in May 1892 under the pretext of wanting the address of a mutual friend. In the same letter, she speaks of what she has been doing and thinking about since she last saw him—though it was only the previous night.

With her sister Renee, Inessa visited the lake near Pushkino where a seemingly contrived meeting with Alexander led to an afternoon boat ride. Alexander made her promise to keep the meeting secret, since a younger sister was hardly an adequate chaperone, but the moment she got home she could not resist telling her mother.

A few days later, Inessa sent Alexander an invitation to a small party for her birthday. "Please come. We'll be expecting you. There will be a lot of young ladies for only four or five young men."

For a year, Inessa and Alexander got to know each other. Although she was callow and lacked experience, her letters are interesting, if voluble and self-condemning. "I am horribly thoughtless. I'm boring you abominably by always asking services from you. I never stop complaining. I have become capricious and nervous."[4]

She seems to have been expecting a flattering denial, which she probably received. However, she constantly attacks men, such as those, invited by her friends, whom she finds "condescending. They think they are masters of creation. They have an absolute disdain for women that finds expression in their respect for feminine weakness. For these men," she mocked, "believe themselves generous, terribly generous, under the cover of amiability, false respect, and a patience with women they would grant to a child. Women believe anything, and men lie endlessly."

For a woman who was to become a leading feminist of her day, this is, perhaps, generalizing and simplistic, but the anger was to remain. She accepts acidly that men believed that "a woman has a little intelligence, just a little bit, and also a soul, like they do themselves" but fears that "on reading this, I know you will take offense, that you will cease to be my friend, but I think it is better that I should tell you the whole truth so that you know the depth of my thoughts. And men in general have good qualities," she asserts, softening the blow. "I hold you, for instance, in great esteem, and I would be very sorry if we ceased to be friends. However, men make me angry, they exasperate me. But enough on that subject. Above all, I don't want you to be upset."

Alexander wasn't upset. Inessa may have been disappointed by young men in general, but she made it clear that he stood out among the crowd as a shining exception.

Inessa's later letters are more concerned with their relationship.

It is true that I do not have a complete trust in you because you do not know me. You know only my good sides, not the bad ones. And because the opinion of others is very precious to me, it would be unpleasant for me to think that (even the bad aspects) were not good in your eyes. What's more I have the impression that, if I disappointed you, you would end our friendship. I would be sorry. See how frank I am with you.

She writes later:

There are people whom I trust more than myself because I know that, even if I became the worst of women, the nastiest and most odious of people, they would remain my friends, but it seems to me that if I became bad you would cease to be my friend. I know what I am telling you will probably be disagreeable. I don't want to cause any bad feelings between us, but I prefer to be sincere with you.

What she is seeking, it seems, is an assurance: He would never cease to be her friend. "Anyway," she ended one letter, "I find I trust you more now than before, don't you find? Well I do anyway."

She is reaching for an honesty between them, even if her aim is calculating, but she guesses he's keeping too much of himself hidden from her.

Yesterday you had a very strange expression, as though you didn't have a happy heart, yet you went on smiling and being friendly. And if you want to know, I find it infinitely disagreeable that you can't tell me (what is worrying you), that you are going to put on a mask and smile when you don't want to smile.

But maybe I am fooling myself and you're (always) going to be smiling when you're sad or angry—and note these future tenses and see how, without noticing it, they are committing us to a future. Marriage, as they say, would seem to be "in the air."

These sentiments were outrageously forward for the period, since it appears that Alexander had not yet proposed. However, they show early signs of the determination Inessa was later to demonstrate.

At other times, she is worried by the reproaches she imagines in his letters and, in contrast to her previous remarks, suggests that "you are a man and I am a woman, and that means that you are more intelligent than I am. I'm always scared of saying stupid things, and this curbs my confidence. Fear of ridicule prevents me from saying all that I have in my mind. I know that you would not deliberately make fun of me, but involuntarily you might do so." Is there an element of friendly sarcasm? Or does she really mean that he is more intelligent than she? Or is there a hint of the manipulative techniques she will develop later with Lenin—and *for* Lenin—who was a master of the art?

Three weeks before her wedding, Inessa wrote Alexander what seems an odd letter:

It is a long time since I have written to you, Alexander Evgenevich. I have all my time taken up with lessons with Anna [her youngest sister] and my other affairs. How are you all in Pushkino? It is such a long time since I have been there, and in Moscow the weather is bad, and everywhere there is noise and chaos. But in Pushkino everything is so good.

What's more I have been a little sad for a while, and I would like to tell you why, but I would bore you. All right, perhaps I will tell you. I won't be so sad if I tell you.

My mother torments me so much. She has such a passionate and violent nature, and her limitless capacity to love so deeply causes her constant suffering that hurts me terribly because I think it is incurable. What will become of her when I leave her?

In me she has put all her love. When I think about that, I have such sadness I feel no tears could express it. I would give anything to appease her, but she is so full of contradictions. She makes demands on me that are totally impossible. She would like me to love no one else. And even if I submitted, she would not be satisfied. She'd find another reason to torment herself.

It is clear from this where Inessa inherited her own agonized conflicts, but she was, in course, to reveal a hard core of intelligence beneath the emotional froth and a formidable will, which perhaps her mother lacked.

Also, the cool tone of the letter from a clearly passionate woman is marked. She is three weeks from a wedding that she does not even mention, and, while it may have been custom to call her fiancé by his formal name, she says nothing about missing him or looking forward to being his wife. However, the last lines of the letter have been lost, and these might have been more intimate.

The real problem with her mother is not clear. Inessa had, of course, seen little if anything of Natalie since she had been taken from her as a five-year-old—possibly blaming the parting on herself, as children often do, for some unknown fault. Now in her late teens, she had been living with her mother for little more than a year.

Natalie is clearly obsessive. To run away from home to live with a lover, as she had with Theodore, was at that time very unusual. And she was to do it again, leaving Moscow just before—not after—

Anna's wedding, to set up house with with a new lover, Charles-Louis-Joseph Faure, of the theater-owning family that had employed her husband. In nineteenth-century terms, it was the behavior of a willful, unstable, and probably unhappy woman.

But did Inessa make too much of it? Presumably Natalie loved her other daughters, too. And what happened to their relationship after Inessa's marriage? Inessa, who wrote at such length to her husband, lover, and children, often discussing very minor details of her life, rarely mentions her mother.

Inessa's relationship with the teenage sisters whom she had effectively met for the first time at seventeen is interesting. Renee was to marry Nikolai, Alexander's brother, and Inessa claims to have gotten along well with her until a bitter quarrel in 1899, the cause of which is obscure.

In this angry dispute, Inessa speaks of Renee's accusation of "her own sister . . . poisoning her against their own mother" and trying to force her to take the side of Anna. This could possibly have arisen from Natalie's decision to leave Moscow so precipitately for Paris and her new lover.

Inessa claims total innocence of Renee's charges and appeals simply to her "sisterly love. But it seems I am such a villain . . . that I can't see how you can ever trust me. We have known each other for eight years, and quite closely it seems to me. . . . Au Revoir, my Renee, I bid you farewell with a very heavy heart," she writes, adding a postscript: "I'll be sad not to see any more of Kolia, my little god-child."[5]

She is being dramatic and obviously does not mean what she is saying. Relations were, in time, reestablished. When later both sisters lived in Moscow, their homes were on the same street in the Arbat district. Renee clearly helped with the children when Inessa was first arrested and almost certainly provided cover for her to meet them in later years when she was in Moscow illegally.

Since 1893, Inessa and Alexander had developed a rare and fascinating relationship. In its early stages, the marriage was traditional enough. Within three months, Inessa was pregnant. A handsome home, in the European style, was available to them at Eldigino, some fifteen miles away from Pushkino, on one of the Armand estates, but they seem to have been slow to take advantage of it, living in the family complex at Pushkino until the birth of the baby—a son, also named Alexander.

Years later, Inessa told her daughter Inna that she had always felt like an outsider among the Armands,[6] but she appeared to join with some enthusiasm in the family entertainments. Two months after her wedding, as part of the New Year celebrations, she had a role in a play, *A Tale of Summer*, that was to have resonance later. The program, beautifully decorated by Maria, featured the cast list in both Russian and French: Alexander's siblings, Eugenie and Nikolai; Inessa's two sisters, Renee, who was soon to marry Nikolai, and Anna; and three who came from other French families: Georges Gautier and Emma and Georges Wilken. Both the Gautiers and the Wilkens were to seek Inessa's help in the chaos that was so disastrous for such middle-class families in 1918. Inessa was listed there, too, of course, under her new status as Madame Ines Armand.[7]

Certainly, she loved the theater. One reason she was happy to stay in the Armand home instead of the somewhat remote Eldigino was Pushkino's location on the railway, with easy access to Moscow. She was, after all, a city girl.

During these early months of the marriage, Inessa seems to have developed something of a new persona. Alexander took her often to Moscow—to plays, concerts, operas, ballets. The Armands maintained a home in the city, where the young couple could spend nights.

She entered into the city's social life, bought stylish hats and dresses, and, more important, became part of an artistic avant-garde set. She was invited with Alexander to the Mamontovs, one of the old industrialist families of Moscow, who owned a theater where Feodor Chaliapin sometimes sang and Chekhov attended rehearsals of his own plays. The Mamontovs entertained lavishly, the guests including actors and writers, at their big home on Sadovaya Koltso and their country mansion at Abramtsevo.

Another important hostess was Minna Gorbunova-Kablukova, who held an open house every Sunday for people with new ideas: philosophers, poets, thinkers, artists. Minna claimed to be a correspondent of Friedrich Engels. In Minna's home, Inessa met such writers as Valeri Brionsov, seen as the "new Pushkin," whose work she was reading at the time in Paul Verlaine's translation.

It was here, too, that there was much talk of "Zhenskii vopros," the woman question, and if Inessa's remarkable transition from giddy young girl to skilled, clear-thinking revolutionary is to be wondered at, then the feminist Minna certainly played a great part.

So, too, did Alexander's married sister, Anna, eight years older than Inessa, who often joined her, in lieu of Alexander, on her social rounds. Inessa was to see a lot of Anna in Europe later in her exile days. And in 1917, Anna was to accompany Inessa in the famous "sealed train" that took Lenin and his party across a Germany that was still slaughtering Russian troops on the eastern front.

Alexander lived the way men often live. He liked shooting in the forest and enjoyed male company at Le Club des Marchands, sometimes preferring this to the fashionable friends of his young wife.

After the baby Alexander's birth, the family moved at last to Eldigino, which was set beautifully on a hill in the forest. A wall plaque there records that Inessa lived there from 1894 to 1904, but much of this time was, in fact, spent at Pushkino—the center of Armand family activity.

Inessa planned to keep a diary, with a red velvet cover and edges of gold leaf. She persuaded Alexander to supply the first entry. "What shall I write to you?" he wrote. "Do I write that I love you, that you are my life, the light which illuminates for me every thing in every place—but all this you well know. I am nothing without you."[8]

Alexander was a member of the Moscow Region Zemstvo, a body that had authority in such areas as education and, in particular, public health. Inessa joined him in visits to the poorest families in the cottages around Pushkino and in the Moscow slums. She was shocked. She knew that such conditions existed, but she had never before witnessed close-up what could have been seen in any developed country at the turn of the century: the homelessness, the dreadful overcrowded housing, starvation, poverty, disease, appalling sanitation, and the effects of despair, such as drunkenness and prostitution (distinct from that found in Moscow's legal brothels).

Perhaps these experiences inspired her to adopt a child, Vladimir, who had been born to poor parents in Moscow's Khitrov Street Market. This was a kind of charity, customary for rich families; Vladimir was raised almost like her own children.[9]

Inessa saw education as the answer to some of the social devastation she witnessed. "Oh what misery in the cottages," she wrote in her diary. "What riches in the books."[10] After discussion with her sister-in-law Anna and two of the Pushkino tutors—a young left-wing Social Democrat named Eugene Kammer and an older teacher, also with Marxist views, named Nikolai Ivinsky—Inessa started a school for the sons of the Armand workers and local peasants.

On one occasion, she matched Alexander's passionate entry in her diary with a scribbled note that must have pleased him. "Dear and beloved Sacha. Excuse my absence but you are late, and I must leave for the school. I love you madly with all my heart. You are my beloved, my darling."[11]

. . .

At about this time, in St. Petersburg, some four hundred miles to the north, an angry young lawyer named Vladimir Ilyich Ulyanov, who would eventually be known to the world by his cover name, Lenin, had just become a member of a small revolutionary group with plans to start a political journal called *Rabotnik* (The worker). For some months in 1895 he had traveled around Europe, meeting the leading Social Democrats such as George Plekhanov, Pavel Axelrod, and Paul Lafargue, who had married Karl Marx's daughter. He returned to Russia with some useful European links and a suitcase with a false bottom that was packed with illegal literature.

While Lenin had been away, another activist, Yuli Martov, had joined Lenin's friends with a group of his own. Lenin had so far worked with his comrades to frame their policies by group discussion, reading the key banned books and writing articles that were hard to get published. Martov, though, was urging direct action, awakening unrest in the factories and helping striking workers.

It was a vision that appealed to Lenin, who nursed a great hatred of the establishment and the bourgeois middle class that was never to leave him. Born of minor nobility, his father had been an inspector of schools in the Volga River town of Simbirsk. His elder brother, Alexander, had been on the fringe of a student plot against the tsar that failed.

Despite the pleas of his mother, Sasha had claimed that he was one of the leaders, which he was not. He was hanged in 1887. As a result, Lenin and his family had been ostracized and forced to leave Simbirsk in disgrace.

Now Lenin ached for revenge, as the St. Petersburg police probably guessed. In December 1895, he was arrested. His friend Martov was taken a few days afterward.

· · ·

In Pushkino a few months later, during 1896, Inessa bore Alexander another son, Fedor, just as the political future in Russia was looking darker. Revolution had become fashionable, openly discussed by people who would not, in most cases, dream of being part of a secret cell—the same sort of people who had once turned their backs on the Ulyanovs. Revisionist writers like Turgenev and Chernyshevsky, with different ideas about marriage and society, were popular.

There was possibly a strain of resentment within the Armands. As well as being classified as second-ranking "honorary citizens," they were also in "trade," which excluded them from the higher social circles. Evgenii Evgenevich, Alexander's father, was a man of liberal views but was hardly radical, unlike most of his children, nearly all of whom became politically active. Anna, Alexander's elder sister, was to be banished—as Alexander was himself for a period, after a short spell in prison, though he was not a revolutionary by nature. His sisters Sofia and Varvara married activist Social Democrats (the party that, after splits, was to become Communist). Maria and Sergei were to join the rival Socialist Revolutionary Party, with its Terror Brigade. Vladimir, who later was to become so important to Inessa, was only eleven in 1896 but would in due course become a dedicated revolutionary.[12]

And then there was Kammer.

Eugene Kammer was a young medical student who had been taken on as a tutor. He was popular with the Armand family, and his sister was to marry Alexander's brother Sergei.

In 1896, Kammer told two of his pupils—Alexander's young brother Boris and his cousin Lev—that he was a member of a university student group that promoted propaganda among the workers, supported political strikes, and was a source of forbidden books. The two boys were caught by Kammer's enthusiasm and were eager to become involved.

It took only a few months for the police to learn from an informer that there was a printing press in the Armand home, together with a secret network spreading illicit literature. With some embarrassment, they approached Evgenii Evgenevich, who was so important in the area, and said they were under orders to search his home. He laughed. "Search if you want to, but you won't find anything."

But they did. Tapping on the floorboards, they noted that some had a hollow sound. On lifting them, they found a hidden part of the cellar, with a full range of equipment, from a printing press to four Linotype machines and a store of illegal leaflets.

Kammer, together with Boris and Lev, was arrested—the first of the Armands to be taken. Kammer accepted full responsibility, insisting that the boys were innocent. The Armands backed him, paying for his lawyers and putting up his bail. With their help, he escaped to Germany. Years later, when she lived near the Kremlin, Inessa was to support Kammer's application to join the Bolshevik Party at a time when it was deemed a great honor.

Lev's father, Emil, was told to send his son abroad for a few months—in lieu of formal exile—and eighteen-year-old Boris had a restriction put on his movements at home.[13]

The Kammer case brought a cold realism into the Armand world, but if anything it increased the temperature of their revolutionary ambitions. And it was not limited to the family; it affected the community at large. Dr. Petchkine, the local doctor, and Valentina Ethtekina, his nurse, were activists. So, too, was Alexander Rodd, who ran the local library. All played roles in the party networks that were soon to be formed.

. . .

It is tempting to wonder what all these rich young people thought they were working to achieve—and not only them, for many of the leaders of the revolutionary parties came from bourgeois and intellectual backgrounds. Most of the Armands were Marxists, though a declared aim of the Communist Manifesto, published by Marx and Engels in 1848, had been state control of "the means of production, distribution and exchange"—which was pretty well everything.

It was, of course, expected that in time change would come to the antiquated tsarist society. It was only forty years since serfdom had ended, and still Russia, with its autocracy and semidivine image of the tsar as a "Holy Father," lagged way behind most western nations.

The Armands were good, progressive employers, but it is doubtful that they accepted that their factories, their homes, their way of life could be stripped away. Or that they considered the possibility of a dictatorship even more rigid and ruthless than the tsar's, that would rule by terror. Probably, they were likely expecting some kind of democratic system, with rule from below, truly by the people, by election.

For some seventy years since the Decembrist rising of young aristocrats in 1825, Russia's history had been marked by men and women who, fighting the autocracy, were seen by many as heroes and by others as tolerable villains. The list is long—including such men as Petra-shevsky, whose circle included Fedor Dostoevsky, who was actually facing the scaffold when amnesty was galloped up; Karakosov, who was tortured so badly he could hardly walk the short distance to the hangman; and Nechaev Neyachev, whose Revolutionary Catechism clothed revolution in a religious color and who, when writing materials were denied him, wrote in his own blood. And there would be others to come.

. . .

In 1898, Inessa bore her third child, Inna. She was accustomed now to motherhood, but her first pregnancy had exposed her to bitter humiliation: She had been refused admission to a church on the grounds that, being with child, she was "unclean." According to her friend Polina Vinogradskaya, Inessa had been devout in her teens, but the shock of this new experience made her question the tenets of her faith.[14]

This may be true, and she became an atheist in time, but the political circles with which she was soon to become involved—already being on their fringe—would probably have made her question them anyway.

She had always questioned much, even in the confusion of her teens, and now the problems of marriage were starting to be apparent. At fifteen, she had been appalled by Tolstoy's description in *War and Peace* of Natasha becoming, with her marriage, a "complete woman," a "samka"—the implication being that a woman needed a man, children, and the world of a wife to be whole. "It hit me like a whip," she wrote, years later, to Inna.[15] She swore she wouldn't become a samka, but now, five years into marriage, she seems to have feared she was getting close to it.

Although a friend of Kammer, Inessa had not been involved with the secret printing press—possibly because she had been spending more time at Eldigino. Also, she was not yet committed to activism.

"Marxism for me was not a youthful enthusiasm," she was to write to Alexander's brother Vladimir in 1908, "but a long evolution from right to left."[16]

She had seen much, though, of Minna Gorbunova-Kablukova, being a fairly regular guest at her Sunday salons.[17] Three years before, in 1895, Minna had asked official permission to start the Moscow Society for Improving the Lot of Women, but the Ministry of Interior refused. What was going on at Pushkino was rife elsewhere, too, and the government was growing increasingly nervous. Philanthropic groups were acceptable to it, but anything that was even remotely political, and could provide good cover, was not. And this included active feminism, which was implicit in the Moscow Society's proposed title.

By 1899, however, the ministry relented, and permission was granted. The society was ambitious, encompassing demands for women's political and legal rights, promoting their education and technical training, as well as trying to divert country girls, who flocked into the city, from prostitution.

Inessa became secretary of the society and tried to broaden it by writing to Adrienne Veigele, secretary of the Women's International Progressive Union in London. The two women exchanged frequent letters and developed a close friendship, though they never met. Inessa told Veigele that, like many fashionable women in Moscow, she had become a vegetarian—and later, rather to Veigele's disappointment, had abandoned it. She described the progress of her new baby Inna.

Veigele suggested that the Moscow Society should become a branch of her organization and even claimed in print that this arrangement was already in place. But, although Inessa—international, even then, in her thinking—was in favor of this, Minna was not. (The police, too, were none too happy, for reasons of control.) Minna had a point: The London union had broad, lofty feminist aims; the ladies of the Moscow Society were out there working directly—perhaps not quite on the streets but near them.

The next year, Inessa was appointed president of the society. She had been watched by the Okhrana, the tsarist political police, ever since the Kammer case, and they continued to scrutinize her actions now. She applied in the name of the society for permission to open a Sunday school for women; to publish a regular news leaflet that might grow into a fully fledged newspaper for women; and to open a library with books of feminine interest. All were approved by the local police and overruled by the Okhrana, believing all could be exploited for "anti-loyal" propaganda.

The Okhrana were to play an ever-growing role in Inessa's life. They were the descendants of Ivan the Terrible's Oprichniki, who wore black uniforms and rode black horses, with dogs' heads attached to their saddles. Their order had been to exterminate treason, which remained the aim of the Okhrana, though their brief was now somewhat wider. They were often ruthless—and, although some of the information gathered by their surveillance can now be seen to have been hopelessly wrong, their success at getting spies into the high levels of the main revolutionary parties was formidable.

Inessa decided to break with Minna and set up her own Society for the Protection and Emancipation of Women, as well as a Sunday school where prostitutes were welcome. Neither the police nor, surprisingly, the Okhrana took exception, seeing this mistakenly as a society for fallen women, with no political elements.

A decade earlier, Moscow had 105 brothels and 1,178 registered prostitutes. A member of the society approached Tolstoy for advice on what action they could take to persuade girls to renounce the life. He was gloomy: "It was thus before Moses. It was thus after Moses. Thus it was. . . . Thus it will always be."[18]

This was ultimately Inessa's reluctant conclusion, too. It did nothing to help her morale. "I'm a little unhappy," she wrote in her diary. In 1898, she took the children for a holiday in Yalta, where she read the agrarian socialist Peter Lavrov's *The Problem of Understanding History* and was impressed by his radical answers to the peasant problem. "It's been a long time," she wrote Alexander, "since I read a book which more closely conforms with my own opinions."[19]

Within months of her return, she left again, this time for the Swiss resort of Montreux, taking one of her sons for medical treatment. "Darling, it's wonderful here," she wrote to Alexander,

> but I'll be glad to be back home again in Eldigino. The sunset was beautiful today. I walked along the bank of the lake for quite a long time. The water was tranquil. The sun was just below the horizon lighting up the mountains in different colors, and you can't imagine what this sight did to me. It seems that the mountains are like one's soul which grows high above everything. They make me feel unformed and immature, small and lacking in harmony. I want to cry.

She was reading Jerome K. Jerome. "He says that we are never content and happy with what we have. He says that even Cinderella, once she'd got her prince and all the riches, would still have wanted more."[20] As, of course, Inessa did herself. She was thinking of studying chemistry and of helping with a workers' association, presumably linked to the Armand factories. "Then I intend to write something."

Meanwhile, Alexander was taking on more responsibilities. In 1901, he became a member of the Moscow City Duma. Already he was working for the Moscow Forest Protection Committee. He had his place on the Zemsto, was supporting several charities, and, of course, helping his father run the Armand companies.

Inessa, who was becoming busier with her work and who was now pregnant for the fourth time, began to spend more time in Moscow in an apartment the Armands owned at 6 Ipatievsky Lane in the Arbat, the district favored by artists, writers, and intellectuals. Any of the family could use this on visits to the city, but Vladimir, the Armands' youngest son, lived there most of the time, since he was studying biology at Moscow University.

With Vladimir, everything would change.

CHAPTER 2

MOSCOW 1902

The process of change was not fast. In 1902, Vladimir was seventeen; Inessa was twenty-eight and, since bearing her second daughter, Varvara, in October 1901, the mother of four. She had known Vladimir since he was a child.

While thoughts of revolution were affecting the younger generation in such families as the Armands in Pushkino, students in Moscow were even more and obviously militant. Vladimir had started to arrange meetings of the students' Executive Committee in the family apartment. Sometimes Inessa would be present at these, probably briefly while passing through, since she spoke later of becoming involved with "underground revolutionary people" in 1902. However, the police learned of these meetings soon enough, and in February 1901, they raided the apartment and arrested several students whom they believed to be planning illegal protest marches.

Vladimir, or Volodya as Inessa called him, was a quiet, serious, rather frail young man with a short beard, sincere brown eyes, and what a friend described as "an uncommon, apostolic simplicity." He was a radical activist but no leader. He wouldn't be out there at the front or storming the barricades, but he *would* be doing the political thinking. At this early stage, he had not made up his mind whether to join the Social Democrats or the Socialist Revolutionaries.

The SDs and the SRs had similar aims. They both sought revolution and an end to the evils of society, which is why they could sometimes work together, but they had radically different views about methods and theory.

The SDs were Marxists who believed that capitalism had within it the seeds of its own destruction, though force, in the form of revolution, might be needed to provoke its final collapse, when those in power might try to cling to it. The SDs' main purpose was to educate the people, and the workers in particular, so that they would be ready to exploit that collapse when it came, which was why it was illegal to hold meetings promoting this idea or to publish books, journals, or leaflets that discussed it.

The SRs, with deep agrarian roots and a vivid revolutionary tradition behind them, believed by contrast that the road to socialism lay in the peasant communes. They were committed to terror, and the "People's Will Party," its predecessor, had indeed shocked the nation with the successful murder of Tsar Alexander II in 1881. As a result, five people had been hanged in public in Semenovsky Square in black clothes on a black scaffold. Two of them, Andrei Zhelyabov and Sofia Perovskaya, had been lovers, she the daughter of an aristocrat, he the son of a serf. He had been allowed to kiss her farewell before the executioner, dressed in scarlet, had put the noose around her neck. She was the first woman in Russia to be executed in public.

But the executions didn't check the killings. In fact, the actions of the SRs' Terror Brigade were to hinder by association the Marxist SDs, who saw violence as achieving nothing. Also, it colored the attitude of the police, who were not always sure which party they were dealing with.

Even so, the authorities could be punitive to excess. Soon after the raids on the Armand apartment in 1901, the students of Moscow University went on strike. In response, several hundred were herded into the riding school and charged by mounted Cossacks, who flogged them with their knouts. Some of the girl students were raped.[1] This cruelty turned one easygoing nonpolitical student, Yegor Sazonov, into an active SR terrorist who was later to murder Dmitry Plehve, a particularly brutal interior minister.

Inessa, like Volodya, was still a long way from joining either party, but she was growing disenchanted with her societies, which were only a slight improvement on the usual "good works" of many rich young wives.

By contrast, she found the meetings of excited and courageous students, intent on creating a better world by revolution, extremely attractive. Drawn by this emerging cause, she grew closer to Volodya.

The large age difference between them perhaps blinded them to the emotional dangers. She was a mother and well-read in the mainstream literature, but Volodya was probably more acquainted with the works of Karl Marx and other radical thinkers. The two elements merged in them, each finding the other highly stimulating and attuned to a common purpose, maybe intellectually in the early period, when each may have seemed out of reach to the other, and then at last with recognizable emotion.

The fact is that, during the course of 1902, they formed a deep attachment that, though unusual in certain aspects, was clearly demanding.

Inessa has often been compared to Vera Pavlovna, the much-admired heroine of *What Is to Be Done?*, Nikolai Chernyshevsky's novel, written while he was in prison in the Fortress of Peter and Paul. The book caught the imagination of a Russian generation before being banned. It so impressed Lenin that he gave a major work the same title.

Vera Pavlovna lived on equal terms with her husband and had her own room in their home, where she could entertain her friends and lovers. When she decided to leave him—and, in time, his successor—

the parting was without jealousy or rancor, both being seen as de-grading emotions. Personal freedom overruled everything else, partic-ularly the repressive institution of marriage.

Certainly, Inessa and Alexander were about to behave in a way of which Vera Pavlovna would have approved.

Exactly when Inessa told Alexander of her emotional involvement with his brother is not clear. But she had for a while been discon-tented, and her behavior reflected this. She began to quarrel with Alexander, according to an old family servant named Ivan, often screaming at him and stamping her feet with a petulance that seems childish and is, again, in striking contrast with the strong character that emerged in her.[2] While she was to be petulant at times with Lenin, who certainly didn't spoil her, it was more calculated, a weapon of maturity that she deployed with some skill.

Inessa and her husband were playing out a drama that is common enough. With all Alexander's new activities, he was often away from home, and Eldigino, in its forest, was remote. Also, her life was in stark contrast to her somewhat simple past. On her marriage into wealth, with a husband keen to please her, she could have anything she wanted. She could buy any clothes she chose. She had servants. She was able to travel abroad on a whim. It was enough to go to any young woman's head.

Whether or not Volodya was a factor, she took to suddenly run-ning away from the house, often not returning until hours later. More than once, though, she did this after dark in her nightdress. A desper-ate Alexander, terrified she might take her life, would summon teams of local workers to help search for her with lanterns, systematically scouring the immediate area—the park, the forest, even the wells. Then at sunrise, she would emerge unharmed from an outhouse or a barn, having been listening all night to the commotion of the search.

And while many husbands would have reacted with fury, Alexan-der would fall to his knees in front of their servants and beg her to forgive him for whatever he was supposed to have done to provoke this behavior. "She just wanted to punish the master," said Ivan.

"What a character she was!"[3] And Alexander should not be dismissed too easily as weak, for, like his capricious young wife, he, too, was later to reveal a character of some steel and even acumen.

The crisis of Inessa's new passion for Volodya came to a head, and Ivan, who speaks of them as "wonderful people," witnessed the scene in Eldigino. "The three of them were sitting on a couch for hours, with Inessa between them, and all of them were crying. 'I can't divide myself,' she kept insisting, 'I feel so sorry.' " Ivan, who sounds as though he was a little in love with Inessa himself, remarks, "She wasn't just crying for herself. And all the servants in the house were crying too."[4]

Like Dmitri Lopuklov, Vera Pavlovna's husband, Alexander accepted the fact that his wife had fallen in love with another man. But instead of leaving, as Lopuklov did, he continued to maintain her, support her various causes, pay her bail when necessary, and, despite her requests for no favors, use what influence he could to gain her release from prison. He aided her escapes when she had to cross borders illegally. He brought up the children when she was away in exile or prison and made sure that the Pushkino home was always available to her as a haven. He became a stalwart friend, as she recognized repeatedly with gratitude.

There was little doubt she felt love for him, though it differed in character from her feelings for Volodya. When Alexander was away, she would keep him chattily up-to-date with the progress of the children, and when she herself was away from them, she would often express anxiety to him about them, ranging from their teachers to their health, and ask him to take specific action.

In January 1903, the lovers left Russia for a holiday on the Neapolitan coast that had all the color of a honeymoon. They visited Capri and went east to Sorrento, traveling on south to Amalfi and the high cliffs of Ravello. There, she became pregnant with Volodya's child.

They returned to Moscow, living together in the Armand apartment as an unmarried couple with her children.

In July, when her pregnancy was becoming evident, she left for Martheray-Lausanne, Switzerland—with all the children but without her lover. "When are you coming to join us?" little Fedor asked his father, Alexander, in a postscript to one of Inessa's letters from the Alps.

They stayed in the mountains for almost a year, and although part of the reason may have been the imminent birth—a last discreet nod to the bourgeois life and perhaps concern for Alexander's position—she seems to have needed a period of peace to sort out the direction of her life.

This possibly explains why she was willing to be parted for so long from a lover who had overwhelmed her enough to leave her husband. Before leaving Moscow, she had broken off all connection with the Moscow Society and her other philanthropic projects, a last step in creating a clean slate.

In the mountains, Inessa went for mule rides, took long walks. There are pictures of her sitting with her children against rocky, cave-like backgrounds. She took trips to Geneva, where there were many Russian exiles, and visited Georges Koukline's famous bookshop, where Russian books and, it was rumored, Russian passports could be bought or borrowed. It was also a place of meetings and lectures, one of which she attended to hear Anatoli Lunacharsky, a rising young Marxist whom she would come to know well.

She read Lenin's *Development of Capitalism in Russia*. He was a new name to her, but the book made a huge impression. Later, she wrote that it caused her to become a Bolshevik. If so, she was one of very few, since Lenin had only coined this name for his faction in August.

• • •

This was a crucial time, too, in the life of the SDs. Three years before, in 1900, Lenin, Yuli Martov, and Alexander Potresov had started a new journal titled *Iskra* (The spark), which was to form the tactical backbone of a cohesive SD Party, which until then had consisted of a series of independent groups. They moved their headquarters to Munich because of Okhrana activity. Martov had toured Russia for agents while Lenin had gone to Switzerland to seek the backing of prominent Social Democrats of the older generation, which was vital to the project.

But by 1903, the close friendship of their youth between Lenin and Martov had faded with their differing views on strategy. Lenin believed the party should be a tight organization of highly disciplined, full-time, secret workers, controlled by a small central committee on a semimilitary basis through local cells and area commands, as spelled out in his pamphlet *What Is to Be Done?* Martov was more of a western-style democrat. He wanted a broad party open to anyone who gave it "regular personal cooperation." To Lenin, this was too mild, too open to compromise, too "soft." He wanted "full-time dedication."

On this membership question, the young party backed Martov, despite aggressive behind-the-scenes campaigning by Lenin. The division colored the congress, reflected as it was in other issues. The delegates split into "hard" and "soft" and eventually into "Bolsheviks" (men of the majority) and "Mensheviks" (men of the minority).

Even the naming was clever opportunism, *Bolsheviks* being chosen by Lenin because on one issue his faction had won a majority vote. The fact that Martov accepted the minority labeling was proof of an attitude that was "soft." They were to be political enemies for the rest of their lives, though their mutual respect was never to fade.

So, just as Inessa was arriving in the mountains, Lenin isolated himself politically. Trotsky, hesitating since he was an independent, had eventually gone with Martov, as had Plekhanov, the most prominent of the old Social Democrats. Lenin was to start building his Bolsheviks with only twenty "hards."

Coincidentally, just after Inessa left Switzerland in 1904, Lenin, who loved the mountains, arrived in Montreux—just up the lake from Lausanne. Had she stayed another few weeks, she would possibly have met him, perhaps in Georges Koukline's bookshop in Geneva.

• • •

In October 1903, Volodya's son, Andre, was born. And again Alexander behaved like a saint, granting the boy the treatment and status of his own children, including his own patronym, registering him as Andre Alexandrovich Armand.

Inessa returned to Russia at last in May 1904, with illegal literature, doubtless obtained through Georges Koukline, hidden in the false bottoms of the children's luggage. This was to be the base of a revolutionary library that she had planned with Volodya. Among the journals were old copies of Lenin's *Iskra*.

Naturally, they were not searched at the Russian border. After all, she was a lady of status returning from a holiday in the Alps with her children and a nanny.

• • •

What Inessa had decided during those long months in the mountains was to devote her life to revolution.

This need was to be the key to all her relationships—including those with her beloved children. Her letters are marked with angst, with loss for them, with plans to be reunited. But the partings were her choice—a result, at least, of the life she chose.

Her conflict was fascinating: Her letters are partly those of a devoted middle-class mother and partly those of a revolutionary whom the police would soon be watching like hawks. Some are coded with secret messages concealed in references to the children.

For Inessa, revolution, like religion for some people, was to come first—something she would be prepared to die for. Now, both because she had readied herself during her long months in the Alps and because the cause had suddenly become more possible, and therefore more demanding, she entered the fray.

Times were changing fast and so was the scope of potential revolution. Since February 1904, Russia and Japan had been at war, started by a surprise attack by the Japanese navy that sank much of a Russian fleet sent east to impress them.

Since that first brilliant assault, a model for the sudden bombing of Pearl Harbor nearly forty years later, the Japanese had won battle after battle in the field and at sea. At first, the war had inspired an outburst of patriotism throughout Russia, but this was fading with the failures of the military forces and the reality of the trains bringing back the thousands of dead and wounded. The rumblings of dissent were growing.

Against this darkening setting, Inessa returned to Pushkino with the children and, one suspects, a degree of trepidation. How had her behavior gone down with the family now that they'd had time to digest it? Since she had left Alexander, Eldigino was no longer her home, and as of May 1904, Alexander was in the Far East in charge of medical relief for the Moscow Duma.

She had always gotten along with her mother-in-law, Varvara Karlovna, but she could hardly expect her to approve the breakup of a marriage with one son in favor of an unconventional liaison with another.

She was welcomed back, though, and the new baby took its place for the time being in the crowd of children that always swarmed about the Armand complex. Inessa stayed there impatiently for a while, taking the opportunity to organize the local SD network with the help of Dr. Petchkine, his nurse Valentina Ethtekina, and the local librarian, Alexander Rodd. Her aim was to link this amateur group with the hard-core networks in the city.

She made frequent visits to Moscow, where she joined Volodya at his new apartment in Granatny Lane in the Arbat. While she had been away, he had at last committed himself to the SDs. This had brought him under police surveillance, which meant a life of changing homes with the younger children joining her often wherever she was.

After a few weeks, as the winter came and snow covered Moscow, the lovers decided to settle despite the police and rented a house,

8 Ostozhenka Street, a big building with an archway opening onto a courtyard and, most important, with two exits. From a few yards up the street, she could see the Kremlin in the distance, with its towers and cupolas and high walls that extend for a mile and half. Inessa and Volodya's house became a refuge for "wanted" politicals, which confused the "Nannies," as the surveillance teams were known. Who, in fact, was living there?

Inessa moved in with the children and, to help with the rent, Ivan Nikolaev, another student, known as Vanya. He was in fact an SR and thus carried weapons. Vanya's father had been an Armand serf, but the family, recognizing talent, had funded the boy's education, and he was now studying medicine.

Inessa put Vanya in charge of setting up her secret library. To help him, he had co-opted another student, Nikolai Druzhinin. The library actually came into being in the home of Druzhinin's sister, an actress named Alvetina, who was not a member of either party, and therefore less likely to interest the police. Druzhinin called at Ostozhenka every week to collect orders for literature, which would then be passed to various SD cells in the city.

All the time, the going was getting tougher. There was unrest in universities in many Russian cities. And as the possibility of revolution became more prominent, so did the forces of reaction.

In September, a student protest march in Moscow was broken up by police, and there were many beatings. A few days later, as Inessa wrote Alexander, a dissident group arrived in the city from Vologda, three hundred miles north, and there was serious shooting with the police that ended with six dead and fifty wounded.

With members of both the SD and the SR parties living in the Ostozhenka house, the Okhrana put it under full-time surveillance. They had information that the two parties had agreed to join forces to create the revolution. Volodya and Inessa knew they were being watched, which highlighted the growing tension. The Okhrana were preparing to act.[5]

Thirty thousand police were believed to be on surveillance duties in Moscow at this time. They referred to Volodya as "Ipatievsky," after the Armand family apartment, and often tailed him when he was with a girl named Alexandrovna Lipinskaya, known to them as "Kurskaya," whose father was an adviser to the Court. Every detail— what they were carrying, what they did, whom they spoke to—was reported.

Meanwhile, Inessa continued her maternal role. "My dear Sasha," she wrote in October to Alexander,

> there is so much to tell you that I could write a whole book. The children were excited by the photos you sent them and want to reply to you, too. Varya loved you calling her a "rascal." Andrushka has been very ill with acute dysentery, and the doctor told me that there was a danger he wouldn't recover. But he is now getting better all the time.
>
> For some reason, Fedor has not been accepted by the gymnasium. I think it is a misunderstanding. I've placed him in a private school. Zalesskaya, the head mistress, runs it very well, but it is still only a preparatory and I still hope to get him into the best school in Moscow.
>
> Sasha [Alexander] is doing well. There was a parents' meeting which I attended. He has so much to do this year because their standards are so high.

At this time, she was clearly staying at Pushkino, as she often did, for she speaks of sending the three boys to stay with friends. "They were upset because I sent them with Dasha [presumably a nanny]." "So is she going to walk with us and hold our hands?" they complained.

"I went with Inochka [Inna] to Eldigino, and it was snowing for the first time this year, so we traveled by sleigh, and she absolutely loved it. She wants to go again.

"For myself, I'm healthy and feeling much better than I have for the last two or three years, but still I don't work!"

She has been to the theater, on one occasion with the children to see a show called *Snowgirl,* "which they loved." She also went to a meeting of the local Psychological Society and "was so bored I almost swallowed my tongue."

She tells him about the student demonstrations and the beatings in Moscow. "The police were helped by the porters and market-stall owners—those bourgeois who can be corrupted so easily."[6]

· · ·

Now that she was living openly with Volodya, she felt guilty about taking so much of Alexander's money. She wanted to support the children and Volodya. "I did write to you about our plans for Vanya Nikolaev and myself to give lessons at home here, but there are problems."[7] The local police had approved, but the Okhrana had forbidden it, arguing that she "was a member of the Armand family and well known for her political lack of loyalty. . . . The lessons are not recommended, given the propaganda that could take place there."

She was advancing fast as a revolutionary, building her network and educating its members in politics, but the police were usually close. To outwit them, they had taken to holding meetings with workers in the open fields, with lookouts to warn of any approach by government agents. The woods, formerly the usual venues, provided too much cover for the police.

Early in January 1905, Inessa was first exposed at a personal level to the dark side of revolution. In a protest march, Vanya was badly beaten by police and staggered back to the house, bleeding profusely and badly bruised. "I cannot put into words my pain," she wrote Alexander on January 7. "My children will never get over this sight."[8]

She wrote of the rising tension. "There are spontaneous meetings on the streets and in the restaurants." Two days later, on Sunday, January 9, the new mood came to a climax. In St. Petersburg, a peaceful procession of unarmed men, women, and children were led by Father Gapon, an Orthodox Church priest, to present to the tsar at the Winter Palace a petition pleading respectfully for better conditions for the workers.

As they drew near the palace, the marchers were ordered to disperse, but they refused and marched on. Troops assembled in front of the palace, though the tsar was absent.

The marchers streamed into Palace Square. The sight of the approaching crowd unnerved the officers. The order was given to fire. Hundreds of innocent people were killed. The whole nation was appalled. "Bloody Sunday" was written into history, and strikes broke out in all the major Russian cities.

"Now [in Moscow] we have a sort of revolution, an unusual state of agitation," Inessa wrote to Alexander five days later. "Beyond the Moscow River everyone has stopped work. Not only the factories but workrooms and small companies like laundries. Also printers, which means there aren't many newspapers left in St. Petersburg, not a single one. And what do you say about the nomination of Trepov?" Trepov was Moscow's iron police chief whom the tsar had ordered to St. Petersburg to establish calm there.

"These days in the streets of Moscow there are notices that are really funny. The strikes, they say, are the work of the Japanese, who are spending millions of rubles on provocative propaganda. This information is said to come from a western agency that, of course, does not exist. Isn't that the peak of stupidity?"[9]

She would not be talking of funny things much longer. On February 4, the governor general of Moscow, the Grand Duke Sergei, was murdered by Ivan Kaliayev with an SR bomb. It was the second attempt. On his first, Kaliayev had seen two children in the carriage with the duke and had been unable to bring himself to commit the act. On the second attempt, the duke was alone. Immediately the police reacted to the assassination by arresting radical students and known SRs, such as Vanya Nikolaev.

At 4:00 A.M., they raided 8 Ostozhenka Street. "I was awoken that night by a sudden noise," Inna, then six, wrote years later, "and found police searching our room, turning everything upside down, even the beds of us children. Mother stood nearby, absolutely calm. She smiled at me and made a sign not to cry."

Horrified, the child watched as the police worked. Inessa had warned the elder children of this possibility. " 'Do not show you are scared, and do not say anything. If necessary, look after the little ones.' Varya and Andre were crying. They didn't understand what was happening."[10]

The police uncovered illegal SR literature and conspiratorial letters in Vanya's room. Then they searched Volodya and Inessa's and, among her possessions, they found something that was far more incriminating: a revolver and bullets that belonged to Vanya.[11] Inessa, being an SD, was presumably hiding them for him, but this tainted her record, and for years afterward the police believed she was an SR. That night they arrested all three of them.

"Don't tell anyone I have been arrested," Inessa whispered to Inna as she kissed her good-bye. This was asking a lot of a six-year-old, but Inna did keep the secret. It served her well, for three years later she was trusted to see Inessa several times when she was living illegally in the city and police were searching for her.[12]

Inessa's sister Renee, who with her husband, Nikolai Armand, did not live far away, is mentioned in the police report of that first night. She was summoned to take care of the children when their mother was removed. There would have been a nanny, but a person of greater status would be needed for family decisions.

It was the start of the first big test for Inessa. As she was driven away in the darkness of the police van, the sounds of the horses muffled by the snow on Ostozhenka Street, she must have been very aware of this.

CHAPTER 3

MOSCOW BASMANNAYA JAIL 1905

It was worse than anything she expected. "I am among drunken men who scream and make a lot of noise," she wrote to the governor of Basmannaya Jail.[1]

She had been separated from Volodya and Vanya, who had been sent to the Miasnitskaya Prison. Basmannaya was normally a woman's detention center, but following the riots sparked by Bloody Sunday in St. Petersburg, the demands on all the prisons in the city were too great, and men were also being held there.

Inessa was appalled to be held in a large cell with other prisoners, mostly male, drunk, and criminal. "As the prison at Basmannaya is more than full," she complained to the governor, "I have been locked up in the drunkard's cell. I beg you to transfer me without delay to Miasnitskaya, my local prison, or to another place."

Her request appears to have been refused, since she remained there, but she was placed in solitary, probably for her own protection. The next day, she wrote to the governor again. "I beg you to arrange for the return to me of the watch that was confiscated when I arrived here at Basmannaya. I also wish to be able to write and to have baths and to be able to take daily walks."

Young Ilya Ehrenburg, who was to become famous in Russia as a journalist and writer, was in Basmannaya for a time. Later, he was to join Lenin's exile group in Paris at roughly the same time as Inessa. "The station was noisy," he recorded.

> At night the drunks were brought in, beaten mercilessly and put into the "Drunk Box"—that was what they called a large cage of the sort one sees at the zoo. . . .
>
> When he saw me [on arrival], the head warder of the Basmannaya police cells bawled at once: "Off with your trousers!" A "personal search" began. From paradise I had come to hell. A powerful clout over the ear soon introduced me to the new regime.
>
> In Basmannaya we announced a hunger strike, demanding transfer to another prison, I remember begging a cell-mate to spit on a slice of bread. I was afraid I wouldn't be able to resist just the slightest bit.[2]

Inessa had not, by this time, been charged with anything, but the revolver was damaging evidence. Technically, though, she was being held on suspicion, so her requests were not unreasonable.

She was worried about Volodya, which was one reason why she wanted to be moved to the same prison. She feared that his fragile health would not be up to a Moscow jail, well known for cold, damp, and only minimally hygienic conditions. She did her best in the interrogations to absolve him from blame, insisting that she was an older woman, the mother of five children, while he and Vanya were just boys.[3]

The police had subsequently arrested Nikolai Druzhinin, who had arrived at Ostozhenka Street on his weekly call without knowing of the earlier arrests and been caught by waiting police. Unhappily for

Inessa, they found on him lists of much of the contents of her secret library. When they confronted Inessa with Nikolai's evidence, she said she had never met him before, which he confirmed.

There was much confusion among the police about which parties they all belonged to. At first, according to the reports, they believed Volodya and the "Armand woman" were SDs but had been informed that Vanya was a member of a terrorist group "attempting to make bombs and explosives" and involved with "terrorist propaganda openly seeking the death of the Sovereign."[4]

On the day of Duke Sergei's killing, according to the police report, suspects had been seen near the duke's usual route. One was found at the scene of the explosion half an hour before the assassination. It was at Vladimir and Inessa Armand's home that some "suspects," who were, of course, innocent of this crime, "were surprised and arrested."

Inessa's concern about Volodya and the effect of the cold, damp prison was growing. So was that of his mother, who wrote to Inessa often, and fretted about his lungs, fearing tuberculosis.

Inessa got regular news of him via prisoners in transit or warders who knew other warders. She was relieved to hear of his release, together with Vanya, after a few weeks, though they were required to stay near Pushkino. But he was now very ill.

Inessa, however, was charged under article 126 of the criminal code with belonging to an organization seeking the "overthrow of the existing social order" and held in prison awaiting trial.[5]

Alexander, still in the Far East, was appalled at what had happened, but she was allowed to receive his letters, in which she found great comfort. "Dear Sasha," she wrote back,

Thank you for your letter. I was touched by your loyalty and friendship. What a wonderful relationship we have.

Sasha, about your offer to help with my release, don't do too much. If you want to talk to the General Major, I don't know what to tell you. If it's the same for everyone, then perhaps it's all right to talk to him, but if it means treating me as a special case, then I beg you not to do it.

At times I've felt a great need to get out, but now I am under control. I feel fine. I am quite healthy. I am absolutely calm—probably because recently lots of prisoners have been released. And you see they will take a lot of money from you.[6]

Her light dismissal of her time in solitary as merely giving rise to a "great need to get out" is impressive.

Solitary confinement has been described by many. Ehrenburg was to write: "I tried knocking on the walls, but nobody answered. . . . I tried reciting poetry." You perform physical exercises, realizing the need to keep active. You attempt various mental exercises, recalling the plots of books, calculating mathematical sums, playing patience in your mind. You must guard against sleep during the day so that you can sleep at night. Loneliness is, at first, overwhelming, then disorienting.

Inessa was given a gray dress, a straw pallet to sleep on, and fed barley gruel, which only extreme hunger would have enabled her to eat.

In May, Inessa became ill, informing the governor that she had "developed anemia and was in generally poor health." She asked for more fresh air and contact with other prisoners, but the request was turned down.

She wrote to Alexander: "You know, Sasha, there is something I want to tell you. When I was free with the boys, we had a plan to go down the Volga and also to visit the lakes in Finland. So if you want to, and have the money, this wish could come true." She means, of course, that he should take them without her.

I don't think they will release me, not for a year. There is this court hearing in a month, and they say it can go on for four, five, or six months. So you will have to go and return before my release.

In prison, time goes very slowly. I am reading a lot, but the last few days I haven't been able to concentrate because the weather is very good and I think about the meadows and the forests. But enough of my dreams. They say that defeat [in the war with Japan] is imminent. For the revolution it is useful, but when you think of the hungry people who must pay the price, then I have terrible fears, and it seems to me that we are really heading for disaster. We have to shake off this terrible yoke [of the tsar] as soon as possible. This is the only way we can survive.

Thank you very much for the money. Now I am completely provided for, and if I have need again I will tell you.

So ask the children to gather flowers in the woods and meadows and send them to me in the same way as letters. Wild flowers, Sashechka. Something else: I was thinking of giving little history lessons to the boys. I've promised this for a long time.

To prepare for this, she asks for some books such as Ashley and Gibbon's *History of England* and Guizot's *Histoire de la civilisation en France*.[7]

The letter, with its revolutionary despair that would never have passed the censors, must have been sent to Alexander by secret routes. He had returned to Pushkino by now, and despite her request for no special favors, the family influence was at last deployed to get her out of jail. On June 3, some five months after her arrest, she was released, against guarantees by Alexander and his father, but she still faced charges and was under police surveillance until her trial.

The doctors' reports on Volodya were serious. He *had* contracted TB, they concluded, and must move to the temperate climate of southern Europe or the mountain air of Switzerland. The family urged Inessa to go with him. But she had been deprived of her children for months, and her revolutionary zeal had hardened, so she was at first reluctant. Then, aware of the Okhrana "nannies," she decided it would be wise to stay out of sight for a while.

It seems odd that, still facing trial, she was allowed to leave with Volodya for Nice. Presumably the family bought permission for her, as they had for Kammer. Perhaps the police welcomed it as a form of exile, often a regular sentence of the court, and were glad to see her go.

In July, at a time when the repercussions of Bloody Sunday were looming greater every day, the couple left for the south by train. For Inessa, it would be only a pause. She was becoming a veteran, well along the path from right to left, from rich young wife to seasoned revolutionary.

CHAPTER 4

NICE 1905

The news came in bits, partly because of the censors. Each day, Inessa and Volodya scoured the newspapers. There were reports, mostly unconfirmed, of unrest and rolling waves of revolt in the Russian cities, which was no surprise.

It was a cause for anxiety, though. Pushkino—where the children were, with Alexander and the rest of the family—was probably far enough from Moscow to escape serious danger, but it was on the rail line to Archangel, and control of the railways would be a key element of any revolution.

In early October, the workers in twenty Moscow printing firms went on strike. Because the printers were located near the university, students flocked into the streets in support. When the police acted, because these were illegal meetings, the students pelted them with stones.

The workers in another thirty Moscow printers joined the strike, and Cossacks were brought in to control the crowd. They opened fire, killing ten people. The next week in St. Petersburg, the printers joined their Moscow comrades in a three-day strike.

And so the crisis built. In Moscow, the railroad workers closed the Moscow–Kazan line and marched to other yards to urge their colleagues to walk out, too. Four days later, no trains were running out of Moscow, which was potentially catastrophic, for Moscow lay at the heart of the railway system. And without trains, nothing was coming into the city: no food, no coal, no goods of any kind.

In St. Petersburg on October 13, a workers' soviet, attended by deputies from most of the factories in the city, met for the first time and formed a rough kind of policy to merge their power, discovering quickly that the people would obey the soviet orders.

In Moscow, meanwhile, there was an eerie quiet: no gas or electricity. The trams had stopped. The telegraph system and telephones were unusable; post offices were closed. The water system was feared to be polluted.

On October 15, Police Chief Trepov, who now had wide powers in St. Petersburg, issued an ill-advised order that only escalated the tension: Police were to disperse illegal meetings. If crowds did not obey, the police "were *not* to use blanks or *not* to spare bullets."

This had defiant crowds heading for the streets in their thousands, especially around the university. Oddly, the police and troops did nothing in response. Two days later, the tsar offered concessions in a manifesto that included freedom of conscience, speech, assembly, and union; an enlargement of the voting franchise; and the right of a new state duma to approve laws.

This was greeted with jubilation throughout the nation and was in theory a huge gesture, not that far from an offer of constitutional democracy—except for the revolutionary parties who didn't trust it. On a balcony before a huge crowd at the university, Leon Trotsky dramatically tore up the manifesto. The tiny Bolshevik faction of the SDs declared that "tsarist freedom is the freedom of new tsarist guards and the Black Hundreds to kill and rob peaceful citizens."

The Black Hundreds were a civilian force that, campaigning

under the banner of God and the tsar, had often led pogroms against the Jews with the tacit approval of the police. Now they were ranged against anyone they deemed to be enemies of the sovereign.

But not many shared the fears of the revolutionaries. A wave of optimism swept through the two cities. In Moscow, a crowd of fifty thousand people gathered in Theater Square to hear speeches about the manifesto. Many wore red ribbons. A huge red flag was raised bearing the words "Freedom of Assembly," and all the men doffed their hats.

Someone started humming "The Marseillaise." Others took it up. More joined them, with streaming tears, until soon the marching hymn of the French Revolution was echoing, in haunting tones, across that great square near the Kremlin.

The elation of the two capital cities spread through the nation. Not many had expected success so soon. The St. Petersburg soviet still refused to call off the strike, fearing this would be seen as approval of the manifesto, which they still had to consider. But unplanned strikes are hard to maintain, and already the fervor had started to wane. On October 20, the soviet, fearing it could be wrong-footed, ordered the strike to end before it faded on its own and urged workers to "discuss" the decision in their factories.

From Nice, a frustrated Inessa wrote to Alexander:

My dear Sasha, I started writing this letter a long time ago, but could not continue because Russia was completely cut off. We had neither letters nor telegrams.

The news has deeply worried us but we are glad for Russia. We would love to be there and make to this great national cause our small contribution. At such great moments it is hard to be able to do nothing. . . . We have been very worried for all of you—for you, for Vanya, for Boris and other comrades. . . .

I admire the way the working class has performed. They are real heroes. What strength and grandeur and what a splendid fight. And now in Moscow the Black Hundreds are acting. I am terrified for all of you—this systematic beating of the intelligentsia. Yes, I would love to be there, and Volodya as well, but [presumably because of his illness] we have to wait a little.[1]

. . .

Two days after Inessa posted her letter, Lenin and Nadya arrived in St. Petersburg from their exile in Geneva, where the SD party journal had been printed since 1903. He had planned that they should register under their real names and operate openly, but on detecting the Okhrana agents who were tailing them, he decided they should use aliases, and they moved constantly, staying in various safe houses. He kept a low profile, in contrast to Trotsky.

But as always, Lenin was the tactician. Before coming back to Russia, he had made fiery demands of his new Bolshevik faction: "For God's sake, there has been talk about bombs for more than a year and yet not a single bomb has been made." He had urged the creation of detachments of workers and students that would kill spies, blow up police stations, and rob banks to gain the funds they needed for an armed insurrection.

Lenin had these rages when his anger boiled over and his imagination ran wild. His new demands hardly conformed with Marxist policy. Rather, it was what the SRs did. But he was soon calmer, though again changing policy, urging them to exploit the manifesto's legal avenues and put up Bolshevik delegates for the new Duma. He was overruled in conference by his comrades. This would be collaboration with a hated system.

Lenin persisted, seeing the potential for greater influence, even proposing conciliation with Martov's Mensheviks, which astonished everyone in the faction he had created: For a year Menshevism had been a heresy. Anyway, his suggestion was only temporary—to exploit the immediate opportunity. Lenin was always one step ahead of his comrades.

Meanwhile, as the revolutionary tension in the capital eased, the tiger showed his claws. On November 29, troops surrounded the St. Petersburg soviet and arrested its president and several deputies. It looked like the end, but there was worse to come.

In Moscow, the SRs and both factions of the SDs had agreed to work together in a new uprising. Lenin himself had ordered the Bolsheviks to take part and approved the funding. A civilian force of militiamen had been armed, and on December 6 the newly formed Moscow soviet called another general strike. Within two days, eighty thousand workers responded.

In Pushkino, Alexander led his own workers out of the factory on strike with a red ribbon in his lapel, which must have bemused the authorities in the city. He was supposed to be a hardheaded industrialist.

There was a short, tense period in Moscow when there were few casualties, as both sides were holding back. Then the governor general of Moscow ordered action, the revolutionaries responded, and the killing began in earnest. The government troops began to use artillery, most unusual for civil control, and the rebels responded with hand-thrown bombs and guerrilla tactics. Their sniper units had orders to fire at officers and Cossacks but not ordinary soldiers (who might become supporters) or police, except those known for their cruelty.

Barricades went up in the streets, strengthened with ice, as the battle developed. The rising confidence of the government was evident. The famous Semenovsky Regiment arrived from the capital and poured shells into the Presnya textile district, which had become the rebels' base area.

This truly was the end—anyway for 1905—and the cost was high: more than 1,000 dead, including 137 women and 86 children.

"I remember that December," wrote Ilya Ehrenburg, a teenager at the time. "That was when I first saw blood on the snow. . . . I shall never forget that Christmas: The terrible heavy silence after the singing, the shouting, the firing. The ruins of Presnia stood very black."

The events of 1905, though, were to serve as a dress rehearsal. The revolutionaries, and Lenin in particular, learned valuable lessons in tactics and the psychology of crowds and the state. The soviets were closed down, but they'd be back.

· · ·

In Nice, the news of hope and disaster eventually filtered through. For an impatient Inessa, the conflict was hard. She later wrote to her friend Anna Asknazy that "friction between personal and family interests and the interests of society is one of the most serious problems facing the intelligentsia today."

She stuck her voluntary exile out through January, and Volodya made good progress in the Mediterranean climate. In February, when he seemed well enough, they returned to Russia, joining the children and Alexander in Pushkino.

If the question remained as to why she was allowed to leave Russia, there was none now about her return. The government was swinging between the use of carrot and stick techniques. A political amnesty had been declared, canceling such charges as Inessa still faced, so she was safe for the moment.

But she was careful, for the climate after 1905 was uncertain. She began to be a serious revolutionary, building the networks cell by cell, and tutoring the recruits in political theory. And the police watched her closely. According to their records, she and Volodya moved often, usually in the Arbat district but also back to Pushkino where she revived the old ring of A. N. Rodd, the librarian, and Dr. Petchkine.[2]

This consisted of three circles with a total of fifty-five members. Illegal meetings were held in Dr. Petchkine's house or the Armand family home. Leaflets were printed on the factory hectograph and left at night by the village well for the women members to circulate.

Inessa often had her younger children with her in the city when she was there—to the astonishment of Elena Vlasova, a young activist student, who could not believe how she could find the time to be a good mother.[3]

On March 10, barely a month after Inessa and Volodya had returned, they arrested Vanya Nikolaev at a Railway Union meeting where a strike was being planned but freed him days later for lack of evidence.[4]

Inessa was put in charge of SD propaganda in the Lefortovo district—although she was not yet formally a member of the party. R. C. Elwood explains that being both "respectable" and female, she was well suited to this, since a "well-dressed lady was less likely to arouse police suspicions" and more easily accepted as a circle leader by male workers.[5]

"Our meeting places," wrote Elena Vlasova in 1920,

were the Annenkova Woods and the Ismailov Zoo for daylight meetings and the banks of the Yauza, a backwater of the Moscow River, for more secret gatherings.

The workers in our district were from the confectionary factories, bakers and textile industries. . . . Many were illiterate, living in great poverty. Inessa had a simple direct way of getting through the distrust and awakening their interest. She would talk about the differences between the Bolsheviks and Mensheviks.[6]

She was also able to simplify Marxist theory without seeming to condescend. Already, too, her talent for organization, which was to impress Lenin, was becoming clear.

That autumn, 1906, she enrolled in Moscow University in the study of law, recently opened to women, though they were still forbidden to practice. Most female students were taking humanities and science courses, which could be put to practical use, though Inessa wasn't interested in being a lawyer but in knowledge. It was a gesture really, pressed as she was, but it was to come in useful.[7]

By then, she was aware she was followed every time she went near the Lefortovo district, where she had focused on the important railway unions that were still legal. She was also a member of the SD "Lecturer's Commission," a pool of experienced propagandists.

At the end of February 1907 and the Russian winter, Volodya began to suffer new attacks, and he left Russia for his old sanatorium on the Mediterranean. It devastated her to see him suffering, with constant coughing into bloodstained handkerchiefs.

But now that Volodya had left, she was alone in the city, and, by March, the children were back for a time at Pushkino. Inessa was never easy without people around, although oddly she seemed well able to stand her periods in "solitary" in jail, which most prisoners find intolerable.

Not that she was alone for long. Refugee politicals were often staying with her—as they were when in April the police swooped again. They found no suspicious literature and showed little interest in others there, but they arrested Inessa because they had her listed as an SR. Vanya's revolver, found in her room back in 1905, remained on record.

They held her for only a few days, which clearly surprised Volodya. "Don't worry about me any longer," she wrote to him on May 11. "I have been at large for some time. I am rejoicing in the thought that you will soon leave there and come back to us. I work a lot. Sometimes I just don't feel my feet. I kiss you. Your Inessa."[8]

A few days later, they arrested her again, this time for attending an illegal meeting, under the guise of a reunion. She refused to answer banal questions about her children, husband, or parents, declaring simply "I haven't taken part in any [political] meeting." She was only there socially with a friend she'd met in Ekaterinsky Park. Ten days later she was released with a fine of three hundred rubles.

However, at last, she had accepted what had been obvious to anyone else: The constant danger of police raids, to which her life exposed her, made an unsuitable background of fear for the children.

Discussing this with Elena Vlasova, the young girl urged her to move in with her. "Quite a bit older than me," Elena wrote, "Inessa was an experienced revolutionary . . . and for a young militant like me to know a woman like that was priceless." But they got home "too late and too tired" for much in the way of talking.[9]

For Inessa, though, the tides were not good. The reaction to the critical events of 1905 was growing, and Inessa was more exposed than she realized. General Reinbot, governor of Moscow, had decided that "Elizaveta Fedorovna Armand [her legal name] is a danger to public order, deserving imprisonment until complete enlightenment about the circumstances of her affairs."[10]

Her cause was not helped by a four-day strike at the Armand factory. When Alexander agreed to all but one of his men's demands, unusual for employers, this strengthened police suspicions of his perplexing political sympathies. They arrested four of the local party members—but their watch on Alexander, too, became closer.

In early July, the Okhrana raided an SD meeting in the offices of an employment agency—which gave Inessa, who arrived late, a chance to say she was there only to hire a cook.[11]

It wasn't accepted, of course. Under interrogation, she denied everything as usual and wrote a statement, which did not really match her original claim: "I have been retained as the result of a misunderstanding and with no official charge. I was arrested as I entered 30 Kolossov Lane to rent an apartment. But I am innocent."[12]

This time it would be no brief visit. She was taken to Prechistensky Jail where she shut her eyes shut to make the police mug shots less usable. She lied about her age, saying she was twenty-eight, being, in fact, thirty-three, and when asked for the names of her children gave those of her sisters.

It would soon be summer and conditions in her new prison were a great improvement on Basmannaya in the winter of 1905. Volodya, too, was back—living in their old apartment in the Arbat. "My dear Volodya," she wrote,[13]

I feel completely cut off . . . and sometimes the most crazy thoughts come into my head. I wonder if maybe all of you are ill. . . . Especially, I am worried for Andrushka. When we saw each other last time he was not well and you didn't tell me anything about him. . . . I am frightened that he is getting worse and you are keeping it from me. It is terrifying for me to have these horrible thoughts.

My life here is not too bad. . . . We sit at open windows and eat well. We take turns to cook and wash the towels. . . . I was very worried about my soup, but it was all right, though the vegetables were all half cooked.

Witnesses for her trial were being interrogated in the prison, but she claimed: "My file doesn't seem to move. I was told I would be freed in three days but I'm still here."

Inessa realized that everything was now different but she displayed spirit, again writing to the prison governor, pleading innocence and a lack of any evidence.[14]

Elena Vlasova was in the same cell as Inessa, together with several comrades. "And at once she organized our communal life." Inessa was missing her children. "She never spoke of them. But we knew that all the embroidery and knitting was destined for them." The notion of Inessa knitting seems strange until her education, aimed at a good marriage, is recalled.

Meanwhile, the two men in her life fought hard for her release. Volodya had already had trouble, being only a brother-in-law, in gaining visiting rights.[15] But he wrote to the city governor, asking for "the exact grounds for the detention of my brother's wife. . . . Would you please explain why she has not been freed."

Alexander demanded her release stating that "during interrogation, she was told she was to be tried in three days' time."

But neither supporter made much impact on the course of events. The police had no case, but they had a dossier. The head of the gendarmerie wrote to the minister of the interior on September 1 requesting her exile for three years, since she had long "been engaged in agitation of the workers and communication with extreme parties."

The minister agreed but reduced the period. In October she was told her sentence: two years' banishment to the Russian North, under the control of the Archangel authorities. The next day, she passed on the appalling news to Alexander, who wrote at once to the governor of the city and asked that she should be allowed to serve her exile abroad—and was refused.

And so on November 21, Inessa, in handcuffs, entered Moscow's Yaroslavsky Station with two guards to board a train. To her delight, Alexander, carrying a large bouquet, was there to see her off with all the children. Much moved, she was allowed to embrace them all.[16]

Volodya, despite his frail health, was to travel with her.

Just over an hour later, the train passed through Pushkino, and she would have looked out of the window at the Church of St. Nikolai with its pale blue cupola, where she was married, and at the two tall redbrick chimneys of the Armand plant.

The next day, the Armand workers struck again—this time in an openly political protest at the trial of SD deputies in the Duma. The police acted fast. Twenty-four workers were arrested and shortly afterward they took Boris, Alexander's brother, A. N. Rodd, the Pushkino librarian, and then Alexander, who, to Inessa's alarm when she heard the news weeks later, was to be jailed prior to foreign exile. The family home was raided, as Rodd put it, "like an invasion of barbarians."

. . .

Meanwhile, as the train traveled to a frozen north, far colder than anything Inessa had ever experienced, Lenin was in trouble, too, not all that far away and for the same reason: the wave of reaction in November 1907 with a government growing harsher. The dramatic points of Lenin's and Inessa's lives were again coinciding.

In 1906, Lenin and Nadya had moved to Finland. It was a cautious retreat from St. Petersburg, since he could see the way the political wind was blowing. Finland was part of the Russian empire, but it was to some extent autonomous. Even so, the Okhrana had right of entry, and in November 1907 they were exercising it.

A message arrived at Lenin's home in Kuokkala that the police were searching the town. At once, he packed and left, making for Helsinki, 240 miles away, leaving Nadya and several comrades to move the Bolshevik headquarters abroad. They burned all files that could not be transported, and Nadya, who had lived this life for a long time, carefully buried the ashes, knowing they could cause suspicion.[17]

Lenin's flight was typical. He would never risk his life or security because of the destiny he believed was his. Lesser people, like his wife, comrades, or even, later, his mistress, could be exposed to any risk he deemed necessary, but not the future leader of the world revolution.

It was a stance that was both far-seeing and arrogant, for at that time he had lost control of his own faction of the party, having failed even to be elected to the Bolshevik Central Committee. But the Moscow uprising had whetted his appetite for the role of outrageous revolutionary, for whom nothing was barred if it served the cause.

Early in 1906, he had persuaded the SD Central Committee that defensive actions should be conducted against the Black Hundreds, who were dangerous in certain areas. Exploiting this vote, Lenin had set up a secret center and treasury within the party—secret, he insisted, because of the (real) danger of Okhrana infiltration.

His squads of the Combat Bureau, under the control of L. B. Krasin, had mounted two hundred "expropriations" in January and February 1906 alone, mostly in the form of bank holdups, attacks on customs houses and ticket offices, and train robberies. They had often used criminal gangs and thus provided them with a more respectable "political" cover. Much of this revenue had gone into Lenin's secret treasury, which he used to finance Bolshevik interests.

Several raids were handled by a cross-eyed Caucasian bandit later known as Kamo, who was a friend since boyhood of Joseph Stalin. Kamo's most dramatic operation was to hold up a carriage on the way to the State Bank at Tiflis and take from it 341,000 rubles that he then smuggled across the Russian border in a hat box. But the notes were all of high denomination—500 rubles—which could attract attention and be easier to trace.

To reduce this danger, Lenin thought up a clever plan. The notes would be presented in small quantities at a number of banks in different cities on the same day and time. As was to happen so often, one of Lenin's men was an Okhrana spy, and the police were waiting, but not everywhere, so funds were still raised, albeit not on the scale Lenin had hoped.

The bank raid and others provoked a violent reaction from the Mensheviks. "How can one remain in the same party as the Bolsheviks?" Pavel Axelrod asked Yuli Martov. Georgi Plekhanov declared that it "was so outrageous that it is really high time for us to break off relations." Lenin coolly shrugged off the attacks: "When I see Social Democrats announcing . . . 'We are no anarchists, no thieves. . . . We are above that . . .' then I ask myself: Do these people understand what they are saying?" This method of fund-raising, however, had shocked many Bolsheviks, too, and Lenin had failed to gain election to the Central Committee of the faction he had created. The members knew they needed him, but there were limits for them, if not for him.

In November 1907, while Lenin went into hiding in the village of Olgbu, near Helsinki, Nadya finalized party business in Kuokkala, arranging the transfer of *Proletarii,* the Bolshevik newspaper, to Switzerland, and she even returned to St. Petersburg to set up new communication channels with local activists.

Lenin, still uneasy about his security, decided to move on to Stockholm, leaving instructions for Nadya on how to catch up with him. The plan was for him to take the ice-cutting ferry to Sweden from Turku, but Finnish comrades warned that the Okhrana were watching the boarding stage and advised him to pick up the ferry at its next stop at Nauvo Island, twenty miles to the southwest in the Gulf of Bothnia.

He left Turku by carriage, switching to a boat to Kuusto Island. From there he island-hopped to Lille Meljo Island, from which he had to go on foot across the ice to Nauvo Island. That early in the winter, the ice had not settled, and he had to keep jumping the gaps between the floes.

He had two local comrades to guide him, but they were both drunk. At one point, the ice broke up beneath him and only by a huge desperate leap did he manage to get onto a solid floe. "What a stupid way to die," he thought, so Nadya recorded. He reached Nauvo Island despite this and boarded the ferry without detection by the police. The next day, he arrived in Stockholm, where he was joined later by Nadya.

It was to be ten years before Lenin returned to Russia. By then he would have honed his Bolsheviks into a fighting force, capable, as he was to claim to mocking laughter at the Congress of Soviets in June 1917, of taking over the government of Russia. It would be a hard period, marked by frustration, poverty, furious arguments, and moving, always moving, from Geneva to Paris to Poronin, near the Russian border, and back to Bern and Zurich, but always developing his vision, building his control, cheating when he felt he had to—for the end, for Lenin, always justified any means.

And for seven of those years, Inessa would be working with him, loving him, sharing the tactics, doing the dirty work, going to jail. For his vision of the future was her vision, a disaster, some might say, considering the millions who died in its cause, but one that was to have a huge, continuing influence on the social and political development of the world.

. . .

Some three weeks before Lenin reached Stockholm, Inessa's train had reached Archangel, which had been Russia's only seaport until Peter the Great had built St. Petersburg, and was still an active trading town for timber from the vast forests that surrounded it, as well as for fish and flax. But in winter, the sea was frozen, as was the Dvina River, which flanked the railroad. Inessa saw a city cloaked in white as the train slowed and the Troitsky Cathedral with its five great domes came into view.

The dread at facing two years in this arid country seemed intolerable. Worse, she would not be in the city but far further north, where it could be even more than forty Celsius degrees below zero; a cup of hot coffee would freeze in seconds. But the usual stoicism marked her letters, except for those to the authorities in which—as usual, too—she demanded improvement of the conditions.

Her gratitude to Volodya for coming with her, despite his damaged lungs, was immense. He was able to help, of course, because he was free and could negotiate with her captors, though in truth he did not achieve much. His efforts during this period of prison, both in Moscow and in Archangel, reveal a more definite personality than normally emerges from Inessa's correspondence and other evidence. He usually appears as a shadowy, rather colorless figure, which Inessa's letters do little to embellish. Her letters home from Mezen refer to "I" rather than "we" except when she is specifically describing him doing something or accompanying her.

Later, she thanked him effusively for his guidance of her into Marxism and clarity of thought, the suggestion being that she could not have matured without him. It was a strange relationship. She could, it seems, live for long periods away from him, often by choice, which suggests a lack of passion. But she appears totally content when she is with him. She needs him, but he doesn't have to be there in person, providing she has other company.

There was no sign, even with the faraway excitement of 1905, that she resented his keeping her from it in the tranquillity of the south of France.

If revolution was Inessa's religion, then it seems that Volodya was her priest, a very young one, but quiet and ideologically strong.

. . .

In Archangel, while her onward passage was arranged, Inessa was held in a local jail, which she called the castle. She was not in the holding cells where exiles were normally kept but in solitary confinement, possibly for her own protection, in one of the only two cells designated for political prisoners. The conditions were worse than any she had so far experienced in prison.

She had now learned that she was heading for Mezen, a small port just below the Arctic Circle. Their route would be circuitous, a rough, arduous journey by horse-drawn sleigh. At once, she wrote to the governor claiming that she "suffered from fever weakness and complete exhaustion and could not survive the long journey to Mezen. I am asking for a medical examination and to stay in Archangel or a nearby town."

It was a good try, but as usual it didn't work. And nowhere in her letters is there any sign of a weakening in her beliefs or concern at the price they might demand. With the help, perhaps, of Volodya, she was still a fervent revolutionary.

CHAPTER 5

MEZEN IN ARCTIC EXILE 1907

"I n the second cell in Archangel," Inessa wrote to Alexander, "there was a girl who had been there nine months and was now a nervous wreck. She had hallucinations. She saw faces moaning and screaming. I was so sorry for her because, at eighteen, she was so young."[1]

It was a chilling harbinger of what to expect. Conditions at Mezen were likely to be worse.

For two weeks, Inessa was held at Archangel. She wrote to a member of the Moscow Duma, saying she was imprisoned in the castle without the right of visitors, asking him to intercede on her behalf. Volodya, who had rented a local furnished room, complained about the prison conditions to the SD members in the local Duma, though without much effect—possibly because such requests came too often. He appealed to the authorities to allow her, on account of illness, to stay in Archangel or in a nearby town, such as Pinega or Kholmogory.

Volodya had caused some confusion because he was her brother-in-law, and this robbed him of authority. Normally, exiles were accompanied by their married partners. His complaints achieved nothing.

As Inessa requested, she was examined by a doctor. "She is suffering from malarial fever," he reported. "She needs special treatment for a month." The governor still took no notice. On December 7, when Inessa was dispatched with Volodya to Mezen by sleigh, he wrote to the Mezen chief of police: "She has agreed to pay for comfort on the journey by sledge." He added darkly: "I recommend that you watch her very closely on the convoy."

The conditions of the journey were primitive. Along the route were uncomfortable stations where horses were changed and travelers could rest. "All stations were the same," Inessa wrote to Alexander. "One sofa or double bed that was so dirty that we preferred to sleep on the floor."

The journey made her yearn for "civilization" and appreciate the railways to an extent she never had before. However, the stations did have huge stoves at which they could dry their clothes. These had ovens decorated in wood in semicircular patterns of yellow and red. They also had steps so that people could sleep on platforms above them. Washing facilities were limited, with no drains from the basins; copper scoops were used to remove dirty water.

The sun was up for only four hours each day, from 10:00 A.M. to 2:00 P.M. While they presumably traveled much in darkness, Inessa was caught by the beauty of the region, the unbroken stretches of forest and the vast expanse of snow, blue in the northern light. She was also intrigued by the *malitsas* worn by the coachmen and also by the Mezen inmates—"marvelous garments" of fur that were put over the head like ponchos.

At every station, they had to compete with other travelers for fresh horses, sometimes having to wait hours for replacements, and at one stop as long as a full day.

Despite the problems, Inessa was impressed by their progress. Although it normally took seven to ten days, she told Alexander, her convoy made it in five, which, at more than forty miles a day, plus the delays, does seem remarkable in that territory. But sleigh travel, often along the courses of frozen rivers, was fast.

The journey, demanding as it was, especially for a person who was ill, perhaps eased the first formidable impact of that "mean little town," as she described Mezen, that was to be her home for two years. It was excruciatingly cold, a country of dense forests stretching for vast distances, set close to the White Sea with lakes and an estuary. Wolves and bears roamed in the distant timber. On the far sea ice were polar bears.

■ ■ ■

The long, hard winter, with its white Arctic nights, lasted from October to May, when the sea ice would at last allow occasional ships to enter Mezen's little port for a few months. The thaw turned the land into a quagmire for six weeks, and frequent floods made sleigh travel impossible. This meant no mail at that time of year.

Inessa did not make too much of the harsh conditions of her sentence, though depression would come later. "On the eve of our arrival," she wrote Alexander,

> it was minus thirty-seven degrees [Celsius]—warm by their standards. They were planning to send me even farther [to Kodia, about seventy miles away], but I was unwilling to go. There were no politicals there—just criminals—and the whole village has had syphilis, which wouldn't be very amusing, would it?
>
> Up to now, I have managed to stay here where there are about a hundred politicals.

Volodya had telegraphed the Archangel governor, who had rejected all previous requests, asking that Inessa remain in Mezen, where there was a hospital. This time, the governor agreed. He also said that since she had no occupation, being the wife of an "honorary citizen," she would receive an allowance of twelve kopecks a day, the rate being set by her background; noble exiles received fifty, ordinary people eight.

Exile, in general, was better than prison. "To start with we had to share," she told Alexander, "and then we were given our own place. There is a local-style kitchen which I like—a big room with practically no furniture so it looks like a barn and a large larder."

She was writing of the roughly made *isbas* rented out by Mezen's permanent residents to supplement their incomes from fishing and forestry. These were roughly made huts with ill-fitting doors and windows that let in icy drafts and had no running water. Theirs had three rooms, including the big barnlike kitchen, where they probably also slept.

"I cannot say much about my life here," she continued to Alexander.

> My thoughts still go back to Pushkino. I think of you a lot and all you have done to help me. . . . I was delighted to find you all at Moscow Station [on departure]. It was a great joy for me. I am keeping your bouquet as a souvenir. I don't know how I will manage two years here without my children. But I hope I may be allowed to move to Archangel, where they could come to me.
>
> How did you settle down with the boys and Inna? I want to hear all the news. It's not worth writing about my moods. They keep changing all the time. When I was at Archangel I was very depressed, which was worsened by the fever. At first, when I got here, it was good to be able to move around and see people . . . but now I'm not very happy. I can't complain, though. I'm better off than some people, but I do miss my children.

Volodya got up first on those dark mornings, fueled the stove, broke up the ice in the water buckets, and set up the samovar.

"Strictly speaking," Inessa wrote to her children, "I should get up the samovar, but I am famous for being lazy. I get up late, and . . . it always seems the samovar is ready."[2]

She cooked, but she wasn't very good at it, as she had long been surrounded by servants. She made blini with yeast and hoped they "would be able to hack through it."

In the afternoon, when it was dark again, the couple gave lessons to their comrades, Volodya teaching mathematics and Inessa tutoring them in languages.

With so many "politicals," they soon made friends. The range was wide, SDs being outnumbered at that time by SRs and others, including anarchists. Some were totally disenchanted with the revolutionary activity that had landed them in Mezen or with socialism altogether. "Others drink and carouse," Inessa wrote. "In general, hard drinking is very great here."

In the general store, there was a piano that she was allowed to play.

Alexander received her early letters but by then he, too, knew he faced the possibility of prison.

In December 1907, Inessa sent her children a descriptive, cheerful letter: "Dear Sasha, Fedya, Inessa and Volodya [Vladimir]," she wrote,

> The road [on the journey] was very beautiful, hilly country, and . . . we traveled much along rivers.
>
> On clear days . . . the snow reflects many colors, such as rose and blue and green. Some places are such a bright blue that I could hardly believe my eyes.
>
> Mezen consists of two parallel streets with side streets crossing. It is not bigger than Pushkino, maybe two thousand inhabitants. But there's a school, hospital, post office, and telegraph. The mail comes twice a week.
>
> Today there was a more severe frost than we expected, and we had let the stove go out. I told off Volodya, but it was

probably my fault. Anyway, it was desperately cold, and our hands were frozen.

I dream about the summer, when you can come here because the ship arrives then. . . . At that time, we can hunt and fish, but [I am told] there are lots of mosquitoes.

Andrushka, you have mumps so you must be very careful not to get cold. What about you, Inessa [Inna]? Have you moved to Pushkino? And Volodya, you do not eat gravy and are probably as thin as a rake. You're almost in the sixth form now, so what are you reading?

I love to curl up in bed at night, cozy and warm with a book. If it is a serious book, I fall asleep immediately. I implore you, though, not to follow my example. Only in this. In all other ways, as is well known, I am perfection.

With lots of kisses—please kiss the young ones on my behalf, and don't forget to write about them.

In January 1908, a new governor was appointed to Archangel Province. He was rumored to be hostile to "politicals," which seems accurate. An idea was broached that the exiles should celebrate January 9, anniversary of Bloody Sunday, with a demonstration. Inessa and Volodya said they would have nothing to do with it; she considered it stupidly provocative.

As it was, she did not escape suspicion, being sharply warned that, unless she took care, she would be celebrating the anniversary far away. Her plea of innocence was eventually believed. "The situation here is not suitable," she said. "It's like making war on war."

Writing to her friend Anna Asknazy, she said: "The locals here are quite wild. The men have dangerous and difficult professions. In winter they fish, when it is minus forty. They catch them with their bare hands. It is terrible to even think about it." The local women stayed at home, she explained. "There is no respite for them, like the slaves of the past. Since there are no mills, they have to grind the grain by hand."

The number of exiles was rising fast, mainly because of enforcement of the stronger government policies, and by February had doubled to two hundred. A meeting, attended by the new arrivals, was called in the apartment of a local named Minkin to decide where they were all going to live. Single people slept in dormitories and ate in a refectory, serviced by exile volunteers, including Inessa, despite her poor cooking. Couples were normally given their own quarters. Helping to organize this was Polish exile Saul Zubrovich.

At 8:30 the meeting ended. The first six people to leave ventured into the dark and were horrified to find themselves facing a mixed detachment of Cossacks and police formed up in the street, visible presumably from the light of the moon and their lanterns. At once, they attacked the exiles, some of whom ran back inside, only to be pursued by Cossacks who hit them until Minkin's shocked wife insisted they stop.

According to Zubrovich and the account in a Moscow newspaper, *Rech,* the district inspector ended the street beatings but placed some of his men in the passageway to the front door so that anyone leaving would have to pass between them. At the same time, other men were positioned outside the rear entrance.

Minkin told the inspector that the scared exiles had been having merely a housing meeting. The inspector appeared to accept this and ordered all the exiles to leave. He promised no one would touch them, but in the passageway his waiting men struck them as they ran.

Others were in the front yard of the house, where the worst assaults were inflicted. The exiles panicked. There was terrified screaming. Some ran for the back entrance, only to find the Cossacks there. Others made for the attic, but they were cudgeled out of it. Others still, like Zubrovich, headed for a nearby ravine, aiming for concealment in deep snow.

Zubrovich was found, stamped on, beaten unconscious, and left with blood streaming from his mouth. He was carried to Inessa's *isba* nearby. "I came to," he wrote, "in a house I didn't know. I was bandaged, covered [with blankets], and lying on the platform above the stove. It was then that I made the acquaintance of Inessa," who had not been at the meeting.

The reason for this violence remained obscure. Possibly the authorities believed the gathering had a political purpose, though housing meetings were officially approved. Perhaps the new governor had ordered a deterrent example for the future.

There were signs of a cover-up of an official plan that had gone wrong. The most badly wounded had been taken to the hospital. On leaving, each had asked the doctor for a certificate they could pass to the district prosecutor. The doctor refused, saying it was illegal for him to do this without police permission.

Telegrams were sent to Governor Sosnovsky in Archangel, with copies to the district prosecutor. And it would appear that the incident was seen in Archangel as an error of judgment, for the Mezen police were transferred to Kholmogory. When a vivid account appeared unsigned in *Rech,* sourced from Archangel, everyone believed it had been written by Inessa.[3]

By now, she'd heard that Alexander had been imprisoned in Moscow's Taganka Jail together with Alexander Rodd and Boris. She was appalled. "I was so glad to receive your letter," she wrote to Alexander on February 16,

> but I'm sorry that it arrived only after you were sent to prison. Every day, I am waiting for the news that you're free. It makes no sense for them to keep you. . . . There is nothing against you. Write to me, please. What are your views? They have to explain your arrest. How is your health?
>
> Here, we live as before, the same gray life. The days don't pass but somehow imperceptibly slide by like pale, bloodless shadows. We try to convince ourselves that there is life here.
>
> Of course I am better off than others because I am not alone. On the other hand, I am worse off because there in Moscow are the children I miss and worry about.[4]

In March, as the days grew longer, Inessa established a routine. "I do a lot of housework," she wrote to Inna, now nine,

> and I have two lessons, so up to 4:00 P.M. I'm usually busy. In the evenings, Uncle Volodya and I either read together or go to see people or simply talk. Guests also visit us, but we have only three chairs and one bench, so when it is more guests than we can seat . . . they have to sit on the floor, but no one seems to mind.
>
> I have portraits of some of my new acquaintances. When at last I see you, I will show them to you. There are no photo studios, . . . but one of the post-office staff has a camera but charges a lot, probably because he has a monopoly.
>
> Volodya brought his camera here, but he has no paper or plates or developing methods. . . . With the last mail I received pictures of you all, and I was so glad that I cannot express it. They are not of very good quality, but all the others that I have on my desk are of when you were little, and they don't look like you are now.
>
> Thank you for your drawings, . . . my dear sweet girl.
>
> I am so sorry Papa has been arrested. I don't think they'll keep him long. Write to me if you've been allowed to visit him. He will be dying to see you. Write and tell me how his health is, whether he hasn't gotten cold there.
>
> I hug you warmly, my dear Inushka. Uncle Volodya sends you many kisses.[6]

Inna had attached a letter from Andre, now four—written, of course, by her. "I don't kill bears," Inessa replied to him.

> I don't have a gun. There *are* bears but far away in the Arctic Ocean, which is covered with ice now, but we do have reindeer here. They are so beautiful—brown, gray, and even completely white.

Ask Grandmother to show you the deer on the tapestry. They are harnessed into little sledges, and they run very fast, not only along the road, but also directly over the snow.

You say you have had a good haircut. I cannot see you, but I know you are my sweet boy.

Back in April, because of a relapse in Volodya's health, he was forced to leave Mezen. She dreaded his departure, but she was delighted to hear from him in Pushkino, where he called on his way south. "Thank you," she wrote to him in May, "for describing your meeting with the children. I so vividly imagined you with them."[7] Volodya's absence was made more bearable, she wrote Alexander, because she had found "two new comrades she liked to have dinner with, so I don't have to cook myself anymore."[8]

One of these comrades was almost certainly Ivan Popov, a Bolshevik. Zubrovich recorded that he was present at many of the talks Inessa had with Popov but couldn't understand much of what was said.

"She tried to teach me Russian," he wrote,

> but I was lazy (and didn't study). So she would scold me. She wore her beautiful hair in long plaits, and I'd respond by grabbing them. She'd scream but was never offended. If I had known what kind of family she came from I wouldn't have behaved like that, but it was only when I arrived in Moscow with her that I discovered she came from the most bourgeois of bourgeois. Among the Poles at Mezen were working-class people, and she got on well with them.[9]

Inessa's study circles were partly political. Since she was very short of party literature, Zubrovich arranged for some books to be smuggled into Mezen by a kulak he knew, together with some old issues of *Iskra*.

. . .

In April 1908, when Mezen was still blocked by sea ice, Lenin was in the bright sunshine of the Bay of Naples on Capri. He was staying in the villa of Maxim Gorky, and he went fishing and played chess with Alexander Bogdanov, his rival within the Bolshevik faction.

Lenin wasn't on holiday. He was there with a special purpose. Bogdanov was the only person in the party who was his intellectual equal if not his superior. But their views on strategy were in total contrast. Lenin was still keen to use the existing institutions of the state, like the Duma, to extend their influence.[11] Bogdanov opposed this, even insisting that all Bolshevik deputies in the Duma should resign or face expulsion from the party. His target, which took him to the fringe of Marxist historical theory, was armed insurrection by the working class, which would have its own cultural development. To Lenin, this ignored political realities. Intellectual guidance was vital, something Bogdanov shrugged off as impossible because intellectuals were enmeshed in the bourgeois culture of the individual.

So Lenin finally decided that there wasn't room for both of them in the Bolshevik faction. Bogdanov would have to go. The planning of this was why Lenin was in Capri playing chess with apparently jovial cordiality, unless he lost, when Gorky would be astonished at his "angry and childish" behavior. Lenin's decision was bold. Owing to his criminal approach to the raising of party funds, he now had few important supporters among the Bolsheviks.

Bogdanov, too, was finished with Lenin and bored by the endless conflicts within the party. After returning to Paris from Capri, he resigned from the board of the Bolshevik newspaper, *Proletarii*, as Lenin had planned. But he kept his place on the Bolshevik Centre, which, for Lenin, made him dangerous, given the animosity in the Central Committee.

Gorky had hoped that the meeting on Capri would ease the divisive tension between the two men. Certainly, he didn't think Lenin would split the Bolshevik faction. But this was exactly what Lenin had in mind, and what made it possible was a new source of funds that shocked his comrades even more than the bank raids. The matter of the Schmidt funds would long echo throughout the party and would, in time, involve Inessa.

N. P. Schmidt, nephew of a wealthy Moscow industrialist and a revolutionary sympathizer, had died at the hands of the Okhrana in 1907, leaving a fortune to his two sisters. Lenin ordered two young Bolsheviks to woo the sisters, marry them, and contribute their inheritances to his faction.

Astonishingly, the plan worked, in part at least. The two men succeeded in marrying the girls. One then decided to keep the funds, but the other, Viktor Taratuta, while retaining some of his wife's money, handed over a considerable sum, enough to give Lenin independence.

The Schmidt funds, like the bank raids, were to cause Lenin a stormy few years of internecine fighting, which Inessa was to help him ride out.

Lenin's response to the shocked flood of criticism was revealing. Viktor Taratuta "is good because he'll stop at nothing," Lenin said to one comrade. "Tell me, could you go after a rich merchant lady for her money? No? And I wouldn't either, I couldn't conquer myself, but Viktor could. . . . That's what makes him an irreplaceable person."

But Lenin was deceiving himself or his listener. He, too, would stop at nothing to achieve an aim.

In May, Inessa made another plea to the governor to allow her to spend the rest of her sentence in foreign exile. She provided official certification that her conduct in Mezen had been satisfactory, but her health was not. She attached a medical certificate confirming that she "suffered from gastritis and malaria and that her state required a change of climate and a cure by thermal waters." This was met with yet another rejection—though the fact that, in a moment of rebellion, she had put this in the form of a demand and failed to address the governor as "Your High Excellency," as protocol dictated, may not have helped.[10]

. . .

Lenin had returned to Geneva by June, when the sea ice had broken up at Mezen. A white ship, the *Barty*, arrived in the port, and
Inessa was delighted to find Volodya on board.

His presence greatly cheered her. "The weather is very warm and
sunny," she wrote to Inna in July,

> and we walk a lot. We especially like to walk toward the
> Mezen River, which is about five miles. There are many lakes.
> The blackberries are already ripe and we got a lot yesterday.
> We plan to go tomorrow for the whole day. Maybe we will
> camp.
>
> For some time, it has been very light. At night you can
> read easily—and night is only different from the day because
> of the freshness of the air and the mosquitoes. You can't
> imagine how awful the mosquitoes are here.

She had hoped that Inna could join them, but she had since
learned that the autumn weather was marked by "sharp changes from
very cold to very hot," and "the wind whistles through, and it is easy
to get cold—especially for you my fragile Inushka. I realized then that
bringing you here was not a good idea." She added optimistically:
"Maybe I will be able to move to Archangel. The climate and conditions are better there."[12]

By the next month, she was gloomy again. "We have just got
through the six weeks 'no road' period when we are completely cut
off," she wrote to Anna Asknazy, referring to the thaw, with its quag-
mires and floods.[13]

> And then I was ill with fever. Mezen is a town of the spiritu-
> ally dead and dying; there is nothing particularly shocking or
> terrible here, as for example in penal servitude, but there is no
> life, and people fade like plants without water. Those from

the cities, with their intense life and richness of interests, cannot settle down and adapt themselves to this bog, and they spiritually decline. It is sad to see how the comrades arrive here full of energy and life and then waste away. And it is unpleasant to notice the same process happening in yourself.

In August, Alexander was in France. He had been released in May but banned for two years from the Moscow region and other major Russian cities. He had tried to run his business from Dmitrov, some forty miles north of Pushkino, but found this impractical. He applied for permission to spend his exile abroad and opted for Roubaix, near Lille, France.

Roubaix was a textile town, where he had spent much of his training, and he wanted to study the most modern methods of dyeing wool. Also, Inessa was keen for Sasha and Fedor to improve their French, so he took the two boys with him.

First, they had a holiday in Switzerland where in August Inessa wrote to him.

> I was so glad to get your letter and little Sasha's. I am glad you are high up in the Swiss mountains with the healing winds. . . .
>
> About schools in France, I agree it's important to be careful. Good schools are [usually] only available [there] to rich children and could be ultrabourgeois. For the first year, while you are looking around, it's better to keep the children at home with private lessons.
>
> I'm glad they are with you since they were missing us both in Moscow. They are such affectionate, loving children.[5]

In early September, Volodya again fell very ill, and it was obvious he could not spend the winter in Mezen. He was forced again to leave her, with more than a year of her sentence remaining. After he left, she wrote to the governor again, requesting even temporary transfer to Archangel, where Inna could join her. "Further separation is completely inconceivable," she had written to Inna. She complained to the governor of toothache, malaria, and swollen glands. There were no dentists in Mezen. The police, she said, would confirm her continued good behavior. Doubtless she addressed him this time as Your High Excellency, but again her request was refused. This made her feel desperate.

She had often talked to Zubrovich of escape while Volodya was away. The plans, though vague, centered around one of the fishing boats.

Suddenly, however, martial law in Poland, under which many of the Poles had been exiled, was lifted. They were free to return home. "Because there were so many of us," Zubrovich wrote, "we could hide Inessa and take her with us to Archangel. I told my friends about the plan and everyone supported it. So I hurried to Inessa and said 'Get ready.'

"There were several women among us, so Inessa was not the only one. And we dressed her in the fur *malitsa* worn by the local women."

They had "documents and three sleighs." On the morning of October 20, they set off across the early snows. It took a lot longer than her five-day outward journey of the previous year, but no one stopped them. "Everyone knew that a big party of Polish exiles was returning to Poland, and they didn't even count us. In Archangel, Inessa and I went to a former landlady of mine and waited until evening. Then we crossed the River Dvina to the station." They caught a train to Vologda, where several lines merged. There, they changed onto a train to Moscow, arriving on November 3.

Amazingly, M. Lapine, the officer in charge of Inessa at Mezen, did not notice she had gone until November 8, when he reported her disappearance by telegram.[14]

Inessa did not underestimate her danger. As soon as her disappearance was noticed, she would be a wanted woman. The Moscow police would be searching for her, and the border posts would be put on alert.

On November 10, Inessa wrote to Volodya at Beaulieu in the south of France, where he was now in a sanatorium. The letter was almost childish in its colorful joy at freedom.

> My very dear Volodya, So I have managed to extricate myself from the ends [of the earth] to return to the center at last. It is with great pleasure that I listen to the noise of the carriages as they rumble by, of the moving crowd. I look at the multistory houses, the trams and carriages and [think], My dear town, how much I love you. How closely I am connected by all the fibers of my being. I am your child, and I need your bustle, your noise, your commotion like a fish needs water. . . . I am very happy and excited.
>
> I know you understand amazingly and are glad for me. I feel quite well in general and am quite joyful and excited in spite of the fact I've been here about a week, but I'm restless. It takes time. I think I'll stay in Russia until after the summer. Then it'll be apparent what to do next. I'll take the children with me. I haven't seen them yet.
>
> Tomorrow I'll be meeting Inna, and I'm so emotional in advance and so rejoicing at the thought. . . . The other children I won't see yet for the reasons you know [presumably because they were too young to be trusted with a secret].[15]

Altogether it was an excited cry, even if the Okhrana were searching for her. That she should feel euphoric after the long, dull, unpleasant months of Mezen was understandable, but it apparently hadn't yet occurred to her in all her elation to ask how Volodya was. Also, her proposal to stay away from him until after the summer—some eight or nine months—can hardly have cheered him.

Again, it is strange behavior toward a lover, especially one who had shared her harsh Arctic exile despite his deplorable health. She may have been a Vera Pavlovna, but she was no Anna Karenina. If she had been, it is unlikely she could have achieved the heights of influence that she did. However, there is no question Inessa loved Volodya.

She wrote to him again the next day, perhaps nagged by a little guilt.

> I am writing again, my good one. All the time I am thinking about you. How are you? How do you feel?
>
> Up to now everything is going well. Soon I will leave. I am in a comparatively good mood, and I feel more alive because my social life is awakening.
>
> In my town I have found very big changes. It's more alive, and it's becoming more important. In the evening in the streets it is so beautiful, so many lights, so lovely. I've got used to riding on a train. I've been three times to the Moscow Art Theater, twice to a cinema. I attended a lecture about symbolism.[16]

Her excited description of her high life in the city cannot have been welcome news to a lover in a sanatorium.

He didn't reply. By the end of November, she was getting worried. "For a long time I've had no news from you, and I'm afraid you are not getting my letters. I am still at the same address. Every day I am going to leave but something always keeps me. . . . The last time I saw all of my family [though not the two youngest], which is a rare exception, they were all in good health and asking about you."[17]

Meanwhile, she kept a low profile, living at a secret address, reading and writing in the Rumyantsev Museum, which was safer than the university library, which she would have preferred, and meeting women who had been coprisoners in the Prechistensky Jail. The news of some of them was not good. One had become insane; two others were in bad straits; a third, still only nineteen, had come out of the Butyrki Jail with wrinkled lips and a haggard face, probably due to severe dehydration.

Inessa was trying to form plans, her immediate intention being to move to Kiev with the children. She presumably believed that a smaller city, where she was not known and the Okhrana were likely to be less thorough, would be safer.

First, though, she decided to risk traveling to St. Petersburg to meet Anna, her sister-in-law, to attend Russia's first All-Women's Congress. This conference had at last been reluctantly permitted by the SD leadership, despite the party's antifeminism. For all their ideas for social change and their gestures in the direction of Chernyshevsky, they still believed that a woman's place was in the home. Alexandra Kollontai, destined to be both a comrade of Inessa and a rival, would be attending with a forty-five-member women workers' group and was certain to be prominent.

The police would be watching the congress, so Inessa had to keep a low profile—no speeches, even if she had been asked to make one; no official position, since this would have been listed. Even without the fear of the police, however, it is unlikely she would have been playing much of a role. Despite her work for the SDs, she had still not formally joined the party.

Instead, she just observed proceedings. She was interested mainly in the "Women and the Family" sections and the discussions on "Free Love," the arguments hinging on the conflict between the need for freedom of love with the fact that most women had such small incomes that this was unattainable. "They went around in this circle like a squirrel on a wheel," she wrote Volodya.[18]

The congress was not successful, and the women workers' section staged a walkout over procedural issues. Anna and Inessa soon had enough themselves.

Anna left the city, but Inessa decided to stay on until after Christmas. Clearly, it would be unwise to join the family at Pushkino, tempting though this was. Also, Kiev no longer seemed a good idea. St. Petersburg had advantages: The city was big enough for her to stay hidden. It was near the Finnish border, and the party was well established there with a good underground organization.

So Inessa rented an apartment on Kolpinsky Lane, writing to Alexander in Roubaix that her plans had changed, though she couldn't find a large enough apartment for the children. "To think," she wrote, "that for a year and a half I haven't seen them."

It was not a happy Christmas for her. "I had a terrible time," she wrote Alexander.

I felt absolutely lonely, completely despondent. I did not know such loneliness in the north as I have experienced here because, even after Volodya left, there was our circle which, through living together, became one big family.

I quite understand how spoiled I have been by life and how used I am to being surrounded by people who are close to me. But when I found how hard it was I thought that there were so many people who were alone all their lives.

However, she remained positive about the future. "I greatly hope something good will develop in my private life."[19]

It was going to be a while before things got much better for her. "The news I have of Volodya," she wrote to a friend, "is not very good. He is better, of course, but he has to stay in bed, and he's bored. He was very pleased to get your letter." She urges the friend to write again since several of Volodya's friends were out of contact for one reason or another. "Send your letters to the old address, care of Anne."

To Volodya, she wrote a deeply affectionate and grateful letter, reflecting on her gradual political ripening. "During the last stages of this, you did so much for me," she said.

It is thanks to you that I came to understand so much better and quicker the different problems of Marxism because your approach to these was so true and so deep. Finally, it was because of this last reactionary year, when I lived with proletarians, unlike previous years, that I became stronger [in my beliefs]—and because of you and your conception of the world that does not seem to have been dictated by any kind of obsession but by mature reflection.[20]

These were almost certainly the last words she ever wrote to her lover. A few days later, in early January 1909, news reached her that his condition had suddenly worsened. He had been moved urgently to a clinic in Nice for an operation, but to her the gravity of it was played down, as though the procedure would be "like piercing an abscess."

She had an anxious intuition, though, and left immediately for the south, crossing the Finnish border and then into Sweden, first by train and then by sleigh over the frozen lakes. By the time she reached the south of France, his operation was over, but he was declining fast, to the "surprise even of the doctors." Two weeks later, he died in her arms, possibly from blood poisoning.[21]

She was absolutely devastated and fled to Roubaix, to Alexander and her sons.[22] After a few weeks, she moved on to Paris, perhaps finding it easier to grieve on her own.

"His death was for me an irreparable loss," she wrote to her friend Anna Asknazy, "because he was all the happiness of my life—and without personal happiness the path of life is so very hard."[23]

Years later, when Inna was eighteen, Inessa explained to her:

I think, my dear Inochka, that everything ends with death. . . . You know, it seems to me that you only realize this when you lose someone. It is hard to believe that everything is finished and that you will never again meet the person you love. I remember that when your uncle Volodya died how distressing I found this and how much I envied your Babushka [Varvara Karlovna], who believes in an afterlife and for whom death is only a temporary parting.

But in general, down here [on earth], it seems to me that this knowledge [atheism] imprints on us the necessary spirit to fight and wrestle for a better life for us and for others.

If you believe there is an afterlife, it is easier to resign yourself to the adversities of existence in the hope of finding compensation in a better life beyond. But if you only admit to a terrestrial existence, then you want to make this as good as possible and, even if you cannot improve it for yourself, because of the time this may take, you can at least make it better for future generations.

Life for most people is today so horrible that on arriving at the end of their time on earth, they can only think of it with bitterness and wonder why they have lived.[24]

This, of course, is an argument for socialism over religion, written long after the scars of loss had healed. But Inessa had developed as a socialist, as Volodya had, and it is likely that she would have taken the same view even in 1909 when she was in desolate mourning.

Following family tradition, Volodya's parents gave ten thousand rubles in his memory toward the building of a biological-research station in Murmansk. There has been some speculation within the Armand family that Volodya committed suicide, but it has not been substantiated.

For Inessa, the future now seemed both dark and uncertain. She could not go home to Russia for fear of arrest. She had long since parted from her husband—anyway *as* a husband—and now her lover was gone. She faced a life in exile devoid of emotional stability.

"On the question of work," she wrote to Anna Asknazy,

I'm doing nothing, for it demands courage and energy, and for the time being I have none. I drag along here. I am living in a little French town until Easter. I have moved [my base] to Paris, where I hope to find something to occupy me. I would like to get to know the French Socialist Party. If I manage to do this I will at least have got a little experience and wisdom for my work when I return to it.

In Paris, she gravitated toward the avenue d'Orléans and the Café des Manilleurs, known for its Russian émigré clientele. There, she met Elena Vlasova, her fervent young friend with whom she had shared both an apartment and prison in Moscow. Elena was shocked by how "melancholy, pale and drawn" Inessa seemed. In answer to her questions, Inessa explained, "I've had a great sorrow. I have buried in Switzerland someone very close to me, who died from tuberculosis."[25]

The café allowed its Russian customers to hold meetings in a large upstairs room and to hear speakers. And it was on one of these occasions with Elena that Inessa at last met Lenin.

CHAPTER 6

PARIS 1909

Inessa had never met a man like Lenin. She had known revolutionaries in prison and at Mezen, but none for whom revolution was his whole life; none who had Lenin's knowledge and intellectual powers; none who believed it was his destiny to reshape the world. In a sense, Lenin was what Inessa had been looking for from the start, the figure of authority and dedication for whom Volodya could be seen as a necessary predecessor, since he had given her the knowledge that had prepared her for Lenin.

Inessa was thirty-five; Lenin was thirty-nine and an odd figure, for either a world leader or a lover. He had a round head that was bald except for a ring of red hair; small, dark Mongol eyes; and a short, pointed beard. Always, his clothes were crumpled, his trousers baggy and a little too long. "To look at," his friend Gleb Krzhizhanovsky once remarked, "he is like a well-heeled peasant . . . a cunning little *muzhik* [kulak]."

Most people found him unimpressive on first meeting. Later, it was always his eyes, which narrowed into slits when he smiled, that gripped them. They gave him a mobility of expression that could display an exceptional scale of emotion, ranging, according to Valentinov, an early comrade, through "thoughtfulness, mockery, biting contempt, impenetrable coldness, extreme fury."

"There is no such person," said the Menshevik Fedor Dan, "who is so preoccupied twenty-four hours a day with revolution, who thinks no other thoughts except those about revolution, who even dreams in his sleep about revolution." There would soon be competition in his thoughts, since to love Inessa, as Lenin did, after his fashion and deeply, was probably a new experience for him, despite rumors of past affairs. It is trite to say they were made for each other, but the relationship was to have that color. Certainly, she was the only woman who ever made Lenin cry even if only by her death.

As it was, this first meeting, in the company of others, seems to have had no great importance for Inessa beyond showing her the man whose works she had read and probably knew as a kind of maverick of Social Democracy. Certainly, Elena Vlasova, writing of this encounter after both of them were dead, when the Lenin hagiography was in full flood, reported no admiring comments.

Soon after this, Inessa left Paris for a holiday at Sables-d'Olonne, a resort on La Côte Sauvage in Vendée, south of Brittany. Alexander rented a large villa, named La Favorite, for the whole family. Possibly, with Volodya gone, he hoped Inessa might now return to him and live a family life, structured on more than deep friendship. It was a vain hope. He could not match what was now her basic demand of a man. He must be a revolutionary, ideally a professional, totally committed revolutionary, which Alexander, though leftish in his views, could never be.

Before the end of the holiday, Alexander suggested she come to live with him in Roubaix with the boys until his exile ended in 1910, but the thought of returning to that gloomy industrial town did not appeal to her. Instead, she proposed to take a course in political economy at the Université Nouvelle in Brussels, not far from Roubaix.

This would serve several purposes. First, the course would concentrate her mind; second, she would be away from the émigré community where, in her present emotional state, she did not feel at ease. Third, she wanted to improve her knowledge of Marxist theory, which was important to senior Social Democrats and displayed by such female highfliers as Alexandra Kollontai and Rosa Luxemburg. Inessa spoke much of the intelligentsia, of which she considered herself a part, but she knew she did not rank as a serious intellectual.

After the holiday, she moved to Brussels with the two younger children, Andre and Varvara, renting an apartment on avenue Jean Volders not far from the university. This institution had been founded only fifteen years before with something of a bohemian, radical reputation, attracting many foreign students. It was open to women, and its faculty tended to be socialist. Even so, Inessa cheated a little on the application form, suggesting that the few lectures she had attended at the University of Moscow were a year of full-time study.[1]

She was accepted for a two-year license program, but she worked hard, gaining her diploma after only ten months, on July 30, 1910. A week later, she joined Alexander with the children for a celebration in the Hotel de Graeff in Brussels. His two years of exile were over, and he was about to return to Russia. It would be some time before she saw him or her sons again.[2]

During her studies, Inessa had done some occasional work for the local Russian Social Democrats. She had also agreed to forward to Russia the party journal, *Sotsial Demokrat,* and other party literature, printed in Paris, since Brussels-sourced mail was less likely to attract attention of the Russian postal authorities.

The eighth Congress of the Socialist International was soon to be held in Copenhagen, and Inessa wrote to her main SD contact in Paris, asking if he could arrange tickets for her. To her surprise, Lenin himself wrote to the organizers to ask that Inessa's name be added to the list of official invitations.

It was an important congress, attended by most of the European socialist stars: Trotsky, Luxemburg, Martov, Lunacharsky, Plekhanov, and Chernov. Inessa was probably joined there by Anna, her sister-in-law. Lenin was, of course, in Copenhagen, and alone, although Nadya had planned to accompany him. This has tempted speculation that this period was when the affair with Inessa first started.

There is nothing to support this. Three years later, she wrote to him of the awe in which she held him for the first few months after their meeting, rendering her nearly speechless merely by coming "into the room to speak to NK [Nadya]. I did not know what to do with myself. I felt awkward and stupid. I envied those brave people who just walked in and talked with you," though this seems oddly unlike the Inessa who wrote insolent letters to prison governors and who shut her eyes to spoil mug shots.[3] Inessa's relationship with Lenin seems to have developed slowly, as had hers with Volodya.

Certainly, in September 1910, Inessa returned to Paris rejuvenated. She was in her mid-thirties, a pretty, elegant woman with luxuriant auburn hair and an aura of confidence. She was dressed in stylish clothes and interesting hats, for which she had a special fancy, presumably funded by Alexander. Her comrades spoke of her "cheerfulness" and "happy dynamism." Some went farther, maybe too far. "Life in her," reported G. N. Kotov, "seemed to spring from an inexhaustible source."

"I see her now," wrote another comrade, quoted by Louis Fischer, "leaving the home of our Lenins. Her temperament was impressive. She was a hot bonfire of revolution and the red feather in her hat was like . . . its flame."

Paris was in the belle epoque, and Ilya Ehrenburg wrote a vivid description of the city.

> I had never seen so many people in the streets. . . . Cabbies shouted at their horses and cracked their whips. In the boulevard de Sebastopol I saw a steam tram; It was hooting tragically. . . .
>
> I was amazed by the number of "pissoirs"; On them was written "Meunier Chocolate is best. . . ."

The men wore bowlers, the women huge hats with feath-
ers. On the café terraces, lovers kissed unconcernedly. . . .
There were bright posters everywhere. I felt as though I was
at the theater.

Inessa joined the Russian émigré society on the avenue d'Orléans,
of which young Ehrenburg was a member. *Sotsial Demokrat* was
produced at number 110, and the Bolsheviks met at the Café des
Manilleurs at number 11.

"I asked Savchenko [a comrade] what I should order," wrote
Ehrenburg. "She said: 'Grenadine. We all drink Grenadine' . . . red,
sickly syrup to which they added soda water. Only Lenin ordered a
mug of beer."

He heard Lenin's speeches. "He spoke calmly, without rhetoric or
emotional appeal; he slurred his *r*s a little. . . . His speeches were like
a spiral: Afraid that people wouldn't understand him, he returned to
a thought he had already expressed, never repeating it but adding
something new."

Inessa was filled with a new, exciting sense of purpose, with a
man she much admired and even, as she said, came to "love," although she wasn't "in love with him then."[4]

She soon showed her value with her languages, and Lenin, whose
French was weak, began to ask her to do his translations, notably his
oration at the funeral, after their joint suicide, of Laura Lafargue,
Karl Marx's daughter, and her husband, Paul. Inessa became close
friends with Nadya and took over from her the correspondence with
party members across Europe, while Nadya concentrated on the contacts within Russia.

Inessa moved with her two youngest children, Varvara, now nine,
and Andre, seven, into an apartment on the rue Reille, overlooking
the Parc de Montsouris, not far from Lenin's home on the rue Bon-
nier, where he lived with Nadya, her mother, and, for the present, his
favorite sister, Maria, who was ill at the time.

It is significant that Inessa, concerned as she was with the working classes, rarely refers in letters to the servants who must have moved with them, doubtless with local support, and probably tutors, for Inessa to live the life she did. In Paris, we know from her letters that there was a Russian nanny named Savushka.

When Varvara went home to Russia, probably with Alexander, Inessa moved with Andre to a boardinghouse on the rue Barrault, owned by a Russian émigré couple named Mazanov.

Meanwhile, for the first time, she joined the Bolshevik faction, being elected in due course to the Paris Committee. She also became a Bolshevik representative to the French Socialist Party, which pleased her.

At a personal level she used her fluent French to help new arrivals find work and accommodation. In early 1911, Russian exiles were flocking from all over Europe into Paris, which had become the heart of émigré activity.

Over the nine months after the Copenhagen congress, Inessa became close to the core of the Paris Bolshevik community, with Lenin and his two lieutenants Grigori Zinoviev and Lev Kamenev—known with him as "The Troika"—and with Nadya, who shared Inessa's strong feminist sympathies.

Then in June 1911, she played her first major role in Lenin's life, in the most serious fight he'd ever had within the party. At first sight, with all the factions and conferences and conflicts, like Lenin's with Bogdanov, this little world of exiles had a lilliputian quality. Few people even in Russia had ever heard of Lenin. The émigrés were almost all poor and frustrated, one even drowning himself in the Seine, and lost in fierce, passionate arguments in the street cafés about the new society that the revolution would create. *If* it ever came.

That, however, was the one thing they could all agree about, as they had to: It *would* come. The events of 1905, though six years before, had given them new hope, colored always by sentimental dreams of home. What some people might regard as failure in 1905, since the government had regained control relatively fast, the exiles saw as a standard of what could happen. The 1905 upheavals had not been planned, they reasoned, and therefore they had not been fully exploited.

Next time, Lenin would argue, they must be ready for the opportunity when it came, learn the lessons. Nineteen hundred and five had "taught the masses . . . to fight for liberty. . . . The second revolution must lead them to victory." He had flung himself into a study of military tactics, poring through General Cluseret's *On Street Fighting* and Clausewitz's *On War*.

Many of the more prominent characters in this tiny, taut community would achieve great power in the Russia that was to be created in 1917, or die in challenging it. So what Lenin did in Paris, together with his associates and his ever-growing number of opponents, would in time be reflected in his success in the revolution and on the world political stage.

The Okhrana, at least, did not underrate the exiles. The events of 1905 had been a shock for them, too. The Paris surveillance bureau reported to St. Petersburg a running account of the conflicts in Paris, as well as useful information about the parties' counterparts, legal and illegal, within Russia. They had several well-placed spies and, as it was to be discovered years later, were even covertly supporting Lenin because he was a divider, and the police encouraged division.

In Russia, though, censorship was easing. Left-wing party newspapers could be published, as long as they weren't provocative, although conversely the parties themselves remained illegal. Lenin was not slow to take advantage of this, and plans for a domestic newspaper were forming fast.

In Paris, Lenin was in severe trouble. When Inessa was still in Brussels, Lenin had faced a showdown with the Social Democratic Party, with many Bolsheviks lining up alongside the Mensheviks against him.

At a meeting of the united SD Central Committee, even with Bolsheviks in the majority, he was ordered to close down the Bolshevik Center. The Bolshevik journal *Proletarii* was to cease publishing. The leadership of the party was to be moved to Russia. The Schmidt funds were to be handed over to a group of trustees, accountable to the Central Committee.

Never before had Lenin been so diminished. When Inessa came into his life, he was still surveying the ruins. Not that he appeared to be in disarray, apart from lashing out as usual at "the liquidators," as he called those who were disenchanted with the conflicts and favored a return to legal activities. Lenin knew what must be done. He would create a new Bolshevik Party with the makeup and discipline that *he* wanted, whose members would do what he ordered, though he didn't actually admit openly that this was his purpose.

His first move in an elaborate scheme was to set up a revolutionary school in Longjumeau, a few miles south of Paris. The comrade entrusted with its organization was Inessa. This was Inessa's first step in an escalation of assignments, some linked and of growing importance. Her role at the school surprised the comrades.

There had been two similar schools before, controlled by others, in Capri and Bologna. Lenin's purpose was the same as theirs: the training of inexperienced workers in propaganda, agitation, and organization. But Lenin's aim was also to create more Bolsheviks, screened and brainwashed in his specific line, to add to the small group of supporters that still remained with him, before moving on to the next stage of his plan.

Longjumeau, in the valley of the Yvette River, was "a straggling French village stretching along the high road," as Nadya described it, "over which cartloads of farmers' produce rumbled all night to fill the belly of Paris." Lenin knew it well because he was a great cyclist and had often escaped there on weekend jaunts. Accommodation would be cheaper than in Paris, and covert surveillance, by his party rivals as well as the Okhrana, would be harder in a village than in a crowded city.

Inessa, with the usual help from Alexander, rented a house on the "Grand Rue," where everyone ate food prepared by Katya Mazanov, her Russian Paris landlady, in a communal dining room. The house had bedrooms for Inessa and Andre, as well as for three students, in-

cluding Sergo Ordzhonikidze, who would rank high after 1917, playing a special role in Inessa's life. She also rented a metalwork shop next
door, where classes were held. Inessa provided the furniture and super-
vised the daily curriculum.

The school opened on June 11, in weather that Nadya described
as "unbearably hot," with only eighteen students, including Georgi
Safarov, who would become a close comrade of Inessa's, and almost
as many lecturers, if including the part-timers, some of whom came
for barely a day. Still, future eminent figures were among them.
Meanwhile, the locals were "surprised" that "our teachers would
walk around barefoot."

Lenin and Nadya, as Nadya points out carefully in her *Memories
of Lenin,* lived at the opposite end of the village but dined with the
others in Inessa's house. Nadya seemed to have very little to do with
the school, returning often to Paris to keep up her correspondence
with members and sympathizers in Russia. She gave Inessa full credit
for "the comradely atmosphere which was created."

Lenin and Grigori Zinoviev were the two main lecturers, and
Inessa was the only female teacher. She was inexperienced, but her
university diploma and her solid experience of illegal activities in Russia provided some background.

Lenin always gave the day's opening lecture at 8:00 A.M. on aspects of Marxism, his vision of the party, and political economy before leaving for business in Paris. Inessa then conducted a class
discussion about what Lenin said.

She also gave straight lectures on political economy and various
other subjects, though Lenin would not allow her to speak on prostitution or the organization of women workers, despite the fact that
Alexandra Kollontai had run a similar course at the Bologna school.
Women's interests were not a priority for Lenin, certainly not at this
point of a new campaign.

It was not all work. "Some evenings," Nadya wrote, the students
"would go out into the field where they would sing or lie near a
haystack and talk about all sorts of things. Sometimes Ilyich would

accompany them." On weekends sometimes, students and some of their lecturers "took cycling trips or walks through the hot country-side, went swimming in the Seine, or made excursions to Paris where they saw the landmarks of the French Revolution." The closest group—"Ilyich, Armand, Sergo [Ordzhonikidze], Anatoli Lu-nacharsky—went to a theater on the outskirts of Paris," to see avant-garde or proletarian plays.

· · ·

If Lenin had been growing close to Inessa during the spring, working together at the school was to bind them further. Although there had been suspicions in Paris, many comrades believed that Longjumeau was where the affair between Lenin and Inessa developed. Inessa gave her own version when writing to Lenin in early 1914. "Only at Longjumeau in the summer and the following autumn when I did your translations did I get a bit used to you. I loved to listen to you and especially to watch you as you spoke. First, your face was so animated and then you were so absorbed that you did not notice me observing you." In the same letter, she wrote, "At this time, I was not in love with you, but I already loved you very much."[5]

Her dating may not be exact, for she wrote this letter in a state of deep and desolate sadness, very soon after their first big parting in late 1913. A degree of self-delusion has to be suspected, for again this picture of timid restraint hardly fits the Inessa of 1911 who was already Lenin's trusted colleague.

By that autumn they may not have been lovers, but Lenin was engrossed by her. The French socialist Charles Rappaport commented on how they went alone into the cafés on the avenue d'Orléans and "Lenin with his little Mongol eyes gazes all the time at this little 'Française.' " Nikolai Valentinov, another associate, reported that the affair was "never a secret for [Lenin's] old comrades such as Zinoviev, Kamenev, and [Alexei] Rykov."

Stefan Possony wrote of contemporaries who saw Lenin drinking with Inessa in a bistro in Longjumeau, where the prices were too high for most émigrés. They noted, too, "at lunch at the school how [Nadya's] mother manifested open indignation whenever Lenin conversed with Inessa."

Alexandra Kollontai told Marcel Body that Lenin "had been very much attached to Inessa" and that Nadya knew of the affair and offered to leave him "in the summer of 1911." It was not the only time Nadya made such an offer, but Lenin always asked her to stay.[6] However, according to Lidia Fotieva, one of his secretaries, Nadya gave up sharing his bedroom and moved in with her mother.[7]

Over the years, during the periods they lived apart, Lenin was to write more letters to Inessa than to anyone else, often several a day, usually about politics, since politics were his life, but also with personal concern. When Inessa died, his revealing, tear-marked grief at the funeral astonished several of his female comrades. The romantic Kollontai even suggested that the loss of Inessa contributed to Lenin's own death, four years later.

Inessa was the only person, other than his family and Martov in their early days, whom Lenin ever addressed with the intimate pronoun *ty* instead of the usual *vy*, equivalent to the French *tu* and *vous*. She addressed him in the same fashion. Even Zinoviev and Kamenev, his two nearest comrades, were *vy*, as indeed were their wives, whom he saw several times a week.

Certainly, Lenin came to rely on Inessa at times even more than on his lieutenants in the Troika. She was, of course, a veteran. They had all been in jail but not as often as she had and not in near-Arctic exile. Nadya had shared his passion and his vision but in a plodding kind of way. She understood him completely and provided him, in their endless traveling, with a base.

Inessa, on the other hand, touched his passion, flared it both intellectually and emotionally, reducing him at one level to a normal man but enlarging him at another by providing him with another voice—eventually taking his place on the platform under tight briefings—with her fluency in languages. The organizational and rhetorical talents Inessa demonstrated at Longjumeau ensured a closeness that was both emotional and professional.

On their return to Paris in September 1911, Inna and Varvara arrived back in Paris and Inessa needed more space. She rented an apartment at 2 rue Marie-Rose, next door to the Lenins' new home at number 4.

Both Nadya and Lenin enjoyed Inessa's three children, who would often pop next door. Polina Vinogradskaya, a postrevolution comrade, suggested that they were even a surrogate family for the childless couple. The story is told in Armand circles of Lenin, who came upon Andre, then age eight, and a friend as they played. "You're a Bolshevik," he told Andre. "And you," he said to the other boy, whose father he knew, "are a Menshevik."

After Inessa's death, when Lenin and Nadya lived in the Kremlin, they became informal guardians of Andre, who was then sixteen and in poor health, and Nadya retained a close friendship with Inessa's two daughters.

Inessa's relationship with Nadya is almost as intriguing as that with her husband. For despite the affair, the two women appeared to get along. Nadya came from the same sort of background as Lenin, with parents who were minor nobility. As a young girl, she had heard of his Social Democratic group with Martov and joined it. Yet their relationship lacked passion. They shared a deep faith in revolution, and there is little personal emotion in Lenin's letters to her.

When Lenin was exiled in 1897 to Shushenskoye, near the Mongolian border, Nadya applied to join him, saying she was his fiancée. He didn't argue. The taunt later was that he married her for her copperplate handwriting. She never got along with his mother or his sisters, something that was not helped when she failed to bear him children.

She was a year older than Lenin, and by 1911 she had become plain. She had put on weight with middle age, and she had bulging eyes, owing to a thyroid condition that had caused Lenin's sister Anna to comment that she looked like a herring.

The marriage had always been a working relationship—marriage anyway being deprecated by revolutionaries as bourgeois—but they shared a common sense of humor as well as common ideals. It was not unhappy.

If Lenin's relations with Inessa came to a head at Longjumeau, it would seem he convinced Nadya that he was not going to leave her, possibly because of a lingering bourgeois past or of a belief that a broken marriage was undesirable in a future statesman. Maybe, too, he was comfortable with a wife who provided the stability he lacked.

At any rate, she clearly accepted Inessa in their life, and until 1916, Inessa was to live near them. Inessa shared their holidays, and they shared her children on their frequent visits.

This, then, was the situation in the autumn of 1911. Lenin was planning his next move, and again Inessa was put in charge of organizing it. Incredibly, he proposed to seize control of the whole Social Democratic Party.

To achieve this objective it had to be agreed to by vote in an SD Party conference, where, on the face of it, there would be no chance of success. Not only was Lenin at odds with all the leading figures in the SD movement, but many of his own Bolsheviks were now opposed to him, too. His tactic was to keep the attendance thin and to load it with his supporters, especially Longjumeau students, who had been exposed to brainwashing about the Lenin line.

There were SD groups in cities all over Europe. Some were split into the Menshevik and Bolshevik factions; some still operated as one party. And until Longjumeau it had been Inessa's job to maintain contact with them—which was to have its uses now.

Lenin's plan was to call a party conference in January 1912, in Prague, which was not the easiest place to get to and required a passport, not then needed in some countries. Lenin gave very short notice and shrugged off criticisms that he was rushing the conference for no good reason, though Lenin's reasons were always suspect. And why Prague, in mid-winter, for Heaven's sake? He persisted, and Inessa made arrangements. She was skillful, ensuring a pro-Lenin Bolshevik majority by sending invitations to only a few sympathetic Mensheviks and "forgetting" the more critical of the Bolsheviks. Trotsky, who edited his own newspaper in Vienna, saw what was happening and angrily announced his own conference to be held later, which suited Lenin and Inessa because many Mensheviks who might otherwise have come to Prague uninvited opted to wait for Vienna instead.

In the event, only eighteen people attended Lenin's Prague conference, and eight of these had been "indoctrinated" at Longjumeau. Only two Mensheviks turned up. But despite his substantial majority, Lenin did not have too easy a time. He was opposed on some issues, especially by Sergo Ordzhonikidze, who lived in Russia and believed the leadership should be sited there. He was supported in this by a majority vote. But Lenin achieved his principal aim—an overwhelming vote that effectively empowered him to appoint a new SD Central Committee, all except one being Bolsheviks. But despite this triumph, he was forced to concede that only two—namely, himself and Zinoviev—could live abroad in exile.

There was an outcry across the whole movement, but it was technically a Party Conference decision. Soon, too, there would be a new party journal, to be named *Pravda,* which Lenin would also control—at least so he thought, though this was to be more difficult than he expected.

Prague was not, really, accepted as a fully legitimate Party Conference. Lenin's opposition knew exactly what he had done and how he had done it. It was dirty work that Inessa had been doing for him, but although the party, in its new form, faced a shaky few years of challenge, it would survive.

Lenin expected the Mensheviks to wither, which never quite happened, but they did lack the disciplined virility of the Bolsheviks and a leader of strength.

One of the members of the Central Committee of the new party was Roman Malinovsky, whom Lenin much admired. But Malinovsky, soon to be a Duma delegate, had also become an Okhrana spy. This, in fact, aided Lenin for the Okhrana was backing his divisive policy and increased his control of the Central Committee in Russia by arresting those Bolshevik members who were not total supporters. With each arrest his influence grew—as did Malinovsky's—since this gave him an opportunity to promote their replacement with activists he could rely on for support.[8]

. . .

A few weeks later, in March, Inessa wrote to Alexander in a curious way. She enclosed a letter to a lawyer named Malyantovich, who'd had past contacts with wealthy industrialists. "Please read this," she instructed him, "and intercede with the two people mentioned in it . . . and take it yourself to Malyantovich and tell him that this letter is from Lenin and that he has signed it as Ulyanov only for conspiracy purposes in case the letter falls into the wrong hands. . . . Say that the affair will go forward in the very near future—i.e., between March and May."[9]

One "affair," which took place between March and May, R. C. Elwood speculates, was the launch of *Pravda* on April 22, adding that the Central Committee had been informed that "the heir of a certain factory owner" had promised three thousand rubles. "It is reasonable to conclude . . . that Inessa's husband was actively involved in raising money for the paper."

"Good-bye, my dear Sasha," she ended rather intriguingly, "write to us quickly. . . . Anya is worried about your acquaintance, and she would like to know what is going on with her. We read your letter two or three times. And, because we are women with imagination, we have two interpretations, and they are radically different." Could this be Anna Arbels, the widow of a friend of his, who became his first postmarital lady friend? Or his sister Anna, who was often called Aunt Anya?

. . .

By now, Lenin was making plans to leave Paris, which, with all his angry party critics, was a trial for him at this time. The furious arguments, at which he excelled and so often provoked, were becoming tedious. In June, he moved his base to Cracow, close to the Russian border. Once the capital of the Kingdom of Poland, it was a beautiful city that was now in Austrian Galicia. Zinoviev, with his wife, Zinaida, and their little son, Robert, moved with them. Kamenev remained in Paris.

There were other reasons for the move. Lenin was better positioned there to exploit the fact that, though the party itself was suffering from arrests, party newspapers could, with care, be published in Russia. Correspondence, too, was much easier. "Peasant women from Russia," Nadya recalled, "would come to market in Cracow and for a small fee would take our letters across and drop them into the letter boxes in Russia." Without foreign postmarks, the letters were ignored by Russian police.

Also, the comrades could cross the border with *polupaska,* special semipassports permitting locals to cross. At the frontier, the names of the passengers were called and each had to answer "present" in Polish. A comrade, Nikolai Krylenko, who lived in Lublin, near the border, supplied addresses they could go to on the Russian side. "Once, we got Stalin across that way," wrote Nadya.

Perhaps the best aspect of life in Cracow was that unlike the French police, who cooperated willingly with the Okhrana, the Polish police "did not spy on us, nor intercept our correspondence and . . . had no contacts with the Russian police."

Which is not to say that Lenin was without problems. The editors of *Pravda* were not publishing some of his articles and were changing the slant of others.

So someone would have to go to St. Petersburg to persuade the editors to conform with the new party line. Lenin decided to send Inessa, his troubleshooter, even though this would expose her to extreme risk, since she was a "wanted" woman in Russia. With the Okhrana infiltration that was always feared, the chances of her arrest were very high. As usual, Lenin did not allow personal considerations to guide party decisions.

Lenin briefed her on her mission, which turned out to go far beyond dealing with the *Pravda* rebels. He wanted her to repair the St. Petersburg Committee, the most important in Russia, which had been badly fractured, both morally and numerically, by Okhrana activity. He also wanted her to take charge of the plans for the elections to the Fourth Duma. Again, the local Bolsheviks were joining forces with the Mensheviks in joint Social Democratic campaigns. Didn't they know that this was forbidden?

The best person for such a mission was clearly Lenin himself, but no physical risks could be expected of the future leader of the revolution. With the aid of Nadya, Lenin gave contacts in St. Petersburg to Inessa and her comrade Georgi Safarov, a veteran of the Longjumeau School. Inessa did not hesitate. She was proud to take on such an important, top-level duty for the cause, a bigger task even than fixing the Prague result, and one which clearly reflected Lenin's trust in her.

With Safarov, she crossed the border, using a passport in the name of a peasant woman named Frantsiska Kazimirovna Yankevich that aged her at twenty-eight (not thirty-seven). She dressed for the part in old boots and tattered shawl.

Lenin had calculated the danger. He wrote Kamenev: "The two of them are already on their way. If they are not arrested, this will be useful." Inessa was valuable to him, but perhaps more easily spared than the other senior members, who were men.

There was no chance of their avoiding arrest. Their orders were to contact Nikolai Krylenko in Lublin. He would provide the help they needed to get to the capital. They reached St. Petersburg without trouble, but already an Okhrana dossier had recorded the return from abroad of Elizaveta Armand, together with her assumed name and her disguise as a Polish peasant.[10]

But they didn't arrest her. Not yet. She could be a useful lead for some time.

CHAPTER 7

ST. PETERSBURG 1912

There was something quaint, even farcical about the clandestine venture of Lenin's two recruits as they crossed the border into Russia. They were doomed before they started, given the Okhrana's information, and though Lenin didn't know this, his decision to send them—either of them—is strange.

He was clearly very worried about what was going on in St. Petersburg. The city party was in a total mess as a result of Okhrana raids back in May, provoked by strikes. These had also eliminated many of Nadya's secret addresses for correspondence or foreign-printed party papers. And bringing the dissenting *Pravda* editors into line would require a heavy hand.

Yet to deal with these big problems he sent a boy of twenty-one and a woman, elegant though she was, dressed as a Polish peasant. And Inessa, with her criminal background, long wanted by the Okhrana, was dangerous to anyone she met. Neither of them had any formal ranking in the party beyond their ties to Lenin, whose current standing was itself in question.

However, they reached the capital without any dramas, which, since the Okhrana was waiting and watching, was not strange. It is not clear where they stayed. Georgi Safarov's father, an architect of some note, lived in the city, though his home might have seemed a dangerous place to go.

Safarov had been condemned to exile two years before.

At the Longjumeau school, Safarov and his young wife, Valentina, had become close friends with Inessa. Since the two of them were traveling together, the Okhrana drew conclusions, and recorded that Inessa was his mistress.[1] However, it was an area in which the Okhrana's judgments were often faulty. They did not link Inessa intimately with Lenin until 1916, by which time she had withdrawn from him in an almost total, but temporary, break.

Still, a sexual relationship with Safarov was possible, given the dangers they were sharing, and the fact that she clearly liked younger men; but there is no evidence of it. Certainly, on her return to Galicia the following year, she was still deeply in love with Lenin, as she would be for the rest of her life.

Inessa and Safarov faced serious obstacles in their mission. Not only had the police raids broken the party underground into a series of individual cells that lacked links with each other, but they found that many of the Bolsheviks believed that Lenin's policy at Prague was wrong. There were many advantages to collaboration with the Mensheviks. Lenin was too far away, and they did not sympathize with his need to control.

So there was resistance. Safarov recorded that for a couple of weeks they "wandered about Petersburg in vain and at considerable risk," dressed in old, worn boots and clothes—"far away," as V. I. Malakhovsky, a comrade, put it, "from the Paris fashions" of Inessa's past life in Moscow, which would seem to be overstating it a little.[2]

Inessa wrote to Alexander, thanking him for money that "arrived just in time since I was down to my last kopek. . . . The weather lately has been very poor. Everywhere is damp. . . . I have a bad cold and a fever. . . . I take quinine . . . in a few days I will be all right."

Almost certainly the two emissaries met A. M. Korelkov early on, although Safarov doesn't mention him.[3] Korelkov had reestablished underground cells in three areas including, most important, the Narva industrial district, where the factories of the great Putilov Corporation, the biggest engineering complex in Russia, handled government orders for ships and artillery.

Korelkov, too, favored a united party. Even so, he allowed the duo to address Putilov workers about the Duma elections, and many were subsequently reported to be impressed by Lenin's position following the Prague Conference.

This brought Inessa and Safarov into touch with the left of the party in the Narva district. From this, contact was made with cells in other areas, which, after some months, developed into a newly formed St. Petersburg Committee, as Lenin had ordered.

By and large, it was heavy going, though they were making a degree of progress. They had far greater difficulties with *Pravda*, which was ironic if Alexander had indeed provided some of its funding. The editors refused to talk to them, and, according to one report, an associate of the paper "threatened to kick them down the stairs."[4]

Inessa, opting for a less direct approach, made contact quietly with Konkordia Samoilova, secretary to the editorial board, who was to become a leading feminist Bolshevik. Samoilova arranged a meeting with the editors, but this achieved little. They still refused to print many of Lenin's articles.

The shadow of the Okhrana loomed over Inessa and Safarov wherever they went. "The police watched us constantly," recorded Evgenya Adamovich, a close comrade. "We were well hidden, but the circle was getting tighter." The agency even knew that Inessa had seen a dentist named Rogovin. On August 27, police operatives, in the form of Technical Group 1143 of State Security, accompanied her by train to Moscow. Their report mentions visits to the apartment of Renee, Inessa's sister, as well as those of Alexander's brothers Boris and Sergei.[5] They make no mention of Inessa seeing her children, but there is little doubt that she met them, possibly hidden from street surveillance by Renee or one of the others.

Back in St. Petersburg, Inessa and Safarov held Sunday meetings with workers, sometimes more than one hundred, in a field near the railroad track, rich with mushrooms, which they could all pretend to be picking when the police appeared. "The Pharaohs [mounted police] tried to interfere, but they didn't succeed," reported Safarov. He did not explain why.[6]

By this means, Inessa and Safarov were able to influence the decision for six Bolsheviks to stand for election on a separate Leninist Bolshevik slate—instead of being multifaction SDs—to the Fourth Duma. One of them made it in due course, a minor coup, though there were other Bolshevik deputies who were not of the Prague persuasion.

The election, too, was marked by setbacks. Inessa had rather desperately called a meeting at the Women's Mutual Aid Society on September 14 with the aim of raising the preelection pressure. The Okhrana decided to strike, surrounding the building and arresting the fourteen Social Democrats inside.

Inessa was held in solitary in the city's Police Prison. For two weeks she was constantly interrogated, all the while denying she was anyone but the Polish peasant she claimed to be. At last, agents from Moscow who knew her arrived in St. Petersburg with photographs, and there was no longer any point in pretending she was not Inessa Armand.[7]

Once she admitted her real identity, she insisted she had entered Russia undercover only to arrange her children's schooling. Again, she was not believed. In any event, she had long been wanted for her escape from Mezen. It became apparent that she was going to stand trial, which until then, without serious evidence of her revolutionary activities, she had never had to face.[8]

For six months, Inessa was kept in solitary, where, once again, she had to work to keep her sanity, her identity, and her health. None of her letters from this period have survived, except one to Inna in which she requested books. She was allowed occasional visits by Alexander.

The northern winter, however, in a damp prison cell began to damage her health. She became ill with the early signs of TB. Her handwriting suggested deep fatigue. At last, on March 20, 1913, Alexander obtained her temporary release on health grounds until her trial, still five months away, against bail of 5,400 rubles.[9] This was a huge sum. (It is part of Armand legend that the family had to sell a large area of woodland to raise the cash to cover her bail.) Safarov's bail, by comparison, was only 500 rubles.

For the time being, however, Inessa could return to Pushkino and her beloved children, to recover before a prolonged trip with them down the Volga and on to Stavropol in the Caucasus, where they were joined for a time by Alexander. "How pretty is the Volga," she wrote later to Inna, remembering especially "the early mornings at Stavropol. I remember when Sasha and I went to meet Fidia. It was still dark, and then dawn gradually came. When we arrived at the quay, it was already light, and the river and the sky were an unusually tender shade of pink. I loved our time at Stavropol."[10]

At the end of June, she wrote to Alexander that she was awaiting summons to trial, had appointed a lawyer and witnesses, two of whom were Alexander and her sister-in-law Anna. She was looking forward to his joining them in Stavropol. On August 4, she wrote that the term of exile had been shortened and would end on August 6, though quite why is not clear. However, by then she had also received the summons for her trial on August 27. "As you will see, I give you the pleasant news first and the bad news last. I hug you. Did you get back all right? It's so bad without you."[11]

She did not stand trial. By then, apparently at Alexander's urging, she had crossed the border illegally, as she had in 1909, and was in Finland, having jumped bail. Sending Alexander a card in August, she wrote: "I am in a rush to drop you a line. I have been a bit ill, but generally things are going all right, and the doctor assures me that by Monday I will feel well enough. I kiss you hard—and everyone." An archival note says that this is code, indicating she is delayed a bit but hopes to be across the Finnish border into Sweden by Monday.[12]

From Stockholm a few days later, she sent another card, this time bearing a picture of a lady wearing only a body stocking. "I have been here for two days already, but I haven't been to the Post Office since nothing could have arrived from you yet. I am waiting for news impatiently. . . . I am concerned about a lot of things I cannot mention. I will only stay here a few days. I am writing to you now for the third time. Have you received the rest of my cards?"[13]

It was September when she next wrote to Alexander. She had joined Lenin and his group in Poronin, a village about eighty miles from Cracow, in the Tatra foothills.

> My dear, I am already in Austria and will probably stay some time. . . . At last I have received your telegram. I have been terribly worried. I couldn't understand why there was no news from you. . . . There is not much to write about yet. I am staying in mountains of nine thousand feet. . . . Streams are running just below my window. It is raining all the time. . . . I think you are likely to be in Moscow. . . . Has Fidia passed his exam? What about Varya and Inna? Have they started studies with Nikolai Evgenevich [Alexander's brother]? I regret a lot that I obeyed [you]. I kiss you hard. Please kiss Mama and my sisters.[14]

She had arrived at Poronin when a party conference was in progress with Bolsheviks from various parts of Poland and Russia, including most of Lenin's Central Committee. As Nadya put it, "Inessa flung herself into party work with her usual ardor," adding that "Malinovsky was in a terribly nervous state; he would get drunk night after night, would become maudlin and complain he was mistrusted." With good reason, of course, though Lenin would never accept the rumors of Malinovsky's Okhrana connections. These became very dangerous to Lenin, who was his protector. At last, after the revolution, it was forced on him with the opening of the Okhrana files.

They stayed in Poronin for two weeks after the conference. "We walked a good deal," wrote Nadya in her memoirs, "and visited Czarny Staw, a lake of extraordinary beauty. All of us became very much attached to Inessa. She always seemed to be in good spirits. . . . It seemed cozier and livelier when Inessa was present."

Nadya's memories of this period appear strange, but she was writing much later—in this case, 1933. "We had known her in Paris, but there was a large colony there, whereas in Cracow we lived in a small, comradely isolated circle. . . . She told us a great deal about her life and about her children; she showed me their letters and in speaking about them she seemed to radiate warmth and ardor."

Are they strangers then? These children, who lived next door to her in the rue Marie Rose in Paris, who dropped in often to see her? Was Longjumeau not a small circle? She makes a point that Inessa rented a room in Poronin where Kamenev lived, distancing her from Lenin's house.

"Ilyich, Inessa, and myself did a lot of walking. Zinoviev and Kamenev dubbed us the 'Hiker's Party.' We usually took walks along the meadows outside the town. The Polish word for meadow is 'blon,' and it was from this that Inessa assumed the pseudonym of 'Blonina' "—and, indeed, this is why Varvara's daughter is named Blona.

Nadya writes of Inessa's music. "Ilyich was particularly fond of Beethoven's *Moonlight Sonata,* and he always asked her to play it." In fact, although Lenin liked Inessa to play for him, he was not a great music lover and was bored by the concerts she made them attend in Austria. Lenin distrusted music because he saw it as weakening. He confided to Maxim Gorky, after listening to Beethoven's *Appassionata,* that it "is amazing, more-than-human music. I want to utter gentle stupidities and stroke the heads of people . . . who can create such beauty."

Despite her later recital of pleasant sunny memories, Nadya surely must have been aware at the time of a dramatic undercurrent, which can be glimpsed in Inessa's letters. By the end of September, her earlier plan of staying in Galicia was changing. Inessa wrote Alexander that she was wondering where to go, considering Paris, "but most of the people I used to know have left Paris or have died." She wanted to settle soon and have the children with her. But her mood seems good. "Spoil me a little please. Send me 'chewing' candy and even some red caviar if the season is not over yet."[15]

A little while later, she wrote to him again. They were now back in Cracow. She said that the children should now be sent to Vienna, subject to final plans. She asked for some money to be forwarded in Nadya's name.[16]

Soon she was writing with yet another change. She had decided to stay in Cracow. What was his opinion? She had received the parcel, she said, presumably of caviar, but not the money.[17]

Then, on November 22, signs of serious trouble appeared. She asks Alexander to delay sending the children until Christmas. She has not arranged to rent an apartment, although Nadya had been helping her look for one.[18] But the children would not be going to Cracow at all. Three weeks later, Inessa had fled to the Mazanov boardinghouse in Paris. Nadya rationalized that "there was nothing in Cracow which could provide Inessa with an outlet for her abundant energies," but this was clearly a colossal understatement. Inessa and Lenin had been locked in the second big crisis of their affair, if the early stages after Longjumeau when Nadya offered to leave is seen as the first.

It is clear that following her return to Galicia the affair had acquired a new dynamic. Stefan Possony has suggested that all that walking was not as a threesome, as Nadya suggests, but as a couple. In fact, Nadya had recently had a serious goiter operation without anesthetic in Bern or any proper convalescence, and would hardly have been up to such athletic exercise.

Whether or not Possony's speculation is correct, the affair seems to have escalated. This, it appears, became too much for Lenin, who decided to end it—as is spelled out in painful detail in a long letter Inessa wrote over a kind of lost weekend, using the intimate *ty*.

PARIS, Saturday morning.

Dear one,

Here I am in La Ville Lumière [city of light], and the first impression is most repugnant. Everything irritates me here—the gray of the streets, the overdressed women, the casually overheard conversations, and even the French language.

When I arrived at the Boulevard St. Michel and the Avenue d'Orléans etc., memories were seeping from every corner. I became so sad it was scaring. I was remembering old moods, feelings, thoughts and was desolate that they would never return. Everything seemed so "green." Perhaps this is a stage that we have already passed, and anyway it is sad to think that one will never [again] be able to think like this, to feel like this, to approach reality in the same way, and then one regrets that life is passing by.

It was sad because Arosa was so temporary, so transitory. Arosa was so close to Cracow while Paris is, well, so final. You and I have parted, we have parted, my dear, and it is so painful. You'll never come back here again! I know it!

When I gaze at these places I know so well, I realize more clearly than ever how big a place you occupied in my life here in Paris, so that almost all activity has been bound by a thousand threads to my thoughts of you. . . .

Even here I could cope without your kisses if only I could see you. To talk with you sometimes would be such a joy for me—and this could not cause pain to anyone. Why deprive me of that?

You asked me if I am angry with you for "carrying through" our separation. No, for I don't think that it was for your own sake that you did it.

In Paris my relations with NK were very good. Only recently, in Galicia, she told me that I had become dear and close to her, and I myself have loved her from almost the first meeting. She has such charm and softness. Her comrades and friends trust her implicitly with their confidences.

When I was in Paris I liked coming to see her in her office. I would sit by her table and talk about Party matters first and then stay later talking about all sorts of things.[19]

This section of the letter was written on a Saturday morning in Paris and Inessa was to devote many more hours to this confessional document. (Other excerpts from it are cited in chapter 6.)

The letter is a riddle, though, or rather several riddles. First, there is the reference to Arosa, which is the name of a remote Swiss mountain town, with words that are significantly emotional. She says it is "close" to Cracow which, geographically, it is not.

Clearly, it seemed when the letter was released to the archives, she meant "close" in time or, just possibly, in heights of passion. The impression was that Lenin had been with her in an idyllic, stolen few days in the mountains—unlikely though that seemed.

Also, it had always been hard to pinpoint a date when Lenin, whose movements have been closely charted, and Inessa could have been in Arosa together.

There was then no mountain railway, and it took some seven hours by carriage to reach the resort from the nearest main-line station at Chur, which itself was some three hours from Zurich, so this difficulty of access would have put even greater limits on such a meeting.

There were other theories: that Arosa was the name of a village or a hotel or was even code for somewhere else that *was* physically close to Cracow.

R. C. Elwood, one of Inessa's biographers, while on holiday in Arosa, was loaned some old copies of the *Aroser Fremdenblatt*, a weekly newsletter naming the guests staying at the resort. Inessa was in fact listed in the issues of December 23, 1913, and January 1, 1914.[20]

She *was* accompanied—but by Anna, her sister-in-law, not by Lenin. However, the emotional tone of her letter tempts speculation that Anna was a cover for Lenin, but it is unlikely that Lenin spent Christmas and the New Year holiday away from his wife.

So it seems that Inessa was referring to a period of coping with the parting, of absorbing what was clearly a devastating blow, and deciding where the future lay. Her return in January to Paris with all its memories did not make this any easier.

Historians have combed the letter for evidence of the affair, but why is it in the file at all? Then there is the riddle of the letter's date. It was clearly written in January, since she refers in it to her stay in Arosa, not December as is written in pencil on the original. Lenin's records are no help, as he never referred to it—not even in the postscripts of letters in which he did sometimes make apologetic allusions to the pain he had caused her or to the anger he had inspired. Certainly, no other intimate letters to her have survived, with good reason: in June 1914, Lenin ordered Inessa to bring him "our letters" (that is, his letters to her), presumably out of fear of future compromise.[21] He insisted that she not send them by registered mail, since he did not trust the postal authorities. He wanted to destroy the letters, as was the fate of any sent to him by Inessa, except for this letter from Paris, which remains in the file.

The reason for its survival, almost certainly, is that she never sent it. Presumably, Inna found it among her mother's papers after her death.

Without question, it is genuine. Anyone researching her life and reading her letters will know her style, her voluble phraseology, and her small, sharp hand, writing to the extreme edges of her favorite tinted paper.

Also, her insistence of a warm affection for Nadya suggests that she would have accepted an open ménage à trois. Cynics might see the letter as a feminine ploy, a step on the road to something more. This, though, would be out of character. Inessa was never devious or clever in this way.

If she proposed this to Lenin verbally, which is doubtful, or in some other way, he clearly turned it down, either because it would not have looked good for a statesman in that period or out of concern for Nadya. In Russia after the revolution, his special relationship with Inessa was known at the higher levels, and indeed this provided her with unique influence, but it remained as surmise.

Her break with Lenin was not Inessa's only cause for concern at the time, as her long letter goes on to say. Inessa returned to Paris, it seems, still troubled deeply by her possible role in the suicide of a young girl comrade.

Saturday night.

If I am sad it is because my anguish torments me when I think of Tamara. Yes, Tamara's death was a horror that I can't get over, and at the same time it had something tantalizing in it—as some people are affected by passing trains—finding them both frightening and tempting. And the most awful part is my suspicion that I have some guilt for her death. I want to tell you how it happened.

I got to know Tamara in Paris, and we were attracted to each other from the start. She visited us every day, spent holidays with us, becoming something like an elder daughter. She was a lot younger than me, and my feeling for her was maternal. That's certain.

She was very lonely and enjoyed my tenderness. She'd ask me to caress her, and it was like caressing my children. And in her affection for me, there was an element of adoration. We liked spending evenings together. The children go to bed. Savushka retires. And the house is totally silent. We are in my room. More often, she is sitting in my armchair; I am on the carpet close to her, and we talk sometimes until the early hours of the morning.

At times, our conversation was very intimate. We argued, discussed different questions. And these made us even closer. But then one evening the harmony was broken.

The children and Savushka were away visiting, and we were alone in the house. It was a winter evening, and the brazier was on, with the doors open. She was squatting by the fire, and I was next to her on a log basket. We were talking about what the life of Social Democrats should be. She assured me that they should give up everything for the sake of the cause.

I was a bit irritated by that because I thought for her it was only words . . . words which very often vary from deeds. And it was painful for me to see this in Tamara.

From that day, peace was over between us. I found myself repeating often, "These are your words, and these are your deeds." I teased her unmercifully. "You are staying abroad without real need." Our discussions became colored by irritation and anger. . . .

And then the decisive moment came when the words could be turned into deeds. Tamara decided to go back to Russia, but in Paris there was a man she was in love with but who could not go with her. It was a hard conflict: to stay in Paris and lose her self-respect [as a revolutionary] or to lose a man she loved.

And that conflict broke Tamara, and who knows, if it had not been for my interference, maybe that vague dream would have remained a vague dream. . . . I didn't understand that Tamara was a very beautiful but very fragile and tender flower. "Life" was already too hard for her, and she just needed to be petted. Then probably the flower could have been supported. . . . I am afraid that I only helped "Life" to

put a greater burden on her, because I assure you I loved her
so much, and when this thought comes into my head, and it
came in Cracow, I am horrified. I hate myself.

Two aspects of this story are particularly remarkable. Here she
is grieving for her broken affair with Lenin, and she chooses to
speak of this unhappy memory, which clearly still troubles her. Even
now, she is afraid it will bore him, and she marked the start and end
of the Tamara story with crosses, saying he can skip straight to the
end section if he wishes. But why hasn't she mentioned it to him before? Possibly, she was ashamed. Also, there is a hint of a lesbian
color which Lenin, ascetic and at base prudish, might not have approved. (There is no other such indication in her life.) She empha-
sizes that her feelings were "certainly maternal," as if checking his
suspicions.

The story sheds light on Inessa's highly emotional state. She is
more or less alone—though in the familiar Mazanov boardinghouse.
It would seem that she has a great need to confess her grief to Lenin,
almost as though the lover is a father figure.

$$\cdot\ \cdot\ \cdot$$

On Sunday morning, she continues with the letter, though this sec-
tion is about business. It is emotionally important because it indicates
to Lenin that she wishes to continue to work for the party. This is
what Lenin wants, too, as he has relied heavily on Inessa for important assignments attended by much risk, with no glimmer of complaint from her. But he cannot continue with the affair in the form it
seems to have acquired in Poronin. Inessa is indicating that she is prepared to go along with him on this, and she means it. But she is
human, and he cannot rid himself of all emotional interference. At
least not forever.

She reports on people she has met on her return and seeks political guidance (or orders) before adding:

All right, my dear, enough for today. I want to send this letter off. There was no letter from you yesterday. I am so worried that my letters are not reaching you. I have sent you three letters [this is the fourth] and a telegram. Have you not received them? I have various crazy thoughts about it. I also wrote to NK, to my "brother" [Kamenev's cover] and to Zina [Zinovieva]. Hasn't anyone received anything? I kiss you hard. Your Inessa.

If it is doubtful that this long emotional letter reached him, it is perhaps because it could serve no purpose. Only a few days after Inessa returned from Arosa, Lenin arrived suddenly in Paris with Malinovsky, and they, too, stayed in the Mazanov house.[22]

CHAPTER 8

PARIS 1914

eaders are made and developed in the struggle," wrote Nadya. "It is from the struggle they draw their strength." Lenin, she said, furiously resisted any attempt to "back out" from the proletarian cause, dubbing that "opportunism." "He would break off relations with his closest friends if he thought they were hampering the movement; and he could approach an opponent of yesterday in a simple and comradely way if the cause required it. . . .

"The years of exile . . . drained much of Lenin's strength. But they made him the fighter the masses needed."

What room was there in such a man for love?

In the last few days of that December 1913, the letters to Paris came fast, though it is doubtful Inessa was there to receive them. Acutely aware of their crisis, Lenin quickly established their new situation, writing between December 1913 and August 1914 more than forty orders or screams of rage (at others, not at her—not yet), but touched occasionally with soft notes of concern for her and what had happened between them. All his letters up until August 1914 used the informal *ty* to her.

People only write letters when they are apart, and it was not until he moved to Galicia that he was parted from her for any length of time—except after he dispatched her to Russia when he probably didn't write for reason of caution. And she was in no position to serve the cause!

His first letter to her is dated December 18—two weeks or so before she started writing her long letter. "What's happened to the Central Organ? [*Sotsial Demokrat*]. . . . Inquire and get an explanation, please."[1]

In another note, he is furious with Karl Kautsky, the German socialist leader, because he has written in a journal the "rotten phrase that there is no party" (meaning Lenin's new one). He orders Inessa to organize a protest campaign.

Interestingly, his next letter, dated the end of December, lacks a few lines at the start, being torn off in mid-sentence, and also at the end—suspicious, but not typical of later Soviet censors, who just omitted what should not be printed.[2]

In the first, he writes of "the campaign for the working masses in Russia. The majority are for us!" How has that been achieved? "By 'cunning' forms of the underground." And he displays such cunning, urging her, in a final sentence, to "set about the woman's journal superenergetically!" knowing this will please her. He has long given this project a low ranking, like other men in the party. And, in truth, still does, but it is a sop to her that will also appeal to other feminists.

The plan for a woman's newspaper, *Rabotnitsa* (Woman worker), had long been discussed by the party's senior women, including Nadya, Lenin's sisters Anna and Maria, and such personalities as Lyudmilla Stal, Zinaida Lilina Zinovieva, and Konkordia Samoilova, who had tried to help Inessa with the *Pravda* impasse in St. Petersburg. There was much logic to it: The number of women working in the nation's factories had been soaring with the phasing out of child labor. Their wages were nearly half male pay, which made them popular with employers.

Inessa got to work in January 1914 with Stal, who was also living in Paris. But it soon became obvious that Lenin had other plans for her.

He was devious. "Put me down on the list of speakers of January 9 [Bloody Sunday] if it is useful for your success—financially—but with my right to let you down. Privately, I declare that even if I am in Paris on January 9, I won't go." Not with "such a bunch of assorted animals."[3]

In another letter, he warns that

> the conciliators of all shades [who want a unified SD Party] are out to catch us. Bon! We'll catch those scoundrels, those ridiculous mountebanks. They're getting stuck in the mud. . . . Our tactic is: Give [them] time to sink deeper into the mud. That's where we shall catch the scoundrels.
>
> Meantime we've got . . . to learn as much as we can. Paris is convenient for finding out things and for "diversions."[4]

It should be remembered that all these "scoundrels" are political exiles, too, and want broadly the same revolution as Lenin does. At base, his fury is about method, strategy, and, of course, control.

While Lenin was in Paris for a week in January, he focused on helping Inessa whip into line the Paris Bolsheviks and the Foreign Organizational Committee, who were being far too lazy. He enjoyed the visit, writing to his mother that "there is no better or more lively a city to stay in for a short time."[5]

This is surprising, for he had a rough time politically. Malinovsky was "heckled by a large and hostile audience"—about the splitting of the Party, as usual—ending with "Malinovsky in tears and the crowd chanting 'Lenin, Lenin, Lenin.'" At a personal level, though, the visit might have given Lenin and Inessa a chance to try out their new relationship.

After moving on to Brussels for a meeting, Lenin wrote to Inessa as a confidante. She had written to him, after he'd gone, a letter that must have pleased him. He rushed off a brief note about a conference he had attended—"Victory! Hurrah! The majority are for us"—before responding to her at length, starting: "Dear Friend, I was terribly glad to receive your nice, friendly, warm, charming letter. I am inexpressibly grateful to you for it." It is tempting to wonder if the "warm charming letter" that he is so grateful for is an edited version of the long letter she had drafted before his surprise arrival.

He confides that "things here [in Brussels] have gone worse." *Pravda*'s circulation was dropping. The "conciliators" have not been stuck in the mud yet but have gained ground and will now "have it all their own rotten way."[6]

Two days later, he wrote to her once more. (The first two pages are missing from the original.)[7] Excited by a new way of getting literature into Russia—organized with Belgian seamen by Ivan Popov—he demands that she arrange and finance publishing and printing in Paris.

Inessa took on the job, as she took on others, without complaint. She also deployed "her speciality" as a fund-raiser, seeking money for the party in America and Switzerland with some success. By May, the Bolshevik faction had developed a new dynamic with more than ninety members.

By then, Lenin's capricious relationship with Inessa is marked by a slight change. "My dear friend," he wrote from Cracow in early March in a letter that was censored, "you answered my sad letter, but I have completely forgotten when, how, or why I wrote anyway. This is the inconvenience of corresponding from afar, but I will continue talking to you in spite of the distance and time."[8] What could have made him sad? Sometimes he became battle weary, but perhaps he missed her.

Inessa continued to hanker for her children, who still had not arrived. "What an awful daughter you are," she scolded Inna, now nearly sixteen, for not writing.

I think I did not beat you enough. I am glad you have kept your word [studying hard] and not going to the cinema until Christmas. As for dancing, why should you stop it? Losha's circle is not right for you, though I understand very well. You feel as bold as a lion there, but cavaliers and coquette mesdemoiselles are not worth much. With time you will find your own company in which you may not feel a lion, but you WILL feel comfortable—and not just for dancing.

She wonders if Sasha and Fidior can dance, sadly guesses that "too much time has gone by" for the much-loved dog to remember her, and complains that no one writes. "My dear Inushka, I am very upset—nothing from either you or Papa. From no one. Except for a postcard."

It is an old refrain, but then she cheers up. "You'll be coming to me soon." She is still living at Katya Mazanova's but will move when the children arrive. "Tell me where you would like to go in the summer—the sea or the mountains? I think sea is better. What does Papa think?"[9]

Soon, she writes again. "I have found a nice apartment. I will have a piano, and I really want to play, especially in the sad moments. It's so soothing. I hope that Andre and Varya will not be bored here. I have already fixed up lessons."

She dreams much of Russia but is pleased that Inna has a good new friend.

Friendship is very important and should be valued. What do you mean by saying your friend is an idealist?

Are you still reading Belinsky? Did you read the argument between Gorky and other writers about Dostoevsky's *The Devils*?

I see that you are a terrible hunter. I did want to say intrepid [in English]. . . . I wouldn't like to see a hare in its predeath convulsions and hear it screaming. It seems to me a little cowardly for six dogs and as many hunters to chase after one poor hare. This is slaughter.

Indeed, this seems a strange activity for a young girl in 1914 even if she does live in forest country. "This year Tolstoy, yes?" she ends.[10]

Meanwhile, the letters from Lenin keep streaming in, often breaking into English and sometimes French. He issues a whole range of orders: draft a letter, get someone to sign it; find Popov, who's disappeared with a woman; get contacts to write to the Ukraine to start organizing a new party there. He shares with her his delight at the new *Pravda,* now run by Kamenev—"It's getting to be a real beauty!"—and his despair later: "We're having hard times since Kamenev left."[11]

He often offends her, charging on one occasion that she is behaving like "the Holy Virgin," then apologizing profusely.[12] He was, of course, like Marx, an atheist. So, of course, was she.

In a letter about Malinovsky that had been held in the secret files he ends, in English, with a rare mention of the past: "If possible do not be angry against me. I have caused you a great pain, I know it."[13] Repeatedly he asks if she is still angry with him. In one letter, he defends himself against her wounded anger: "Never have I written that I esteem only three women [from whom presumably she felt excluded]. Never!!! I've written that fullest friendship, absolute esteem, and *confiance* of mine are confined to only 2–3 women. That is quite, quite another thing."[14] He suggests they discuss it when they meet, though the difference must have seemed marginal to a woman who surely only wanted assurance that she was one of the three.

Meanwhile, Roman Malinovsky is proving a great worry. The only senior Bolshevik with a working-class background, he has risen high in the party hierarchy and is now on the Central Committee in Russia and is the Bolshevik spokesman in the Duma. Lenin, as has been seen, is a great admirer and is embarrassed now by rumors circulating in Moscow that Malinovsky is in the pay of the Okhrana.

"It is very hard to see him," Lenin writes Inessa, "so useless and helpless now" in the face of the "infamous campaign of slander. Wiring [sic] with Brother [Kamenev] and small understandings. . . . Generally he is very good, excellent—but . . . in such a crisis a little too weak."[15]

Later that day, Lenin writes again: "The Malinovsky affair is warming up. He is not here. Looks like flight. Naturally, this gives food for the worst thoughts." He adds that Russian newspapers are accusing Malinovsky of being a provocateur. "You can imagine what it means," he says, switching to English. "Very improbable but we are obliged to control all 'oui-dire' [rumors]."[16]

Lenin is forced to set up a Central Committee Commission of Inquiry, though he loads it in his favor. It consists of Lenin himself (who will be compromised when Malinovsky's Okhrana links are proved), his longtime comrade Ganetsky (Jacob Furstenberg), and Zinoviev. After several oppressive sessions, the commission rules that the case against Malinovsky remains unproved. "Scoundrels," Lenin was to write later, "were letting blackguards and vermin and skunks, ignored with contempt by the working class, root around in all this."

Inessa, meanwhile, was anxious about her relations with Nadya, who she suspected still resented her. "You haven't written me for ages, my dear," she wrote informally. "Aren't you ashamed of having forgotten me . . . ? Please write soon. I have received a letter recently from [Inna]. I am sending it to you. It's very interesting, and I hope to share the joy in it with you. . . . I strongly, strongly embrace you."[17] Using the emotional appeal of the children?

Nadya was being cool with her even though she had seen off the competition—anyway for a while—but perhaps she was still scarred from the December crisis.

Clearly Nadya was in no hurry to mend any damaged fences. Two months later, Inessa wrote Nadya again from Trieste, en route to an Adriatic holiday with the children. She had heard from her, though it hardly helped.

Dear NK, I was pleased to get your letter, although I did not like it too much. It was very businesslike and didn't tell me anything about yourself. I would like to know all about you. What are you reading? What are you interested in? How are you feeling. Do you go walking? Please write, my dear.

I am again in Trieste with the children. We are stuck here because the children have colds and Andrushka has had a very high temperature. I thought it was typhus, but today his temperature has dropped. . . . Thank you for your copy of *Rabotnitsa.*[18]

Rabotnitsa, the woman's journal, had been published in Russia with the help of Armand money and other sources, but it continued to be down-rated by the male Bolsheviks. The first six issues contained no articles by Lenin, which would have given it authority. Inessa, who had been its leading advocate, seemed to have lost a degree of interest. She had been locked into Lenin's stream of demands, which in July culminated in the biggest task he had ever asked of her: to take his place on the platform facing some of the star figures in the socialist movement, most of whom would be hostile.

He was again playing games, twisting and turning and pretending to support issues that, in practice, he was against. Inessa was to be his mouthpiece, partly on account of her language skills, but also simply because she was not him. The difference was subtle but significant.

At any other time, she would have been flattered, if scared, but she was on this rare holiday with four of the children in the Adriatic town of Lovran. Alexander was joining them with his new girlfriend, Anna Arbels, the widow of a late friend. Anna, Inessa's sister-in-law, was expected.

The Great War was only weeks ahead and, although no one had any notion of how long it would last or how dreadful it would be or was even sure it would happen at all, it was an ominous cloud.

The Brussels conference, scheduled on less than three weeks' notice, clashed with this holiday. So Inessa did not agree to go, but she didn't actually say no.

Organized by the International Socialists Bureau, this was a "Unity Conference." Lenin, the great divider, was not against unity—providing, of course, it was unity of the kind he wanted and of which he was in charge. He knew that this conference would not advance this kind of unity.

For once, though, after years of declining influence, he was "dealing from a position of strength. . . . The Bolsheviks had scored gains in the elections to the 4th Duma; *Pravda* had won vastly greater circulation than the Mensheviks' *Novaya rabochaya gazeta;* and his party was steadily taking over . . . the top positions in formerly Menshevik trade unions."[19] He was planning the sixth party conference for August, which, unlike the Prague sham, would be properly attended and provide unarguable legal status for his new Bolshevik party.

Despite more cheerful prospects for the party, he was vulnerable personally, still facing the scandals of Malinovsky, continuing problems over the Schmidt money, and a furious quarrel with Camille Huysmans, the bureau secretary, all of which were expected to be exploited with glee by his enemies on the platform.

Lenin was probably surprised by Inessa's resistance to attending the conference in Brussels. He understood the value of the children in her life, but they were now getting in the way of the party. So he put on the pressure.

There was not much time—only days, really. He wrote at the start of July, asking her to "consent to be a member of the delegation . . . if you have the slightest chance to fix up the children for 6–7 days . . . or even less." He reasons that she is well informed on the business at hand, speaks perfect French, and reads *Pravda*. "I don't want to go 'on principle.' . . . You are more sure of yourself now . . . and could carry this through perfectly. . . . Consent, do!"[20]

He wrote again, saying he was "extremely glad that you are well [i.e., able to attend], remarking that Lilina Zinovieva is still in hospital [i.e., ruling out the Zinovievs]."[21]

Only hours passed before he wrote once more. "I am terribly afraid that you will refuse to go. . . . You see, it's extremely important that the main report should be read really effectively. . . . Excellent French is definitely needed" and an understanding of "essentials" and "proper tact. . . . You are the only suitable person."

And so it went on—letter after letter, telegrams, flattering, cajoling. Meanwhile, he was planning around her. Ivan Popov, found at last, was to go with her, as was her St. Petersburg friend Georgi Safarov, as secretary.

At last, the campaign worked, though she was still reluctant. Lenin reacted like an excited boy. "My dear and dearest friend, oh, I would like to kiss you a thousand times. . . . I am fully sure you will be victorious."[22]

A week later, he was worrying again. "I am sure that you are one of those people who develop, grow stronger, become more vigorous and bold when they are alone in a responsible position—and therefore I obstinately do not believe the pessimists, i.e., those who say that you . . . can hardly [handle it]. . . . Stuff and nonsense! I don't believe it! You will manage splendidly! With your excellent French you will lay them all flat and you won't allow [chairman Emile] Vandervelde to interrupt and shout."

He has already asked her to come to Poronin after the congress and "bring when You will come [that is, bring with you] all our letters." He tells her not to send them by registered mail since "the packet can very easily be opened by friends." (He doesn't mean "friends," of course.) "Please bring all letters," he repeats for a second time.[23] This explains why no love letters to her have survived. No *ty* this time. In fact, this letter suggests much concern that the letter may fall into the wrong hands.

It could explain the torn pages and partial pages in those letters that have survived. For these, too, could have been compromising in the future, yet he would have wanted to preserve political pages for posterity. (In the event, however, Inessa did not go to Poronin at all, though she would have obeyed his order when she next saw him in Bern.)

And then came the briefing.

> Plekhanov likes to disconcert comrades of the female sex with "sudden" gallantries. You must meet these with quick repartees. "I'm delighted, Comrade Plekhanov, you are quite an old spark," to take him down a peg or two.
>
> Everybody will be very angry (I'm very glad) at my not being present and will take it out on you. But I am sure you'll show them your "nails" and deliver cold, calm and somewhat scornful snubs.
>
> Plekhanov will heckle. . . . Cut him short immediately. . . . "Will you *please* not interrupt me . . ." turning it into "an attack upon him."[24]

Rosa Luxemburg, he says, will challenge the validity of the Prague Conference, as will others. Lenin urges that, if she is brought under pressure, she just quote the party's resolutions, which "they don't like." "We are an autonomous party. Keep this firmly in mind."[25]

In follow-up letters he expanded on the theme, changing his mind on tactics, in one decreeing they should "agree to nothing, walk out" and in another that they should "not walk out" under certain circumstances.[26]

He ordered that she should attend as "Petrova"—since it is not advisable to let the liquidators know the name "Inessa." Why not? Surely the rumors will have reached them, too. And so she went, with Popov and Safarov and two other comrades, into the fire, with Rosa Luxemburg there as anticipated, as well as Trotsky, Axelrod, Kautsky, Plekhanov, and Vandervelde.

Ten Social Democratic groups were represented, and everyone was indeed angry that Lenin was absent. Stubbornly, Inessa and

Popov insisted they were there by decision of the Central Committee. But the anger grew as they abstained in vote after vote. Inessa started to read Lenin's report, in a voice so low that many could not hear, and was warned she was running out of time. Still, she was allowed to give Lenin's agreement to unity, providing they agreed to fourteen conditions that, as he had forecast, were considered "monstrous."

Inessa was standing alone on the platform with no formal senior official role in the party. Before her was an audience that was growing increasingly impatient and outraged. Once she started to read out the conditions there were murmurs, building to interruptions and cries of shocked amazement.

"The majority of the delegates were greatly disgusted," according to one report with delicate understatement. For Lenin's conditions were truly absurd—one demanded the closure of all Menshevik newspapers that competed with the Bolshevik press—and had no hope of being accepted. Plekhanov complained that they were "the articles of a new criminal code." Kautsky called them "a demand for self-destruction." Vandervelde said it would "be impossible to breathe" if they were accepted.[27]

Inessa kept her nerve, though, and continued doggedly to read them out. But the moment when she had finished and looked upon those furious faces with a defiance she did not feel must have been beyond anything she had endured for Lenin before, short of prison.

Even so, they debated Lenin's conditions for the rest of the day. At last, the next morning, the secretary, unwilling to accept that Lenin had successfully bombed the conference, introduced a resolution so mild and vague that anyone could sign it. But not Inessa. Lenin had told her to agree to nothing.

"We abstain," she announced, no doubt provoking another roar of anger.

She had carried out Lenin's orders, and he wrote several letters thanking her. "You have rendered a very great service to our party! I am especially thankful because you have replaced me. . . . You handled the thing better than I could have done. Language apart, I would probably have gone up in the air . . . would have called them scoundrels. And that's what they were waiting for. That's what they were trying to provoke."[28] Lenin seems genuinely to have seen them as the provocateurs, not him, though his letters make it quite clear that he was.

"Are you very tired?" he asked. "Very upset? Are you angry at me for having persuaded you to go?" Inessa was certainly fed up. She had done his dirty work and hurried back to her children at Lovran.

"A very likely result" of the party's behavior in Brussels, R. C. Elwood has written, "would have been the expulsion of [Lenin's] party from the European Socialist movement."[29] But that didn't happen. In fact, none of it mattered for much longer. Archduke Francis Ferdinand had already been murdered in Sarajevo. Ten days after the conference closed, Austria-Hungary declared war on Serbia. "The idiot Brussels Conference can be forgotten in such times," Lenin wrote to her. "Best greetings for the commencing revolution in Russia."[30]

He saw the turmoil as opportunity. All year, Russia had suffered labor strikes. The volcano within the nation was rumbling again. Now there would be war between the great imperial nations that the participants would be unable to end without transforming the conflict into a class struggle, he declared.

He was wrong, of course. It would end in the usual way, with winners and losers. But it would certainly provide the scope he forecast for revolution, and all his political maneuvering—in France and Belgium and, during the dark years to come, in Switzerland—would acquire new meaning.

CHAPTER 9

BERN 1914

Weeks were to pass as nation after nation, bound by alliances, declared war. There had never been a war that was to approach the devastation that lay ahead. Still, memories of the Franco-Prussian conflict, when Paris was besieged, were still vivid, and new weapons had been developed since with far greater lethal potential.

Inessa and her children were in Austria as citizens of that country's major enemy, which was already mobilizing. She moved fast, took the children by train into still-neutral Italy. At Genoa, she put them on a ship bound for Archangel.

Then she returned to Lovran to tidy up the villa she had rented. She did not know it then, but she was not to see any of the children again for nearly three years.

"I went back with a sore heart," she wrote them. "It was so empty and I was sad to see the bare table in the dining room and not to hear your jolly voices and your laughing. I was sad to look at the things you left behind, sad to enter your rooms now so empty."

Inessa, still wanted by the police in Russia, headed for Les Avants, above Montreux on Lake Geneva, near her old Swiss territory of 1903. From there, she wrote to her children again, saying that she had begun to write the day after she was in Lovran, but

> that letter started to upset me so much I decided not to send it, so as not to upset you, too.
>
> I am planning to move to Bern. . . . Today it is very beautiful here. Snow has just come to these mountain peaks, Rochers de Naye and Col de Jaman, and at sunset it was all pink. . . . I kiss you hard, my darlings. P.S. My word, how happy I'll be when I learn you have made it all right and that you are healthy.[1]

Inna wrote to her mother on the voyage home, while anchored off Cardiff, Wales.

> We arrived last night, but we couldn't enter the harbor because the waves were too great, and now we are waiting for high tide.
>
> We left [Italy] on August 9 about midday. The wind was strong, and there was some pitching and tossing. Andrushka, Varya, and I were all very sick. . . . On the third night, we passed Gibraltar and were still unwell. Sasha and Andrushka [presumably recovered] looked after us very well, bringing us tea and bread. We are all getting better now.
>
> We are now entering harbor shouting "Vive l'Angleterre, Hurrah! Hurrah!" And the English [the Welsh?] have been responding enthusiastically.[2]

The letter made Inessa "awfully happy," but in her response she worried whether their woollen clothes would be adequate for the Arctic cold.[3] She knew what it could be like at Archangel.

She had heard from Zinoviev that Lenin had been arrested as an "important spy" since he had not moved out of Austria fast enough. In fact, it was a great shock for Lenin and Nadya to find suddenly that they were on enemy territory and victims of the high emotions that wars inspire. "We witnessed a horrible scene. . . ." wrote Nadya later. "A train had arrived from Krasnik bringing dead and wounded [Austrian] soldiers. I heard some peasant women coming out of a Catholic church. . . . [They said that] even if the authorities released the spy [Lenin], the peasants would put his eyes out, cut off his tongue, etc. It was clear we could not remain in Poronin."

With the help of the Austrian socialist Victor Adler and money raised in Bern by Inessa and wired to Lenin, he was released. Lenin and Nadya then joined Inessa in Bern, renting an apartment at 11 Distelweg. (She had settled into a house at 23 Drosselweg, some ten minutes' walk away, near the Bremgartenwald.)

Nadya later drew a picture of three close friends living serenely together in the autumn.

> We used to roam for hours along the woodland paths, which were bestrewn with yellow leaves, Vladimir Ilyich, Inessa, and myself. . . . Sometimes we would sit for hours on a sunny wooded hillside, Ilyich jotting down notes for his articles and speeches. . . . I studying Italian, . . . Inessa sewing a skirt. . . . She had not quite recovered yet from the effects of her imprisonment [in St. Petersburg]. . . . In the evening we would gather at Grigori's [Zinoviev's] tiny room.

It was hard to imagine that some three hundred miles to the northwest guns would soon be pounding the trenches of Picardy. This would not have disturbed them. Worryingly, the war was producing a new and deeper division within Social Democracy than all of Lenin's wildcat strategies. There were socialist patriots who believed their countries' armies should be supported, and there were Lenin's Bolsheviks, though some disagreed, who saw the defeat of tsarist Russia as the "lesser evil." They urged that the aim should be to "transform the present imperialist war into a civil war"—leading in time to the long-expected revolution. In this new world, of course, patriotism would be irrelevant.

Soon, a new idea was forming in Inessa's mind. During the summer holiday with the children, there had been mealtime conversations when the girls—and Inna in particular—had questioned her about marriage and love. Inessa was an ardent advocate of the freedom of women and certainly experienced in the effects of passion. She decided to write a pamphlet on love and the family, which, as she told Inna, "your questions were largely responsible for spurring me on to write. If it comes out I'll dedicate it to you and Varya."[4]

In January, she left Bern alone for the mountains, to start work. She sent some of her pamphlet to Lenin for his comments and was shocked to get a sharp retort from the man who still occupied her emotional life, advising her, among other criticisms, to "entirely throw out the 'demand for free love.' "

What did she mean by it? He listed ten possible meanings ranging from prejudices of religion or society, to "paternal injunctions" and "possibly adultery."[5]

She defended her work angrily, and Lenin in turn was "astounded" by her "attack." He repeated her words back to her: "Even fleeting passion . . . is more poetic and pure than the loveless kisses exchanged as a matter of habit between husband and wife." Loveless marital kisses were, he agreed, impure. But what did she pose as the opposite? A "fleeting" passion. Why "fleeting," which, he suggested, was by definition loveless? "It follows logically [in her argument, he said] that these loveless kisses, since they are fleeting, are the opposite of loveless kisses exchanged between husband and wife. . . . Strange!" She was not, in other words, comparing like with like, he argued. Loveless kisses, he implied, were loveless kisses.

Lenin, whose kisses had clearly not been loveless, had a logical point, but he seemed to be discounting the fact that sexual passion may indeed be fleeting. He does concede reluctantly that she could add "if you simply must," that a "transient liaison may be vile or pure," but he would prefer that she did not; it muddied her argument.

Some commentators have supported her, attacking him for "prudish" nineteenth-century views. Others, siding with him, have pointed to her way of life—with two known lovers and rumored others—as evidence of promiscuity. But she, too, was on shaky ground. She and Lenin both argued that marriage as an institution was oppressive, though personally she was not oppressed by hers, and he clung stubbornly to his own.

What she was trying to make, it seems from further letters, was a case for the freedom of women throughout all aspects of family life, including making love or not making love. The quarrel, with its underlying hint from Lenin that her pamphlet lacked intellectual quality, to which she was most sensitive, left a note of sourness that was to remain with her.

Inessa had already written at length to Inna about love. With a side reference to the Greeks who "worshipped beauty" and "looked freely at love," she wrote that "love is also a product of culture and civilization. Animals and savages do not know love." She speaks of "today's society" with its background of the highest "manifestations of love," but warns that "there are people who in love feel completely like savages . . . the majority. . . . Everyone marries or indulges in lust but very few love or have loved."

Quite what Inna at sixteen made of this is not known. Her mother seems to be arguing that there is a higher level of love, denied to all but a minority. Most people, she implies, have to be content with lust—which is assuming a lot.

Inna had, as usual, been slow to satisfy her mother's great need for letters. "Of course, you're a pig," Inessa charged,

> because you haven't written. . . . You asked me to be critical, so I hope I won't have to call you a pig again. Mostly, I want to hug you.
> I think you are strong, and you were never a coward as

you call yourself. You don't know yourself well enough yet or know your own strength. . . . In your femininity and softness there is charm, but this is also strength. You do not know how to use it . . . how to direct it.

I remember when you were small that you could keep a secret. . . . I think such firmness in a child is a rare thing, and you were certainly a little hero.

As for strength of will, this should be developed by exercise like any other muscle.

In another letter, she urges emotional freedom. Inna has said that she was afraid of falling in love with someone her mother did not like. "Inushka, you must be independent and make your own decisions."[6]

The year 1915 was marked by socialist conferences, three in Bern in the few weeks straddling March. Inessa attended them all, including a youth conference with her old friend Georgi Safarov and a woman's conference, where she spoke under briefing from Lenin in a nearby café since, being male, he could not speak himself.

In a Bolshevik "Foreign" assembly, however, she stoutly opposed Lenin over a manifesto aim he had promoted: the formation of a "republican united states of Europe." This was impractical, she said, because of conflicts of interest among the nations. Tempers rose in a fierce public argument. Lenin attacked her "as an anarchist," and she fought back as only she could, alleging he was "an opportunist," which struck close to home, as it was what he was always calling other people.

Lenin shrugged off this flare of independence. He asked her to work with him and Zinoviev on the redrafting of his main resolution and actually backed down on the united Europe proposal. This showed his regard for her—though with Lenin there was always a feeling in any concession that his eyes were on the future. Still, the vigor of her fight was a sign of a new attitude. She was not just doing what he wanted anymore.

In June, Lenin and Nadya left for a long summer break at Sorenberg, Switzerland, and Inessa soon joined them. It might seem that they all spent a great deal of time on long summer vacations while Lenin was pleading poverty. However, these were in effect working holidays. Lenin found to his delight that he could order books by post from public libraries in Bern and Zurich.

It must be remembered, too, that illness was a frequent occurrence at this time. Lenin suffered from frequent headaches, and mountain air was universally thought to have therapeutic qualities.

Inessa spent much of her time in Sorenberg working on her pamphlet on love and the family, though it was never published.

"We would rise early," wrote Nadya,

> and, before dinner, which was served at twelve o'clock, each of us would work in different corners of the garden.
>
> During those hours, Inessa often played the piano, and it was particularly good to work to the sounds of the music. . . . After dinner we sometimes went to the mountains. Ilyich liked to get to the crags of the Rothorn toward evening when the view above was marvelous and below the mist was turning rosy.

Inessa missed her children, as usual. "I cannot adjust to the fact that you cannot come to me this summer," she wrote Inna. "It is very hard for me to live by myself. . . . I have been torn away from everything that is dear. . . . We must meet and talk, and somehow I must make this happen."[7]

She made plans to meet Inna and presumably the others in Sweden. "I have asked a friend who is going to Moscow to talk to you about this," she wrote later. The plans, however, came to nothing.

At the time, Inna had other concerns. "Your jealousy toward Varya," her mother insisted,

> has no basis. You're a funny little cuckoo. I love you both deeply, though a little differently because you are different in-

dividuals. . . . Mothers strive to see in their children something better than in other children, but mothers are not blind.
They see their children's shortcomings through a magnifying
glass, sometimes with pain. None of you have given me this
pain.[8]

During 1915, which was a trying time for them all, separated as
they were by the war, Inessa showed more mild signs of disenchant-
ment with Lenin—or, rather, with Lenin's view of her—though some
historians have suggested that there was a renewal of the affair. Certainly the mountain life, with its long walks and doubtless long talks,
could have brought them closer, especially since Nadya's health was
still not up to much walking. But there is not a scrap of evidence of
sexual renewal.

In early September, however, Lenin left Sorenberg with Inessa to
attend a conference in Zimmerwald, near Bern, and Inessa suffered
another blow to her self-esteem. The conference was called in secret
by Robert Grimm, a middle-of-the-road Swiss Social Democrat. The
thirty-eight delegates met at the Volkshaus in Bern to board coaches
that would take them to the nearby village of Zimmerwald; Grimm
claimed they were members of an ornithological society. The Russians
were permitted only eight delegates, a mere two Bolsheviks, the others being SRs, Mensheviks, and members of other groups.

Lenin had intended Inessa to be a delegate, but this limitation
forced him to exclude her, choosing Zinoviev and himself as the two
Bolsheviks. She may have felt he did not try hard enough, but he did
make amends. An international socialist commission was to be set up
in Bern, and Lenin named Zinoviev as the Bolshevik representative
with "Comrade Petrova," her new name, as an alternate. The conference had raised Lenin's status. Now he was seen as head of the "Zimmerwald Left" as an international group, reaching beyond the party,
even though, in this lilliputian world, there were only eight members.
It would grow, though, and, as usual with Lenin's groups, make an
impact far beyond its size.

Inessa, meanwhile, was reassuring Inna again that she "had always been a strong character." She added that "we are watching intensely and emotionally what is happening in Russia now. . . . We can see something bright which is filling the heart with hope."[9]

She was probably referring to strikes, for the party news was dreadful. The Okhrana had arrested most of the Central Committee, *Pravda* and the journals had been closed down, and the networks had been broken up. With a war on, the government wanted no trouble at home.

By the end of 1915, Lenin was keen to build on his new Zimmerwald Left. But the French socialists were firmly against him, taking the patriotic line, so he decided that Inessa must enter the fire again, this time by crossing the border into France, using a false passport in the name of Sophie Popoff. She was reluctant. The will she had displayed in her dangerous return to Russia in 1912 was not there, perhaps because of the war. But she went to Paris, responding somewhat wearily to the call of the cause.

"Crossing international borders with forged documents," as R. C. Elwood wrote, "and preaching defeatism in wartime to a party favouring defensism was at best a risky venture."[10] The Okhrana Paris bureau soon picked up her track in early January 1916 but, as usual, sat back and waited.[11]

Alphonse Merrheim and Albert Bourderon, the French socialist leaders, whom Inessa knew well, wanted little to do with her, refusing to allow her even to address their members. She tried an associated body that was pacifist, only to find that it was not as pacifist as Lenin would like. She did better with the old French Bolshevik workers, persuading them to spread antiwar literature in the factories.

Lenin, as expected, was growing impatient. "Not a scrap of news," he wrote on January 13. "We do not know if you have arrived." Two days later, he wrote again. "I'm rather surprised that there is no news from you. Let me confess, while I'm at it, that the thought occurred to me for a moment that you might have taken offense at my not having gone to see you off the day you left. . . . But I dismiss the unworthy thought." A few lines earlier he had spoken of a sunny walk they had all taken a few weeks back. "I kept thinking of it and was sorry you were not here."[12]

On January 19, 1916, he complained that "this is my third [unanswered] postcard to you, this time in French to make the work easier for the censors. . . . You are causing me great anxiety." Lightly, he ended, "Sincerely yours, Basil."[13] Again, she did not answer him. But on the same day, Nadya heard from her. "The mood in the streets is somber, and there are many women in mourning." She judged it would be hard to achieve anything in the short term.[14]

Was Inessa making a point? She didn't write to Lenin until the twenty-fifth, nearly a week later, but he wrote to her in answer to her letter to Nadya. She obviously was not getting his letters to her poste restante address, he said, so suggested a code. "If you underline the date twice, it will mean that you are receiving my letters."[15]

Inessa's behavior is interesting. A resentment has crept in, possibly stemming from the Brussels Conference of 1914, when she may not have liked what she was asked to do. Or perhaps Lenin's response to her love and the family pamphlet still rankled. Perhaps she is disheartened at her lack of progress. Also, in Paris, she is once more in great danger, and she suspects she will not be given appropriate credit. She will be thanked profusely, as she was after Brussels, but being female, she won't get the status she has earned within the party.

Lenin, sensing her discord, kept the light tone going for a while. "Salutations Cordiales!" were the last words of a letter in February.

Suddenly, Inessa had some success—by lowering her sights—with a youth group and two trade unions. She impressed the Okhrana, who reported that she "won the confidence" of her young audiences "by virtue of her command of the language and enticing manner." Certainly, she was pleased, writing Lenin that she had won some allies for the Zimmerwald Left, not from above but from below.

Lenin's response was frigid. He was unimpressed by youth groups and urged her sharply to try harder to cause a split in the main French

Socialist Party organizations. In response, she sent him an "angry postcard," and he replied on March 19 that "nothing is accomplished, even in a fit of temper, by using rude words. . . . This is not an encouragement to further correspondence."[16]

She could hardly believe what she read. She did not want to be in Paris in the first place and reckoned she had achieved a lot in very difficult conditions. The French, still touched by the old glamour of Napoleon, were not natural pacifists. Even Lenin had second thoughts, writing on March 31, twice congratulating her on her success. It was a bit late, though, certainly for two people who had been lovers and were still linked by deep emotions. If there was resentment, his calculated use of her could only intensify it.

When she went to an internationalist committee, organized by the French Socialist Party, and urged it to "foment unrest in the French army," she alarmed the surveillance police of a nation already shocked to its roots by the horror of trench warfare. She only just avoided arrest for treason by slipping across the border the next day.

For Lenin, this had been just another little quarrel, the kind he was always locked in with someone or other. For her, it was far more.

. . .

Two weeks after leaving Paris, Inessa attended the Second International Socialist Conference at Kienthal as a formal delegate, but she made no speeches, simply translating for Lenin and Zinoviev. Lenin's Zimmerwald Left made progress, its numbers rising from eight to twelve, which, despite the absurdly low numbers, he used like an advance commando hammering at each weakness in the proposals.

Then Inessa left Lenin, but there was no great scene. There was a vacuum of sorts. Lenin and Nadya had moved to Zurich, but Inessa did not join them there. She stayed on for a few weeks in her old home in Bern.

When the Lenins moved to the mountains for their summer break, this time to Flums, there still was no Inessa. Instead, she went with the Zinovievs to their favorite resort at Hertenstein, not far from Lucerne, before returning on her own to her old hotel at Sorenberg until the end of the season.

Then, in November 1916, she headed for Baugy-sur-Clarens, near Lake Geneva and not far from Les Avants, her earlier refuge of 1914. She rented an apartment opposite Nikolai Rubakin's Russian Library, which gave her room for study.

There were other Russian revolutionaries living nearby. In fact, the "Baugy Group" would be a power, acting with Inessa in Russia after 1917. Like her, they were on the "romantic" left wing of the party, and led by Nikolai Bukharin, who lived in Lausanne. But if Inessa saw much of them, as she must have done in the library, she does not seem to have written of them to Lenin.

But Inessa was behaving strangely again. She had always needed company. She had written to her daughters about the importance of friendship. Now she seemed to have condemned herself to a remote existence in a way that was quite out of character.

Lenin refused to acknowledge any kind of break. He maintained an active correspondence during 1916 after her escape from France, with more than fifty letters as well as speaking with her on the phone and sending telegrams.

In fact, while Inessa continued to work for the party, she did only what she wanted. She also started to challenge some of Lenin's views and Marxist interpretations, with the help of the Russian Library, now so close. He didn't like this, but he still commanded the relationship, though sometimes, being Lenin, he lost patience with her.

. . .

The Great War had been raging now for more than two years, and it was more horrific than anyone had forecast. When Inessa moved to her new apartment in the Swiss mountains, the battles of the Somme and Verdun had come to terrible ends, with the death of nearly two million men, and truly had changed little. Millions, too, were dying on the eastern front and in other parts of Europe.

To Lenin, who saw the whole war as a capitalist, imperialist conflict, this carnage held hope for the future. When the ghastly war came to an end, it seemed impossible that the survivors, mostly workers in civilian life, would just go back to their jobs.

With winter approaching in Russia, famine threatened the nation. The breadlines seemed endless. Within only a few weeks that huge nation would explode, but if Lenin or Inessa or any of them had been told this then in late 1916, they would not have believed it possible. Meanwhile, the revolutionaries continued with their little lives, their little quarrels, their taut relationships.

Back in July, when Inessa had been with the Zinovievs, Lenin had again written of her success in Paris, speaking of her "great influence on the French," leaving "enduring marks"—which he thought might cheer her up. He had hoped, as he confided to Zinoviev, to persuade her to go back into Russia for him, but in her present frame of mind she wasn't going to prison for him again. But he knew where she was vulnerable: He suggested she should go to Norway—replacing the Bolshevik Central Committee's representative in Scandinavia—where she could meet the children. Since Russia would then be so accessible, via Finland, Lenin was reckoning that Inessa might be persuaded to risk occasional visits there.

She was tempted but cautious. She did not have a passport, so Lenin tried to get her a false one with the help of Olga Ravich, a comrade who lived in Geneva. When this failed, he suggested she use Nadya's. He urged her to consider going to England as a stepping-off point and even offered to lend her money.

When she finally rejected the Norway proposal altogether, Lenin decided she should help run a publishing business—the Bolshevik official publisher in Switzerland—but she was not taken with the idea, knowing she would perform the menial tasks, oversee printers, and correct proofs, while Lenin did the writing.

In January 1917, Lenin thought that Switzerland, at present neutral, might be drawn into the war, and the French would occupy Geneva. Contact with France's ally Russia would then be much easier.

He had decided, he told Inessa, to transfer the party treasury to her "to be kept on your person. In a little bag."[17] She was quite keen on this because it underlined her value to him. And then, as with many of his other plans, he seemed to lose interest.

But even amid his demands and suggestions, Lenin did, in his fashion, show his concern for her. "Don't stay in Sorenberg," he had urged earlier. "You'll freeze." On November 20 he had written: "Of course I also want to correspond. Let's continue our correspondence," as though there was some question of not doing so. "How I laughed over your postcard. I really had to hold my sides, as they say."[18] That same month, he had written, in a letter that was censored, that he "felt like saying a few friendly words to you and pressing your hand very tightly. You write that even your hands and feet are swollen from the cold. That's just terrible. Even without this your hands were always chilly. Why bring it to that?"[19]

On December 17, 1916, he had asked in a letter sent to Baugy-sur-Clarens: "Do you go skiing? You really should! . . . It's good in the mountains in winter . . . and smells of Russia!"[20]

A few days later, he wrote, again in a letter that was censored, that "your last letters were so full of sadness, and these . . . stirred up such pangs of conscience in me that I simply cannot compose myself. I would like to . . . urgently beg you not to sit in virtual solitude in a little town where there is no social life . . . and shake yourself out of it."[21]

Then he spoiled it with another letter. "I urge you when choosing your place of residence, NOT to take into account whether I will come there. It would be quite absurd, reckless and ridiculous if I were to restrict you in your choice of a city."[22]

Yet he still demanded translations in his lordly way. "Still no article. . . . What is the meaning of this? I demand that you send it immediately." And then, when she did send it, he didn't use it.

What Inessa really wanted was to set herself up as a writer, because writers, in the party and the socialist world, acquired status. She had written two articles for *Rabotnitsa* and one for *Sotsial*

Demokrat. She was expecting to be assigned a piece on women workers, but it went instead to Lilina, the pseudonym used by Zinaida Zinovieva, who was becoming a literary rival. When Inessa prepared a paper, "Who Pays for the War?," it was not published, while one by Lilina was, but then Lilina was the coeditor's wife.

Lenin "had to choose his words carefully or sometimes lie," wrote Alexander Solzhenitsyn of his dealings with Inessa. " 'What could I possibly have against publishing your article in the *Sbornik* [*Sotsial Demokrat*]?' Lenin replied on 20 July 1916. Then afterward he would pretend that unforeseen circumstances had prevented it." Lenin was like a ringmaster, handling the horses, but he constantly took great trouble to keep Inessa in the ring.

In January 1917, she became deeply depressed, and Lenin felt for her, way up in the mountains, which can be gloomy in the winter if the weather is poor. "I know how terribly bad you feel, and I am eagerly anxious to help you in any way I can."[23]

It is easy to see Inessa during these months as sulking, but this would be unfair. She was trying to replan her life. She had bound herself to Lenin, without reservation, seeing him as the light of her future, willingly going to prison for him. But she had fallen deeply in love with him. Her desolation when he had distanced himself in 1913 was profound.

The cause, though, was crucial to her and sacred in its quality. So she had continued working for the leader who she truly believed would conduct her and everyone else to the promised land.

It is not surprising she was confused. Her love as a woman and her devotion to the cause were totally merged. She knew that Lenin confided in her more intimately than he did in any of his male comrades. And she was not alone in feeling undervalued. Rosa Luxemburg and Alexandra Kollontai shared her view and her experience with the revolutionaries in their lives. Kollontai even wrote a novel about it, *A Great Love,* which was widely believed to be based on Inessa's life with Lenin but could well have been about her own.

For Inessa, the one asset about their terrible isolation in Switzerland was that she could challenge the status quo without harming the cause. And it developed into a recognizable man-woman conflict.

Lenin, too, was to some extent confused. He saw her at the Party level as an extremely good personal assistant, useful for her languages and any dirty work or dangerous missions he might need, who could also be trusted to take his place on the platform before a hostile audience. What kind of an assistant was this? She was not, he felt instinctively, as an old-fashioned chauvinist, in the top rank. In later years, though, when he was a head of state, he was to give her rein. She was to become the most powerful woman in the capital but still not as powerful as the top-ranking men.

During these few months, Lenin's and Nadya's lives had been reduced by poverty. In Zurich, they lived in a single room at 14 Spiegelgasse, a steep cobbled alley of close, tall houses that was so exposed to the smells from a local sausage factory that they had to keep the windows closed. It was a bitterly cold winter, and Nadya had been ill for much of it with bronchitis and the effects of Graves' disease.

Their bare room had no heating, and they shared a small kitchen with their landlady, Frau Kammerer. Often for lunch they had only oatmeal that Nadya was always scorching, not being a natural cook. "We live in grand style, you see," Lenin joked to Frau Kammerer. "We have roasts every day."

"I need to earn," he wrote to Alexander Shlyapnikov, "otherwise, we shall simply die of hunger." He urged Mark Elizarov, who was married to Lenin's older sister, Anna, to find him work as a translator. "We shall soon be coming to the end of our former means of subsistence," Nadya wrote to Maria, Lenin's younger sister.[24]

Nineteen-sixteen had been bad for them. Lenin's mother, whom he had adored, had died. His sister Anna had been sentenced to exile in Astrakhan, though she was released under controlled conditions owing to illness. Even his confidence in his future role in history showed signs of fraying. "We of the older generation," he told a young audience in January 1917, "may not live to see the decisive battles of this coming revolution."[25]

It was only a moment of depression but significant. In little more than a month he would be proved wrong. Revolution would break out in St. Petersburg and with the toppling of the tsar ripple throughout Russia.

Early in 1917, Lenin felt trapped. Nadya, conscious that there was "no outlet for his colossal energy," recalled a visit to the London zoo, where they saw a white northern wolf. "All animals," explained the keeper, "get used to their cages in time. Only the white wolf from the Russian north never becomes accustomed to the cage and day and night bangs his head against the bars." Lenin, she knew, was a white northern wolf.

Lenin fought with everyone: Zinoviev, Rosa Luxemburg, Bukharin, Olga Ravich. He would be overwhelmed by almost childish losses of temper and, if provoked by political opponents, would indulge in violent fits of hatred. At these times, according to Nikolai Valentinov, a comrade of earlier days, he "wanted to smash their faces in. . . . Following an attack . . . his energy would begin to ebb, and a psychological reaction set in: dullness, loss of strength and fatigue. . . . He could neither eat nor sleep. Headaches tormented him. His face became sallow, even dark at times."

It was against this setting that Inessa, from her mountain seclusion, was facing him with a growing challenge, marked by the acute sensitivity of an unhappy lover. *And* playing the game of being slow to answer his letters—or ignoring them altogether. And to be fair to Lenin, he allowed few of his many problems in Zurich to color his long correspondence with her.

"Apparently," he wrote on January 9, 1917,

your failure to reply to several of my last letters reveals on your part . . . a somewhat changed mood, decision, or state of affairs. . . . I don't know what to think, whether you took offense at something or were too preoccupied with the move [to a local boardinghouse] or something else. . . . I'm afraid to ask because I suppose such queries are unpleasant for you . . . and, of course [I] will not repeat [them].[26]

Lenin was not always so restrained. "You did not take offense, did you," he queried incredulously in February, "at my writing about your not having gone over the French text? Incredible! . . . Is it conceivable that anyone can take offense at such a thing? Inconceivable! And on the other hand the complete silence . . . is strange."[27]

Well, not so strange, actually, given that she was in serious and barely believable revolt, considering the reverence in which she and the others held him—and doing so, what is more, at an intellectual level, with the help of the Russian Library.

In fact, she was changing the balance of power in their personal relations. It was *she* who failed to reply to his letters so that he, while not quite pleading with her, was asking why. It was *she* who was tossing in the odd firework, to which she knew how he would react. And she was doing this to a man who, within two years, would be one of the most powerful figures in the world.

Her change of mood emerged quietly enough. "On occasion," R. C. Elwood wrote, "she would suggest a point to be added to something she was translating or she would question a particular phrase or term. Sometimes Lenin accepted these suggestions but more often he ridiculed her idea."[28]

In that January of 1917, she refused to translate a few words because "they made her blood boil."[29]

"Thanks awfully . . . ," he wrote back. "As regards the censorship to which you have subjected my French article, I am surprised really."[30]

She had already gone far, far further, but at a different level and softly. It was a climax in their declining relations. She challenged him intellectually, suggesting politely that the master was being inconsistent on political theory. Marx, who condemned patriotism, had stated in *The Communist Manifesto* that "the worker has no fatherland." So why, she asked, was Lenin constantly arguing against the use of the slogan "Defense of the Fatherland" in the current war?

The argument was complex, and it illuminated the new Inessa. Lenin, unaccustomed to such questions from his assistant, replied that there were some exceptions, such as the colonies of the warring imperialist nations, which were being encouraged to fight for their independence—for their own identity or "fatherland." He sent her one of his articles that explained this more fully.[31]

She found this at variance with his earlier work. He was shocked, accusing her of "apparently wanting to establish a contradiction between my present writing and that of an earlier date. Why? Where precisely? What precisely?"

She told him. An article written eight years before seemed to contradict his present position on "defense of the Fatherland."

Somewhat simply, he explained that "you have taken one quotation from the Communist Manifesto . . . to the repudiation of national wars."[32]

But Inessa wasn't letting up and must have smiled to herself to imagine Lenin discussing this esoteric quarrel with his wife, Nadya. Always she was on the side of the women, even if she had gone through some unpleasant moments with this one.

Lenin was getting very irritated with Inessa. Two days before Christmas, he wrote: "I would find it extremely unpleasant if we should differ on this." He said that the international background in 1891 differed from that in the current war and explained why. "Think about this," he went on, as though she were a child.[33]

She didn't like his tone and went back into battle. "We are talking past one another," she wrote, but argued he was being illogical when he said that Germany's defense of the fatherland was justified in 1891 but unjustified in 1914.

And so it went on. It wasn't what the argument was about but the fact it was happening at all. This woman he loved had become a terrier hanging on with her teeth. Eventually, he fell back on a regular male taunt. "You must be in an excessively nervous state. This is my explanation for the number of theoretical oddities in your letters."[34] These oddities, rather interestingly, would crop up a year later when Inessa and the Baugy group became the core of the left Communist opposition.[35]

In fact, it was amazing that this aspect of the correspondence—which lasted months, mixed in with his concern and his orders—was continuing.

For ten days earlier, revolution had broken out in Russia.

CHAPTER · 10

ZURICH 1917

On March 15, Inessa was in the mountain village of Baugy-sur-Clarens, staying now at the Pension Lergive. It is doubtful she had received the news of revolution. There was no radio yet. Montreux, where the newspapers would have carried the news, was down the mountain, on Lake Geneva. Perhaps there were rumors from tradesmen or even exiles from Bukharin's group who might have come up on routine visits to the Russian Library.

It is possible that Lenin's letter was the first she knew of it—a letter, not a telegram, because he was still unsure if it was all a hoax. Even so, he did not mention it until his third paragraph. "We here in Zurich are in a state of agitation today. There is a telegram in the Zürcher Post and in Neue Zürcher Zeitung of March 15 that in Russia the revolution was victorious in Petrograd[1] on March 14 after three days of struggle, that twelve members of the Duma are in power, and that the ministers have all been arrested.

"If the Germans are not lying," he cautions, "I am beside myself that I cannot go to Scandinavia!! I will not forgive myself for not risking the journey in 1915!"[2]

No letters from Inessa have survived from this period. She is certain to have written to her children, though. Like other exiles, she had been waiting so long for revolution that doubtless she found it hard to believe. It seems she did not immediately reply to Lenin, relations between them having reached a kind of nadir. Perhaps she needed time to think.

As Lenin's letter showed, the news had taken him totally by surprise. An excited Polish comrade, Mieczyslav Bronski, had pounded on their door just after lunch. Nadya, as she wrote, was washing the dishes, and Lenin was preparing to return to the library. "Haven't you heard the news?" asked Bronski. "There's a revolution in Russia."

Lenin was totally "bewildered" at the sudden tantalizing glimpse of what they had worked for all their lives. In fact, he refused to believe it. Lenin had forecast that Europe, after three years of war, was "pregnant with revolution." But he had not believed it would happen yet, and he had not expected it to break out in Russia, with its millions of peasants, who were unresponsive militant material, and an industrial economy that, despite substantial recent growth, was still old-fashioned. Germany and Britain, with their big working populations, seemed far more liable to social explosion. But the young Pole insisted that special editions of the Zurich newspapers carried telegrams from St. Petersburg.

It was easy for Lenin and Nadya to imagine the scenes in the city: the crowds surging through the streets; the Cossacks formed up to charge; the drawbridges raised over the Neva, which the tsars had always used to divide this city of a hundred islands. This time, however, the Neva was frozen, and the workers from the Vyborg factory area had crossed over the ice into the city center.

Lenin and Nadya hurried down the familiar lanes of the Old Town to Bellevue Platz, on the edge of Lake Zurich, glistening that afternoon in winter sunshine. There, newspapers were on display be-

neath an awning. Surrounding the stand was a crowd of barely cred-
ulous exiles. Lenin and Nadya shouldered their way through the
throng and, still dazed, confirmed for themselves that what Bronski
had told them was true.

Lenin was still suspicious, but three days later his doubts had
gone. "We are all dreaming of leaving," he wrote to Inessa, concerned
that once again she had not replied to him. "If you're going home,
drop in to see us first. . . . I would very much like you to find out for
me in England discreetly whether I would be granted passage."[3]

On the same day, she did write back and also spoke to him on the
phone. Not that she pleased him. "I must say I'm keenly disappointed. In my opinion everybody these days should have a single
thought—to rush off. . . . I am sure I will be arrested or simply detained in England if I go under my own name. . . . I was certain that
you would rush off to England, as only there could you find out how
to get through and how great the risk is." He assumed, he added, that
she was planning to go to Bern to see the consul, "but you write that
you are undecided and want to think it over. . . . My nerves naturally
are overstrung. No wonder! To have to sit here on tenterhooks. . . .
Probably you have special reasons."[4]

Then came the orders, in this and succeeding letters:

Find some Swiss or Russian in Clarens who would agree to hand
over his passport, without the person knowing it would be for Lenin.

"Run to the German consulate. Be energetic. Pay Zurich lawyers."

Get Anna (her sister-in-law) to go immediately to the Russian
Embassy in Bern to get a visa in order to find out the procedure for
reentry into their own country.

Get some Russian Social Democrat in Clarens to ask the Germans
to allow for the passage of a railway coach to Copenhagen for various revolutionaries. "You will say perhaps that the Germans will not
give a coach. I bet they will! Of course if they learn this idea came
from me or from you, then the scheme will be ruined."[5]

On March 23, he was in despair. A comrade had been told at the
British Embassy that "there is no passage at all through England.

What if no passage whatever is allowed either by England or by Germany! And this is possible!!"[6]

He considered going across Germany in a plane but realized that this was impractical, presumably for the need to refuel or the fear of being shot down. He toyed with going with the passport of a mute Swede—mute, of course, so that he would not be required to speak Swedish. "You'll fall asleep and see Mensheviks in your dreams," Nadya teased, "and shout 'scoundrels' and give the whole conspiracy away."

On March 25, in the midst of all this high emotional activity, he found time to write to Inessa about "the worker [who] has no fatherland," describing this as "theoretical oddities" and continuing the argument that had already lasted months. She must, he alleged, be in an "excessively nervous state." Who was talking, she might have thought? And at what a time! He even ended this letter: "Probably we won't manage to get to Russia!! Britain will not let us through. It can't be done through Germany." This was after hinting that "someone with free time . . . should collect all the press telegrams in all the foreign newspapers about the Revolution." Could he mean her, still in her secluded spot? Despite all the orders![7]

He did not speak of his real problem to Inessa, though he didn't have to: the Russian reaction to his traveling through an enemy country already responsible for thousands of Russian deaths was certain to do him huge political damage—unless he could find some way to make it acceptable.

In fact, the political section of the German Foreign Office had been planning since 1915 to provoke a revolution in Russia—"revolutionizing," as the policy was called—since a resulting mutiny of the army would enable them to switch their million troops engaged there to the western front.

The Germans' main contact had been Alexander Helphand, an astonishing character who had been close to Lenin in the days of the first party journal, *Iskra,* but had since made a fortune by dubious means in Turkey. He had become a millionaire Marxist, which made him suspect to socialists, who saw him as a fat caricature capitalist with an enormous car, a string of blondes, thick cigars, and a taste for champagne at breakfast.

But he knew everyone, even if they didn't like him, and he now ran a company, of which he owned half, in Copenhagen, that sold chemicals, medicines, and even condoms by means of sales teams within Russia. These would be useful for getting money into Russia and communicating, under cover of legitimate business, within her borders. And for two years Helphand had been insisting that the man the Germans needed to back to achieve their object was Lenin, though Lenin would have nothing to do with him.[8]

These were crucially important days for another reason. Before the Russian Revolution in March (February in Russia), Arthur Zimmermann, the German foreign minister, had taken a huge gamble. In order to starve Britain and France, he had ordered Germany's U-boats to sink all shipping bound for their ports, including neutral vessels. On March 18, the American people learned to their fury that three American ships had been sunk. War was now certain to be declared by the United States. Zimmermann's gamble now depended on one issue: Could Germany gain victory before U.S. troops could be deployed in Europe?

So, suddenly, the direction of revolution in Russia became urgent to Germany's broader strategy. Alexander Helphand took center stage, seeing himself as a kingmaker. Oddly, Jacob Furstenberg, Lenin's old partner on the Malinovsky Commission, was the manager of Helphand's company. He cabled Lenin offering him transit to Russia for two people.

Lenin was cautious. "Uncle wants to know more. Official transit for individuals unacceptable," wired Zinoviev on his behalf.

Lenin had hoped to reduce the immense political risk by traveling with a mixed party of exiles, so it was not just Bolsheviks, and by seeking prior approval from St. Petersburg. The second was a dubious hope. Both Paul Milyukov, the new foreign minister, and Alexander Kerensky, a potential highflier as minister of justice, were patriots.

Without question, they would not want Lenin and other antiwar socialists in Russia making trouble.

Martov, in fact, had come up with the same idea of a mixed group—but, as expected, no approval had come through. On March 31, 1917, with Martov insisting on waiting, Lenin decided he would go anyway, though not with Helphand's direct help.

A Swiss comrade had already made contact with Gisbert von Romberg, the German minister in Bern, exploring the possibility of passage by a train coach. Now Lenin confirmed the request by wire. His condition: The train should be "sealed" and have the extraterritorial status of an embassy. No Russian would even speak to a German during the trip. To avoid this, Fritz Platten, a Swiss Social Democrat, would be in charge of the party and do any talking that might be needed.

Then Lenin wrote to Inessa. "I hope we shall be starting out on Wednesday—with you, I hope. I trust you have received the money [one hundred francs] sent this morning by express [for her and Anna]. We have more money for the journey than I thought, enough for ten to twelve persons. The comrades in Stockholm have been a great help. . . . We shall fight. The war will agitate for us. A thousand greetings. Au revoir."[9]

On April 2, three days later, Romberg was ordered from the Wilhelmstrasse to expedite arrangements. The next day, Lenin wired his sisters in St. Petersburg: "Arriving Monday 11 P.M. Inform *Pravda.*"

It was optimistic, but on Wednesday, as soon as he heard that Romberg was trying to contact him, he told Nadya to pack. They were taking the first train to Bern.

Fritz Platten called on Romberg and demanded that "safe transit" of the exiles should be guaranteed, insisted that no names would be given, just numbers, with everyone paying their own fares. The minister agreed, but Lenin remained nervous. He was placing himself completely in the hands of his stated enemy, Kaiser Wilhelm II, at a time when revolution had toppled his cousin, the tsar.

On Friday, April 6, Inessa joined Lenin and Zinoviev and seven others at the Volkshaus in Bern to negotiate a formal list of conditions. Inessa translated them into French and German. Bolsheviks were alerted in the main Swiss cities.

Meanwhile, Lenin's train was causing wide foreign concern. From Bern, British ambassador Sir Horace Rumbold reported that a group of Russian socialists and anarchists, in favor of immediate peace with Germany, were about to be given safe transit. From London, the Foreign Office cabled the news to Sir George Buchanan in St. Petersburg, asking if the new government "intended to take any steps to counter this danger." Lenin, despite his fears, was unknown in British high circles, showing up only as one of many names on a list of antiwar revolutionaries.

In Halifax, Nova Scotia, Trotsky and friends, who had been in America, had been arrested on their way home on a British ship. Would London please discover, requested local officials, if the Russian government would like them to proceed?

There was reason for anxiety in London. A big new Allied offensive was planned for April 9, 1917.[10] While telegrams were being exchanged between the various embassies, troops were moving into position, with artillery and supplies, through the mud of northern France.

For Lenin, the news from Russia was alarming. A French newspaper, *Le Petit Parisien,* had reported that Milyukov had threatened to prosecute on charges of high treason everyone who traveled through Germany. From St. Petersburg, the party leaders could not contact Lenin and discovered to their alarm that their cables were being blocked, on orders of the new revolutionary government.

A courier, Maria Stetskevich, was sent to Sweden to communicate with Switzerland. On April 2 (March 20), she was back in the capital with letters from Lenin and Jacob Furstenberg informing the Central Committee about the sealed train.

She was sent back to Sweden again with letters. This time, at Tornio, the Finnish border town, she was searched and stripped naked. The letters were taken, but she was allowed to proceed to Sweden. It was another ominous sign of what lay ahead for Lenin and his party. For they, too, would have to pass through Tornio on their way to Russia.

The Central Committee was worried by the problem of the train but, like Lenin, accepted the risk. They got a message to Furstenberg in Copenhagen: "Ulyanov must come immediately." Lenin's sisters wired: "Do not force Vladimir to come. Avoid all risk."

Romberg, who understood Lenin's predicament, tried to persuade some SRs to join the party on the train, but they refused, as did Martov and his Mensheviks. They all insisted on permission from Russia.

On Monday morning, April 9, only a few hours after the Allies had launched a new offensive on the German line at Arras, Lenin's party gathered—some thirty-two of them, including two children—at the Volkshaus in Bern.[11] They were a determined group, though uneasy, since they faced danger both at home and within Germany. Despite the promises of safe transit, could the Kaiser be trusted?

They boarded a train to Zurich, where they all had lunch together with Swiss friends. Lenin made a significant speech. "Russia is a peasant country," he declared. "Socialism cannot triumph there immediately." These words conform with Marx's theory, then believed by all Social Democrats, that revolution in Russia would go through two stages: first, a capitalist, Western-style government before progressing ultimately to socialism.

Then they returned to the Zurich Bahnhof, where an angry crowd was waiting on the platform. To cries and catcalls of "Provocateurs! Spies! Pigs! Traitors!" the party boarded the train that would take them to the frontier. At 3:10 P.M., it pulled out, as the protesters struck the sides of the carriage with sticks. One of the travelers defiantly held a red scarf out a window.[12]

. . .

The actual "sealed train" was waiting for them at Gottmadingen, a tiny station in the hills on the German side of the Swiss border. As they approached, the travelers could see the tall hill, topped by woods, that dominated the little town. The train slowed, and they passed the old Bahnhof Hotel, with its curving roof and faded, cracked plaster, and came to a halt at the single platform, which was empty except for two German officers in high boots and green-gray uniforms.

The sight of the officers caused acute anxiety among the revolutionaries peering through the windows. Nearly all of them had been in jail or in illegal situations. Suspicion of men in uniform was rooted in them.

Uneasily, the travelers clambered down from the train and were ushered into a third-class waiting room. The atmosphere was tense, a suspicion, as feared, that they might have walked into a trap. When the men and women were separated into two groups, their unease grew.

The officers completed the formalities, collected the fares that Lenin had insisted on, and invited them to board the train that would take them across Germany to Sassnitz, on the Baltic.

It was not much of a train, just a green carriage with eight compartments—three second-class and five third-class—and a baggage wagon. Two escort officers were to travel with them, occupying the end third-class compartment, the "sealing" concept being met by a white chalk line on the corridor floor. No one was allowed to cross this line except for Fritz Platten. There were toilets at each end of the carriage, so the Germans did not need to enter "Russian territory," and Platten was the only person permitted to speak to them.

The single men in the party accepted the hard wooden benches of the third-class carriages, ceding the brown padded upholstery of second class to families. By common consent, Lenin and Nadya had the end second-class compartment to themselves, so he could work.

Three of the four external doors of the carriage, except for the officers' "German" end, were locked. As soon as the train left Gottmadingen Station, the anxious gloom of the travelers lifted. Spirits soared. There was laughter and joking. Some of the younger ones began to sing the "Marseillaise." It was taken up in other compartments, and the sound of elated voices echoed through the woods beside the track as the train clattered north through Germany.

. . .

The journey to Sassnitz was to take three days. Lenin was not al-lowed to enjoy the peace they had all intended to grant him. Several times he had to quell the noise in the next compartment, occupied by Olga Ravich, the Safarovs, and Inessa, who were joined by Karl Radek and some of the rowdy young men from third class. Eventually, Ravich's screaming laughter was too much for Lenin. He walked in, took her firmly by the hand, without speaking, and led her into another compartment.

Since Anna was on the train with her lover, Abram Skovno, it is odd that Inessa was not with them, but Radek confirmed she was with Olga Ravich and himself. Strangely, the accounts of the journey written by Ravich, Safarov, the Zinovievs, and Radek barely mention her. Especially odd is Safarov's omission, since they had long been close.

But then Zina Zinovieva wrote later of Longjumeau without referring to her, even though she had organized and lectured at the school. This was doubtless because, as time went on—and these were, of course, recollections written years later—Inessa's position became uncertain. She became dangerous to write about.

The fact that she was not with Lenin and Nadya was itself significant, but then, for months, she had been displaying a different personality, resistant to much of what Lenin wanted. It is intriguing that she showed no excitement about the March uprising, though it seemed like the start of the world revolution to which she had devoted much of her life and which meant her return to her children as a free citizen. Lenin had almost had to beg her to join them on the train, even sending her the fare. Nor did she write much about the journey. The impression that remains is of her sitting rather quietly, almost an outsider to her elated companions and the giggling Ravich, though Olga did report that Inessa laughed, too, at Radek.

She did, of course, have much to think about. Lenin was a long way from achieving the revolution he visualized. The Bolsheviks were a tiny party whom no one in the high levels of the Duma or the new Soviet took too seriously. They knew he would be a source of trouble in very unstable conditions, a strident and extreme political voice, which is why they had tried to keep him out. Russia was in enough chaos already, as politicians struggled to establish some sort of order, now that the tsarist regime and its long-established system had disintegrated.

In fact, Inessa must have reasoned, being more experienced with jail and Arctic exile than any of them, there was a clear danger that they might be arrested on arrival, and there was no doubt at all that the journey through Germany would have provoked many enemies. Was not the excitement a little premature? And what would her role be in Lenin's new life, assuming he was not put on trial for treason?

The train ran on to Tuttlingen, where they stopped to change the engine, then diverted to Stuttgart on their way to Karlsruhe, approaching from the east to avoid the main line to the front, which was reserved for military traffic. They went on through Mannheim to Frankfurt, arriving too late for their scheduled connection for Berlin.

The next day, after spending a night in the railyard sidings, they were given priority, the private train of the German Crown Prince being held up for two hours to allow them to pass as they headed for Berlin. To Zinoviev, the city, as they ran through the suburbs, seemed "like a cemetery," and the usually buoyant Olga Ravich found it "deathly still."

Once they came to a halt within the city, security was strict. No one, not even Fritz Platten, was allowed to leave the train. Under the original plan, they should by the evening of that day have been at Sassnitz.

The plan was changed and they stayed in Berlin for nearly twenty-four unscheduled hours. They were, of course, within easy distance of the Wilhelmstrasse, though there is no evidence of any kind of meeting with Foreign Office officials, except for a courtesy call by a junior officer in civilian clothes, who spoke only to Platten. Yet Lenin was important enough for them to invest in the Bolsheviks forty million gold marks, billions of dollars in modern money, according to two letters from the foreign minister to the Kaiser.[13] It was never acknowledged by the Bolsheviks, but German support, plus funding from other sources, is now accepted by most modern historians.

And the fact, which has never been in question, is that Lenin changed his whole plan of campaign on the journey to Russia, reversing his view of revolutionary development that he described in the Zahringerhof in Zurich before boarding the train for Gottmadingen. No longer would he believe revolution required two stages. They could go straight to socialism, which was exactly what Arthur Zimmermann and the Germans wanted them to attempt.

Why did Lenin change his mind on so basic an issue? It must have been because he now knew that the party, which previously had only limited funds, now had the resources to finance a huge Bolshevik propaganda campaign that would bring the masses behind them.

This does not mean that Lenin was a German agent. He was a Lenin agent. He would have done a deal with the Devil had this served his aims.

The next day, Thursday, April 12, they reached Sassnitz, boarding the Swedish ferry *Queen Victoria* and, after reaching Sweden, traveled by night train to Stockholm, arriving there twenty-four hours later. Inessa rushed off a telegram to the children in Pushkino, which suggested that at last she had shrugged off the gloom of the mountains: "Soon I shall be with you. . . . I am endlessly happy. I am already on the way from Stockholm to Peter[sburg]. . . . [I] will be delayed for a week in Peter. As soon as I arrive I will write to you from there. I kiss and hug you firmly my dears."[14] She gave no word, even of regards, to their father.

At 6:30 P.M. on Easter Friday, the group boarded yet another train that would take them the six hundred miles to the Finnish border. On the way, Lenin addressed them all in the corridor on what they should do if they were arrested at the frontier. On no account should they offer any defense for traveling through Germany. Instead, they should attack the government for not aiding their return from exile.

Tornio lay across the frozen mouth of the Tornio River. To reach the town, they had to travel over the ice in horse-drawn sledges. There, at the frontier, they were searched and stripped, like Maria, the courier. All the women, including, of course, Inessa and Anna, were forced even "to take off our stockings," as Zinaida recorded. "All the documents and even the books and toys my son had brought with him were taken."

It was ominous, suggesting that serious opposition awaited them in Russia. Neither was Lenin cheered by what he read in a copy of *Pravda,* obtained in the town. The Okhrana files had been opened. There was no longer any doubt that Roman Malinovsky, Lenin's protégé, had been a police spy.

"Several times," recorded Zinoviev, "Ilich, staring eyeball to eyeball, returned to this theme. . . . He looked straight in my face. 'What a scoundrel! He tricked the lot of us. Traitor!' "[15] Malinovsky was now, in 1917, a prisoner of war in Germany. But with Lenin's record of breaking all the rules—this was the man who had raised funds from the robbery of banks—a link with the Okhrana was not out of the question. It could be another mark against him at a time when he was highly vulnerable.

He learned that a military guard had been sent up to accompany the train, and he queried Zinoviev wryly: "To take us to jail?"

What awaited them, in fact, was a huge welcome at the Finland Station, a welcome out of all proportion to the tiny size of the Bolshevik Party. Even in June, two months later, after much campaigning, the Bolsheviks had only 105 out of 1,080 delegates to the Congress of Soviets.

But given the mood of the city, still ecstatic in the new climate of revolution and freedom, where comrade waiters were insulted to be offered a tip, people did not need much to get them out onto the streets, especially on Easter Monday, when all the factories were closed. And Nikolai Podvoisky and Vladimir Nevsky, the party's Bolshevik military commanders, were brilliant at assembling militant crowds, so brilliant that they were almost to destroy the party in July when their enthusiasm robbed Lenin of control.

That Monday, though, was incredible. It had become the custom to greet returning revolutionary notables with a parade. Only days before, Georgi Plekhanov had been welcomed by a large crowd. But this was on a different scale. "The throng in front of the Finland Station blocked the whole square," reported Nikolai Sukhanov.

> Troops with bands were drawn up under red flags. There was a throbbing of many motor cars. Awe-inspiring outlines of armored cars thrust up from the crowd. And from one of the side streets, startling the mob, cutting through it, a strange monster—a mounted searchlight. . . .
>
> Within the station, triumphal arches in red and gold stretched the length of the platform above the heads of the mass of waiting people. Banners hung above several divisions of guards of honor—soldiers, sailors, and Bolshevik armed Red Guards.

At the end of the platform was a small group of Bolsheviks that included Alexandra Kollontai, holding a bouquet of flowers.[16] Alexandra, who was to become both a partner and rival of Inessa, thrust the flowers into Lenin's hands. The waiting officers rapped out their commands, and the guard of honor presented arms. "That very instant," reported Vladimir Bonch-Bruevich, "the hubbub died down. All that could be heard was the blare of trumpets. . . . Then suddenly, there thundered forth such a powerful, stirring and hearty 'Hurrah' as I have never heard in my life."

Lenin was greeted by two representatives of the Petersburg Soviet—including the chairman, Nikolai Chkheidze, an old adversary—and made repeated speeches as he moved through the crowd, eventually being driven off in an armored car, though he stopped for brief addresses at fifteen street corners. At last they reached the Kseshinskaya Mansion—once the home of Matilda Kseshinskaya, the tsar's ballerina mistress—which the Bolsheviks had taken over as their headquarters.

There, over supper, after Lev Kamenev had made a speech of welcome, Lenin told them of his new concept—"All power to the Soviets," and, instead of Marx's two stages, a one-stage aim for revolution *now*—that had them reeling. It was, of course, the exact opposite of what he had said in Zurich on their day of departure. His other idea of "Power to the Soviet" seemed equally absurd. The Soviet was a loose federation of strike committees. How could its two to three thousand members, torn by political differences, ever rule a nation?

That night, Lenin and Nadya went to bed in the home of his sister, Anna, and her husband, Mark Elizarov, shared of course with Maria, on the sixth floor of 52 Shirokaya Street. The building, in the middle of Petersburg Island, had been constructed on a very sharp street corner. As a result, the apartment was triangular in shape, and the living room, in the apex, gave an impression of the prow of a ship. Lenin, peering out of the windows, must at times have felt like a sea captain. There was certainly rough weather ahead.

CHAPTER 11

ST. PETERSBURG 1917

The next morning, after a meeting with the party leaders, Lenin traveled to the Tauride Palace, which housed the Duma, the Soviet, and some other government offices. His arrival coincided with a conference of Bolsheviks from all over Russia, providing him with a chance to address delegates of much of the party.

As they crossed the Neva, they passed through the St. Petersburg they all knew so well: the Winter Palace, the setting of "Bloody Sunday"; the Admiralty with its pillared tower; the Field of Mars, the symbolic gardens where a month before hundreds of dead had been lowered into the ground, each coffin being marked by a boom from a cannon.

They traveled along the Nevsky Prospect, with its luxury shops and lavish apartments in the center of the city. It bore little sign of revolution, having the same expensive stores, elegant customers, congestion of carriages and automobiles, and hotel commissionaires, wearing sashes of green, gold, or scarlet. Bourgeois babies were still being pushed in big prams by nursemaids dressed in blue if the children were boys, pink if they were girls.

However, even if the revolution was not too evident on that cloudy April day, there had in fact been enormous changes. St. Petersburg, like much of Russia, faced social collapse. The entire nation had, as Alexander Kerensky put it, been swept by "a sense of unlimited freedom, a liberation from the most elementary restraints essential to every human society."

Crime had soared. In the factories, people had stopped working. Discipline had vanished from the army and the navy. In the streets, soldiers forcibly relieved officers of their swords.

The one factor that prevented a complete breakdown was the Soviet. The government ruled in name, but the Soviet made it possible.

Autocracy and feudalism had been overthrown; but because true chaos was so close, the early extremism, with its undertones of the French Revolution, had now been replaced in the Soviet by a belief that order must be preserved. Clearly, some party aims would have to be shelved for the time being. Certainly, the leading Bolsheviks, who had been running the party until then, subscribed to this view, which conformed with Marxist theory. It was seen as the first stage of revolution that Lenin had now decided they did not need.

Ordinary workers and soldiers felt a keen sense of personal achievement. Everyone was called "comrade." Everywhere, there were red flags, and imperial insignia had been ripped from the buildings. The mood of the city, indeed of the whole vast nation, was one of intense pride, a mood colored by a degree of complacency that Lenin planned that day to shatter.

After a diversion to visit the grave of his mother, Lenin arrived at the Tauride Palace. There, in the gallery, he addressed an audience of Bolsheviks, who had also been joined by Mensheviks, for a move toward unity was once more evident in this heady air. Inessa, as Alexandra Kollontai noted, sat with Nadya in the front row.

In ten clear points, to be known as the April theses, Lenin spelled out his new program, intended to catapult 160 million Russians toward socialism. They included an end to the war; control by the soviets of all production and sale of goods; confiscation of all private land; destruction of the bourgeois establishment (army, police, bureaucrats), which would be replaced by Soviet organs, with officials elected by the people; rule from below, as he was to repeat so often, not from above, a cry that in time was to have hollow and macabre echoes.

The murmuring began early. Then Lenin spoke of the Paris Commune of 1871 as a prototype, and the murmuring became a roar. "This is the raving of a madman," yelled Menshevik B. O. Bogdanov.[1] "Sheer anarchy," asserted a Bolshevik from *Iskra* days. Nikolai Chkheidze, chairman of the Soviet, who had welcomed Lenin at the Finland Station, declared him "a man completely played out."

Lenin's whole program seemed wildly impractical, but his mention of the Paris Commune touched a nerve. The people of Paris had set up the commune by elections in defiance of the government on March 26. It was an experiment in crude socialism. Even the officers of the National Guard, a people's militia, had been elected. But it only lasted nine weeks. The French government, nervous that these ideas might spread, had withdrawn the army from the capital but returned to the city on May 21 to smash the experiment in a massacre of some thirty thousand citizens.

Lenin's dramatic comparison seemed insane and even dangerous. In the evening of this raucous day, the British ambassador happily reported to London: "All Lenin's proposals have been rejected." In Berlin, Arthur Zimmermann's liaison officer was happy, too: "Lenin is working exactly as we would wish."

. . .

Inessa went home to her children at Pushkino for the first time in four years—to Andre, now thirteen, and Varya, fifteen. The two older boys were both away in the army. Inna was at university but likely took a train back to greet her mother. Presumably, Alexander, still legally her husband, was also there to welcome her.

There is no record of Inessa bidding Lenin good-bye before she left, but she must have done, if only in a note. She agreed with everything he'd said. She was more of an internationalist—believing revolution would spread like fire throughout Europe and eventually the world—than he was. Later, in 1918, when he was being politically pragmatic, she was to oppose him fiercely from the left of the party.

Certainly, she would have embraced Nadya before her departure. They had both stayed on after Lenin's speech to hear Alexandra Kollontai, who reported that their encouraging smiles had helped to give her confidence with what, after Lenin's shock waves, must have been a very edgy audience.

She must have left St. Petersburg with a degree of reluctance—since it would be the prime setting of the most important action—but she knew Moscow. It was her home city, with a far bigger population than that of the capital. She had worked there for the party in the underground, was well acquainted with its prisons, and had contacts throughout the new hierarchy of the city soviet.

She didn't waste any time. She moved into an Armand apartment at 14 Denezhnyi Lane in the Arbat. On April 19, barely two weeks after her arrival at the Finland Station, she attended a Moscow regional conference of Social Democrats. She took the platform to explain Lenin's April theses since, as Polina Vinogradskaya put it later, with careful understatement, "not everyone understood the worldwide historical significance of Lenin's prognosis and conclusions."

Vinogradskaya found Inessa irresistibly appealing, and also the vivacious force of her argument. "She was so beautiful, and the features of her faces seemed carved. . . . Her eyes were green, expressive, and magnetic. Her hair was fair, voluminous, worn up at the back with a side parting. She looked disciplined. It seemed that nature had given her something extraordinary."[2]

Inessa urged the election by soldiers of army officers and the fraternization of the troops in the trenches with the enemy. "The speech was very important in balancing opinion in Lenin's favor," Polina concluded. It clearly had impact, since Inessa was appointed as one of Moscow's delegates to the seventh All-Party SD conference, due to meet three days later in St. Petersburg.

By contrast, Nadya, who had expected to continue as Lenin's personal secretary, which she'd been for years, soon found herself sidelined. The party structures were already established, with a secretariat run at first by Elena Stasova and then by Yakov Sverdlov. Clearly Lenin thought it unwise to interfere by insisting that a place should be found for Nadya. Maria, Lenin's sister, who had often mocked Nadya, was now in a strong position as editorial secretary of *Pravda,* the party journal, and that made Nadya's situation no easier. After a while, Nadya gave up the struggle for a role in his new life and moved to the Vyborg factory district, where she worked for the party as an organizer and educator.

Meanwhile, Lenin's position was precarious in the extreme. His own party leaders, ranged around Kamenev, were violently opposed to his new plan. The revelation of the sealed train, unknown to the thousands who had welcomed him at the Finland Station, produced so violent a reaction that Lenin's life was in danger.

His new ideas were a propaganda gift to the right wing, in particular to Paul Milyukov, the foreign minister and head of the big Kadet Party, which had a powerful newspaper, *Rech,* and the solid support of the middle classes. Milyukov was liberal but far from revolutionary, and Lenin had given him scope to promote the idea that all pacifists and many Soviet members were in league with the Germans. The sealed train offered undisputed proof that Lenin had accepted help from the enemy.

Together with the right-wing General Lavr Kornilov, commander of the city's garrison of a quarter-million troops, Milyukov made a secret plan using well-worn tsarist tactics. Milyukov's Kadets, including many students, would provide disorder on the streets; Lenin and the Bolsheviks would be blamed. And the troops, if their resentment because of Lenin's German links could be enflamed, would agree to repress the troublemakers. The Soviet itself would then be vulnerable.

Lenin did his best to deflect the danger by appearing with Zinoviev before the Soviet Executive Committee, emphasizing the role of Fritz Platten and the "sealed" concept.

The Soviet, though noncommittal, published Lenin's statement in *Izvestia,* but this had little effect. All the bourgeois press attacked Lenin. Mobs paraded through the streets demanding his arrest. Large, hooting crowds gathered outside the Kseshinskaya Mansion yelling "Down with Lenin—back to Germany." Whenever he left the mansion, he had to be protected by bodyguards.

In several military regiments, motions demanding Lenin's arrest were carried by large margins. Even the sailors, the most revolutionary element in Russia, turned angrily against him. The naval honor guard that had presented arms on the platform of the Finland Station issued a public statement, regretting "our participation in his triumphal welcome to St. Petersburg." "Not a single Bolshevik," recorded Nikolai Podvoisky, the military chief in the mansion, "was able to enter the barracks without risking arrest or even death."

This was the St. Petersburg to which Inessa returned on April 21 to take her place at the SD Conference. She must have been shocked by the scenes on the streets and by the placards branding Lenin a German traitor. She is certain to have gone to the Kseshinskaya Mansion and witnessed the alarm. Whether she saw Lenin there is uncertain, for he was fighting for his life.

Lenin defended himself as well as he could in *Pravda,* but Kamenev had already denounced his proposals in the Bolshevik Central Committee and won unanimous support. He, too, now went public in *Pravda.* "If we want to remain the party of the masses," he stated, "then Lenin's base assumption about Marx's first stage was unacceptable." Stalin, among others, supported Kamenev.

The mood in the *Pravda* office was tense. "It was enough for one of them to read a scrap from an article he had just written," recorded Bonch-Bruevich, "for a violent quarrel to break out." But Lenin, in

argument, was on familiar ground. In the columns of the paper he attacked Kamenev point by point. He was under great strain but standing up to it well.

There is no doubt Inessa talked to Lenin in his sister's apartment,
for he referred to her visit in a letter in May. "With us, life is un-
changed from what you saw yourself here. There is no end to the exhaustion, and I am starting to give way and sleep three times more
than other people."[3]

He was wary even of his own party. His instructions to Inessa
about how she should write to him were very precise and repeated in
more than one letter. In April, he had written that "everything is boil-
ing, although the persecution is getting less" but advised her to send
all communications to him at the *Pravda* office, addressed to Maria,
and to key all letters "For V.I."[4] He spoke in another letter of the in-
termediaries they would use and told her that Sokolnikov, a trusted
comrade, would act as his emissary in the near future.[5]

With Inessa living in Moscow, some four hundred miles away, it
was clearly hard to maintain the kind of contact to which they had
become accustomed over the years. It was easier when Lenin himself
moved to Moscow in March of the following year, but it was not until
September 1918—when he was badly wounded in an attempt on his
life—that their relations again became close. Yet long before then,
signs of Lenin's influence could be seen in the duties assigned to Inessa
by the Central Committee and in her ease of access to him at a time
when he was under great pressure.

Meanwhile, in the spring of 1917, despite the internal opposition
to him and the hate campaign on the streets, Lenin was not as alone as
he seemed. Many of the ordinary party workers below the top hierarchy were as extreme as he was. In the Vyborg factories were Bolsheviks
as rabid as any sansculottes of the French Revolution, as some had
demonstrated back in February.

The party membership in St. Petersburg had been soaring, now
topping seventy thousand. Few of these new party members understood the internal ideological conflicts—or cared about the "stages of

revolution"—that engrossed their leaders, but they were radicals to whom Lenin had offered a rallying point, as became evident very fast. A full conference of the city party's members gave Lenin's new policy an almost blanket endorsement.

Also, Lenin had strong support in the mansion from two important men below the top leadership: Podvoisky and Nevsky, who ran the newly created Bolshevik Military Organization. They were in charge of party contacts within the regiments, as well as the agitators and the Red Guards, those leather-jacketed units of armed workers that had been set up in February with rifles given to them by the soldiers. Podvoisky, at thirty-seven, was tall, bearded, and fine-looking but unsmiling. Nevsky had an easier personality; he was a clever orator and skilled agitator. Podvoisky was the organization man, sending out orders on little pink slips or calling the field leaders by phone. Nevsky was the spellbinder who would speed to trouble spots by car to deploy his persuasive powers as a speaker.

They were militant, romantic revolutionaries. By mid-April, when Lenin arrived, they commanded only a few hundred agitators. The Red Guards were still being formed and trained.

The two men were at the sharp end of the city hostility. Lenin sent for Podvoisky and told him that the daily Kadet Party processions must be answered. "It's vital," he said, as Podvoisky reported in *The Year 1917,* "that you bring onto the streets some troops marching under Bolshevik slogans—even if it's only one company."

In the current mood of the city, this would be difficult, but the First Machine Gun Regiment had been prominent in the February revolution and were close to the party. They responded, albeit with only a few companies backed up by some workers, but they marched under Bolshevik banners.

Also, Lenin was surprisingly willing, given his past caution, to take personal risks. When Nevsky flashed an alarm to the *Pravda* office that the Izmailovskys, one of the regiments that had wreaked havoc in Moscow in 1905, were in a dangerously angry mood on their parade ground, Lenin at once went to them.

"They'll tear you to pieces," someone said as he left.

But they didn't. Although at first he faced hostile yells about Germany, he won them over. When he'd finished speaking, "explaining," as he put it, he was carried triumphantly around the parade ground on the shoulders of two soldiers.

On April 21, two weeks after Lenin's arrival, the Kadet campaign climaxed with a vivid and macabre march of thousands of the wounded from the city hospitals: legless men hopping on crutches, men with stubs for arms, men in bandages with disfigured faces. They crawled along the Nevsky Prospect and the Liteiny toward the Tauride Palace, under the slogan "War to the end. Our wounds demand victory!"

The Soviet was deeply concerned. *Izvestia* attacked "the dark forces" that were exploiting Lenin. The day after the parade of the wounded, Milyukov publicly assured the Allied ambassadors that Russia had not been weakened by revolution. She was determined to fight on, and he indicated that it would still be a full imperialist war, not the defensive war the Soviet had agreed to back.

Lenin, who had been linking the war to the bankers, the arch-capitalists, was delighted. "Fight," he declared in *Pravda*, "because we want the spoils. Die, tens of thousands of you, every day, because 'we' . . . have not yet received our share of the loot!"

The masses rose, as Milyukov had planned, for now the Bolsheviks really could be blamed. But the Soviet leaders met the long processions as they streamed into the city center and urged them to return home. The Soviet, they promised, would force the government to amend its policy. And the crowds did what was asked, but they were aching for action.

Late that night, however, the right-wing press published a scream of abuse. Blaming the Bolsheviks for threatening civil war, they called onto the streets "all who stand for Russia and her freedom" to support the government.

It was a challenge Lenin had to accept, though he knew its dangers. By the next night, the Cossacks could well be charging. But, in the face of a huge Kadet parade under this slogan, he had no option. The party called out the workers for an "organized" demonstration.

Leaning on his military studies after 1905, he ordered strict tactics. The Nevsky would be the focus. As the main worker column marched down the prospect, others should be moving simultaneously along parallel streets on either side, forming a "three-pronged claw." By this technique, they could block off attempts to attack the central force from the cross streets.

Only workers were marching—no troops, for the Soviet had ordered them to remain in barracks, no matter who called them out. Indeed, when General Kornilov ordered guns into Mariinsky Square, the artillerymen refused to comply. Despite Lenin's plan, there were clashes. Some were serious, and many people were injured. There was shooting on Sadovaya, but it was a civilian affair.

Late that afternoon, the Soviet firmly stopped the crisis. The marchers were to return home. There were to be no street meetings for two days. The Bolsheviks backed this call.

The Kadets claimed victory, but Milyukov and Kornilov had won no ground, their purpose now being blatantly obvious. Within weeks, they were forced to resign. The government was reorganized to include six members of the Soviet as ministers. Alexander Kerensky, appointed minister for war, was the new rising star—especially interesting because, out of all the Russias, the two principal rivals in this ever-changing situation came from the same Volga River town, Simbirsk. Kerensky's father had taught Lenin and was answerable to Lenin's father, who was the local inspector of schools.

Kerensky, a melodramatic but mesmerizing lawyer who had won much popular support by his defense of strikers in 1912, headed a small party that worked with the SRs. But he was a patriot who wanted to win the war. And, great speaker as he was, he set out now to rally the army to mount an offensive that would smash its way through the German lines and tap the basic public affection for "Mother Russia."

By contrast, Lenin, commanding a party that was noisy but also very small, was focusing on his ever-growing network of agitators throughout the nation. "Keep it simple," he ordered. "Speak only of bread, land, and peace." At the Kseshinskaya Mansion, orators spoke from the walls all day to gathered crowds. Lenin, too, took his turn.

Meanwhile, deploying their new mainly German funds, the Bolsheviks launched forty-one newspapers and journals throughout the nation, twelve in local dialects, including *Soldatskaya Pravda,* which urged the troops at the front to mutiny.

In Moscow, during these chaotic weeks, Inessa was active. As a representative of the Moscow soviet, she attended an All-Russian Women's Congress, staging a walkout because, she insisted, working women could have nothing in common with bourgeois women.

She was elected to the Moscow Duma, with the help of women, who now had the vote for the first time. She took an instructing role in a school for agitators, with its echoes of Longjumeau, as she had done back in 1905. And in late June she was elected to the seven-person executive committee of the Moscow soviet.

She wrote articles for *Zhizn' Rabotnitsy,* Moscow's sister paper to *Rabotnitsa,* which had been revived in St. Petersburg. She defended Lenin in one important piece against the attacks portraying him as a German agent, which were soon to reach a new peak, less public but more serious. The French Secret Service had produced what they claimed was proof of German funding of the Bolsheviks. There was also other evidence of large sums of money being channeled through Alexander Helphand's company. In fact, Jacob Furstenberg was reported to be on his way to Russia. Kerensky ordered Furstenberg to be held at the frontier.

Back in the capital, a new Congress of Soviets, with delegates from across Russia, was in progress to take over the central role occupied until now by the St. Petersburg Soviet. Irakli Tsereteli, a leading Menshevik, appealed for unity among all factions. "Today," he declared, "Russia has no political party which would say: 'Give us power. Go . . . and we will take your place.' "

A voice rang out from the back of the hall. "There *is* such a party!" Lenin had stood up. "It is the Bolshevik Party!"

The shocked silence was broken by a wave of laughter. To men from outside St. Petersburg, the idea that the minority Bolsheviks could govern seemed absurd. Kerensky answered him, in a reasoned speech. Lenin walked out in the middle of it. The Soviet rejected all the important Bolshevik resolutions.

The city was seething. Podvoisky and Nevsky saw the situation in optimistic but stark terms. In a meeting at the mansion two days later, they warned that they were under heavy pressure from many regiments in the garrison, now in danger of transfer to the front, to mount a demonstration against Kerensky's planned offensive.

Two weeks earlier, Lenin had vetoed this, saying it was far too early. Now, Podvoisky asked him to reconsider because some regiments were threatening to act on their own.

Lenin bought time, helped by the diversion of twenty-eight factories that had suddenly staged a strike. But eventually the Central Committee reluctantly authorized a "peaceful" demonstration in two days' time. His military commanders, certain he was wrong, began planning actual violence.

Only hours before the demonstration, the Congress of Soviets ordered the Bolsheviks to cancel it. How could they refuse? "Power to the Soviet" was Lenin's slogan. After much heated debate, they did what the Soviet ordered. But would the troops and the masses obey the Party?

The result was impotent fury in the barracks and the factories. So somewhat nervously, the Soviet leaders decided to help them by organizing a demonstration of their own, open to all parties, to show the unity of "revolutionary democracy." Lenin and his leaders, but not his militants, heaved a sigh of relief. He could now mount his parade under the cover of official Soviet respectability.

June 16 was a beautiful day, with a clear blue sky and the sun glistening from the golden cupolas and spires of the city. Marchers from regiment after regiment, factory after factory, paraded under red-and-gold Bolshevik banners past the saluting base on the Tomb of the Martyrs in the Field of Mars: "All power to the Soviets! Down with

Inessa's father, Theodore Stephane,
an opera singer of such works as
Rigoletto and *Faust*. After he died he
was honored by an obituary in the
French newspaper *Le Figaro*.

Inessa, age 6, with her Aunt Sophie,
a tutor by profession, who, along
with Inessa's grandmother, educated
her privately in languages,
music, and literature.

Inessa, age 5, with her grandmother
in Paris. All later photographs from
Inessa's youth were taken in Moscow,
thus providing a rough indication
of when Inessa was taken to Russia.

Inessa, age 10.

Inessa, age 15.

Inessa, age 19,
in the year of her
marriage.

Inessa (bottom right), in her late teens, in a playful mood
with Renee (top left) and two unknown friends. This is a
very unusual photograph, since it was taken around 1892
at the very peak of Victorian/tsarist formality.

Inessa, age 19,
with her husband,
Alexander Evgenevich Armand.

Anna Kostantinovich, Inessa's
sister-in-law and close friend, eldest
of the Armand siblings. Anna, who
lived in Europe, traveled back to
Russia in 1917 with Lenin and Inessa
in the sealed train.

The Armand family sharing a meal on the veranda at their home in Pushkino.
Left to right: Andre, Inessa, Maria Armand, Evgenii Armand
(Inessa's father-in-law), Varvara Karlovna (Inessa's mother-in-law),
Vera Armand, and Vladimir (Volodya) Armand.

The Armand family home in Pushkino, which consisted of four houses
linked by covered galleries, with verandas. Within the stockadelike
complex was a huge room used for parties and amateur theatricals.

Eldigino, Inessa's first marital home, pictured today. A plaque on the wall records that she lived there from 1893 to 1904, which is not totally accurate.

Inessa went to the Swiss mountains near Lausanne, on the north side of Lake Geneva, from July 1903 to May 1904 with all four of her children as a last gesture of discretion, since she was pregnant with Andre, Vladimir's son. She also needed time to think over the direction of her life. In 1916, when she quarreled with Lenin, she again ran to the mountains, this time alone, to Baugy-sur-Clarens, not far to the west.

Inessa in the Swiss mountains, 1903–1904.

Inessa, age 28, in Moscow in 1902,
the year she fell in love with
Alexander's 17-year-old brother, Vladimir.

Inessa with Inna
and Varvara.

Inessa in 1910 with her
five children, the year after Vladimir
died. The children ranged from
7 (Andre) to 16 (Sasha)
years of age.

Inessa, age 30, with Andre,
most likely in late 1904.

Vladimir Armand, Inessa's lover and her
husband Alexander's youngest brother.
The photograph is difficult to date, but it was most
likely around 1906, which would make
him 21 or 22. He died in January 1909.

Police mug shots of Nadya, Nadezhda Krupskaya, Lenin's wife, presumably before they were married. Nadya gained permission to join Lenin in exile in Shushenkoye, near the Mongolian border, because she was his fiancée. They married soon after she arrived, in 1898.

Inessa in Mezen, 1908. She is pictured with several fellow exiles. Probably some of them helped her escape.

Fannie (Dora)
Kaplan, who shot
and nearly killed
Lenin in 1918.
Although Fannie
was a member of
the rival SR party,
she insisted that
she was acting on
her own behalf.
With a background
as an anarchist,
she had been
sentenced under
the tsar to
"eternal hard
labor."

Alexandra Kollontai, a star of the
revolutionary movement. A brilliant
speaker with a high sense of fashion,
Alexandra had several lovers, including
Lenin's close comrade Alexander
Shlyapnikov. Alexandra was a rival
of Inessa, who, as head of the Women's
Section of the Central Committee,
ended up as her superior.

Lenin in disguise, age 46, in 1917.
In the "July Days" he lost control of
his militants, and, as he had warned,
the rising occurred too soon. When
his arrest was ordered, Lenin fled
across the border to Finland.

St. Petersburg, 1917.
The occasion of this
photograph is not known,
but it could have been the
first revolution in
February or the period
of the July Days.

Lenin in 1919. In power
for two years, he looks
older than 49. He had
overseen the Red Terror,
murdered the tsar and all
his children, as well as six
other relations, and waged
war on the bourgeoisie.
Civil war still raged in
many parts of Russia.

Grigori Zinoviev, age 34 in approximately 1917. He and Lev Kamenev were Lenin's closest male comrades, who all together were known as "The Troika." Together with his wife Zinaida Lilina, Zinoviev had shared Lenin's exile in Europe and returned with him in the sealed train.

Lenin with his sister, Maria, in 1918.

Lenin in 1920.

Felix Dzerzhinsky, head of the dreaded Cheka, with senior officials.
The Cheka, which took over from the Okhrana, absorbed Nikolai Podvoisky's
Military Revolutionary Committee, and came in due course to be called the
KGB. Dzerzhinsky, who came from Polish gentry stock, had spent much time in
tsarist prisons. He was a revolutionary zealot following his release in 1917.

Lenin addressing
a crowd in 1920,
the year of
Inessa's death.

Inessa in 1920, shortly
before she died. She was
now head of the
Women's Section of the
Central Committee and
had the power to make
laws within her area.
She decreed that all
factory committees
should include at least
one woman. Inessa's
face bears the strain of
long hours of overwork
and illness earlier in the
year. She was close to
a nervous breakdown
when Lenin insisted she
take a vacation with her
youngest son, Andre,
in the Caucasus.

Inessa's coffin, lying in state with a female guard of honor
in the House of Unions, once the home of the Moscow Duma.
Her coffin lay with a sheath of white lilies addressed "Comrade
Inessa from Lenin." At her state funeral the next day,
Lenin's visible distress shocked several close comrades.

the ten capitalist ministers! Down with the war!" And as each con-
tingent passed the tomb, they lowered their banners in tribute to the
dead.

"Soldiers in drab and olive," recorded an eyewitness,

> Horsemen in blue and gold, white bloused sailors, black
> bloused workers, girls in varicolored waists surging through
> the main arteries of the city. On each marcher a streamer, a
> flower, a ribbon of red, scarlet kerchiefs around the women's
> heads, red rubashkas on the men. . . .
>
> As this human river flowed, it sang . . . the spontaneous
> outpouring of a people's soul. Someone would strike up a rev-
> olutionary hymn; the deep resonant voices of the soldiers
> would lift the refrain, joined by the plaintive voices of the
> working women; the hymn would rise and fall and die away;
> then down the line it would burst forth again—the whole
> street singing in harmony.[6]

That night, in the Elizarov apartment on Shirokaya Street, the
Central Committee and the two military commanders sat around the
dining room table. The day had been a great success, but Podvoisky
was grim. "After this," he said, "the workers and soldiers will want
to stage an uprising."

Lenin feared he was right and insisted that Podvoisky curb them.
"At this stage, a rebellion would be doomed to defeat because there
would be no support from the armies at the Front or from the people
in the provinces. . . . This must be explained. . . . Forces must be
alerted for a decisive assault, but the party will indicate the time."

On the morning of that same joyous day, Kerensky's offensive,
which he was relying on to rally Russia and check the Bolshevik threat,
had been launched. At first, it was quite successful, but then it began
to falter. Although the news of the early advances had been greeted
rapturously with Kadet parades, the Bolshevik leadership did not
order any counterdemonstrations. Troops in the capital who might be

ordered to the front were alarmed. They could not understand the need for delay in the Bolshevik takeover of power—nor could the agitators from all over Russia who had been called to a meeting in the mansion, nor could Podvoisky and Nevsky, their commanders.

Lenin addressed them with the same old arguments. "If we seize power," he insisted, "it is naïve to think we would be able to hold it. . . . Events should not be anticipated. Time is on our side."

They didn't believe him. The agitators said they were being used as "fire hoses," damping down the embers of enthusiasm for the party they had ignited on previous orders.

For once, Kamenev joined Lenin in urging patience. But *Soldatskaya Pravda* came out in open challenge: "Wake up, whoever is asleep!"

The mansion was burning with rebellion. Yet, oddly, Lenin chose this moment to leave St. Petersburg for a holiday. On June 29, he arrived at the Bonch-Brueviches' villa in Neyvola, on Finland's Karelian Isthmus. Four days later, he was called back. A revolution had started.

On July 1, two days before, the First Machine Gun Regiment had refused to obey orders to leave for the front. It was a spark in a city that was waiting to explode. The troops and the workers took to the streets. The Central Committee tried to distance itself from the unsanctioned uprising. Then its members decided to take control, glad that Lenin was out of the city, which would make more credible their pleas of innocence. The only people in the higher levels in the mansion that were happy were Podvoisky and Nevsky, who believed, despite Lenin's warning, that now was the time for the uprising.

Glumly, from the cab Lenin caught with Maria on July 3 at the Finland Station on his return, Lenin watched the marching troops and workers on July 3. In the Bolsheviks' rooms in the Tauride Palace, he met the leaders. There was shooting in the streets, Cossack charges, and finally the Izmailovsky Regiment marching to protect the Soviet.

The next day, government forces surrounded the mansion and broke into the *Pravda* offices. Kerensky, at the front, telegraphed orders for the Bolshevik leaders to be arrested. He was planning to put Lenin on trial with the evidence they had collected—even though Furstenberg, sensing trouble, had turned back before he reached the frontier.

Lenin and Zinoviev escaped from the city in disguise, catching a train, with the help of a Bolshevik rail comrade, to a small station near Belo-ostrov, the border town. They hid in a shack in the nearby woods for two weeks. Then Lenin crossed the frontier, dressed as a stoker, riding in the engine driver's cab, while the genuine stoker traveled in a carriage as a passenger. For a few days he stayed in the village of Jalkala, but then he headed for the Helsinki home of a friend who just happened to be the city's police chief. Even so, Lenin knew from experience that it was unwise at such times to remain in one place, so he moved on to other addresses. Meanwhile, Zinoviev returned to the capital, where he stayed in hiding.

In Moscow, Inessa had been active. On June 22, a week before the big Saturday parade in the capital, she urged, in the name of the Soviet Executive Commission, that mass demonstrations supporting "all power to the soviets" should be held in Moscow. But times were changing. By mid-July, all the party leaders had been arrested, except for those in hiding.

There were no arrest orders out for Inessa, and she attended an illegal party congress in St. Petersburg on July 26 but made no speeches. She witnessed the appointment of Alexandra Kollontai as the first woman to join the party's Central Committee, even though Kollontai herself was unable to be present.

Inessa had rarely displayed jealousy, even seeing Nadya, whom some women in her position might have resented, as a friend. However, she cannot have been pleased to see this elevation of Kollontai. She knew much about her, knew, too, she had exchanged a lot of letters with Lenin, especially from Norway, after the start of war. She was aware that Kollontai had been the mistress of Alexander Shlyapnikov, a close ally of Lenin and the Central Committee member in charge of foreign communications.

Also, Kollontai had great style and a fine reputation as a speaker and writer, whereas not many people outside Lenin's immediate circle had ever heard of Inessa. The two women, different as they were, were doomed to be rivals in postrevolutionary Russia.

Inessa, bowing to the new political climate, retreated discreetly to Pushkino, where Andre was ill again with suspected TB.

· · ·

By now, Kerensky's offensive had clearly failed. On July 19, the Germans had counterattacked and checked the Russian Army. In St. Petersburg, the Bolshevik press had been banned, its headquarters taken over, and its leaders indicted.

However, Kerensky was now having trouble with the right. General Kornilov, commander-in-chief of the Russian Army, became the central figure of a military coup supported by all Lenin's old enemies, the officer hierarchy, Milyukov and his Kadets, and probably the Allied governments.

They planned a dictatorship to liquidate the soviets and restore order to the country and discipline to the army. Almost certainly Kornilov allowed Riga to fall to the Germans to create a climate of crisis. Then he telegraphed Kerensky demanding the ceding of all power to himself and ordered his troops to advance on the capital.

Kerensky had no choice but to ask the Soviet for help, and the Soviet had no choice but to turn to the Bolsheviks, the only party with a military organization, frayed though this was by the events of July.

The Bolsheviks summoned the people of St. Petersburg to defend their city. Once more, the Red Guards were issued rifles. Once more, Podvoisky and Nevsky moved onto center stage. The railway men took up the tracks, which stopped the advancing troop trains. Kornilov's communications were broken by the telegraph operators. Bolshevik agitators, now acting for the Soviet, were dispatched to Kornilov's troops to explain how they were being used by the counterrevolution. On September 1, Kornilov was arrested on Kerensky's orders.

The army reacted violently against the entire officer corps. Many were murdered. Kornilov's attempted coup gave a new dynamism to a gigantic movement that was already swinging back to the Bolsheviks. Within a week, the party had gained voting control of the Soviet, and Trotsky was to replace Chkheidze as its president.

To Lenin, in Helsinki, conditions finally seemed ideal for the party to stage an uprising, but he knew the pendulum could swing again to reaction, so he saw speed as essential. But the other party leaders were more cautious than they had ever been. Even the left-wingers were not demanding militancy after their savaging in July. Compromise with other parties was once more the mood of the day.

Lenin flew into one of his old rages. "You will be traitors and scoundrels," he wrote the Central Committee. If they did not take immediate militant action and "arrest all the scum," meaning Kerensky and the ministers, they would "face dire punishment." The leaders were tolerant. Lenin had become temporarily unstable. The embarrassing letter was formally burned.

When Lenin informed them he was returning, they ordered him not to. So he organized it himself with his old friend the Helsinki police chief and Hugo Yalava, the engine driver who had carried him into exile.

On October 10, in an apartment overlooking the Karpovka River in Old Petersburg, Lenin called a meeting of the twelve members of the Central Committee, demanding an uprising before the next Congress of Soviets, which had been called for two weeks later. It took him ten hours, and even then Kamenev and Zinoviev opposed him. They even pleaded their case later in print, certain that success could now be gained by constitutional methods.

But Lenin had won the issue by a large majority. Trotsky organized the rising, with the aid of the two military commanders. They did not, however, meet the deadline.

Kerensky was already taking defensive measures. The bridges over the Neva were raised, and government relief forces were on their way into the city when at 2:00 A.M. on October 24, Trotsky launched his operation.

Units of soldiers and workers, under Podvoisky's Military Revolutionary Committee commissars, took over the rail stations, the electricity plants, the waterworks, the state bank, the food warehouses. Already they had control of the telephone exchange and the telegraph office. The phones of the Winter Palace were disconnected.

One by one, the bridges were captured, with little fighting. The defending troops just surrendered. The cruiser *Aurora* moved up the river within gunshot of the Winter Palace, where Kerensky and his ministers were meeting. He tried to organize a counterattack, but even the Cossacks played for time. "We are saddling our horses."

Soon after daylight on October 25, Kerensky drove out of the city to Pskov, to meet the troops and Cossacks called back from the front. But his ministers remained. The attack on the Winter Palace, under the command of Podvoisky, was launched against little resistance.

In the Congress of Soviets, there was much argument, especially from the Mensheviks and the SRs. The Bolsheviks were labeled "political hypocrites." Martov, Lenin's partner of his youth, declared that "the question of power is being settled by means of a military plot. . . . Comrades, we must put a stop to bloodshed." In response, Trotsky ordered him, in his phrase that would become famous, to "go where you belong from now on: the dustbin of history."

At 8:30 P.M., Lenin rose and went to the podium, "gripping the edge of the reading stand," as John Reed reported in *Ten Days That Shook the World*, "letting his little winking eyes travel over the crowd as he stood there waiting, apparently oblivious to the long-rolling ovation." Then, when he could make himself heard, he declared: "We shall now proceed to construct the socialist order."

After Lenin had spelled out his vision of revolution spreading among the workers of Europe, Kamenev, in the chair, stood up and asked all in favor of the proclamation to hold up their cards.

"Suddenly," Reed recorded, "we found ourselves on our feet, mumbling together into the smooth lifting unison of *The Internationale*. . . . The immense sound rolled through the hall, burst windows and doors, and soared into the quiet sky."

CHAPTER 12

MOSCOW 1917

n Moscow, the coup was not so easy. "The shooting began last night at midnight . . . ," Yury Gautier, who had known Inessa in her Pushkino days, wrote in his diary. "They [Kerensky's troops] took the Kremlin this morning. Right now they are fighting in the center of the city, northwest of the Kremlin, and on the outskirts of town. . . . The impressions are strongly reminiscent of 1905."[1]

Gautier was a professor and bitterly opposed to Lenin. "We spent our time on the telephone," he wrote the next day. "Occasional shots could be heard on Prechistenka and in the side streets. There are all kinds of contradictory rumors. The telephone is our only contact with the world.

"There was an inspection of the attics in our building. Among the officer-volunteers were Fedor and Andryusha Armand [a cousin]; Fedor is making amends for his Bolshevik mama. We treated them to lunch."[2]

Fedor was in the army and had absorbed cadet-school politics, which were at sharp variance to those of Inessa. But rightish views were not too healthy to have in the new order, as he was to discover.

Three days later, Gautier recorded: "The situation is getting worse. Regular firing on the center from the outskirts has begun. . . . The Bolsheviks have artillery and people who know how to shoot."

The fighting went on for some ten days. A grenade dropped into the courtyard of Gautier's home exploded and broke the windows. It wounded a cook and tenant of the block.

> There is no news from the outside world. . . . The new regime is publishing decrees. . . . Apparently the victors are routing the Kadets, locking them up in prison [with] taunts from the barbarized soldiers. . . . The situation in Moscow is reminiscent of Rome under Marius or Sulla. . . . Rumors proliferate. . . . Minsk, Dvinsk, and Reval have been taken. . . . [Generals] Kornilov and Kaledin are surrounding Moscow. Where is the truth? It seems that we are approaching the final catastrophe. The banks are closed. . . . Apparently everyone who can is quitting Moscow.

The resistance ended at last, a relief to an anxious Inessa in her apartment in the Arbat. Finally, it was all justified: all that planning and dividing that she had helped Lenin develop in exile as he rigidly carved out his tight, disciplined Bolshevik Party; all the intense, studied opposition he'd maintained to those who had disagreed with him. Yet she knew that for all the triumph at the Congress of Soviets and the peace now established in Moscow, the Bolshevik success was fragile.

Danger lay in several directions—ranging from the SRs, which were so big and deeply rooted, but also from the Mensheviks and other SDs who wanted an elected multiparty government; from Kerensky and the generals; from the German armies; and ultimately from the threat of civil war that would soon break out around the disaffected officers supported by many Cossacks and other dissidents, including peasant forces. In time, too, there were the Allies to worry about. Even the right-wing Bolsheviks who had gathered around Kamenev were now opposing what they realized was Lenin's plan for dictatorship.

And overriding everything, now with the winter upon them, was the specter of famine, aggravated by transportation chaos, which made Lenin suspect the kulaks, the more prominent peasants, of hoarding grain. But there was nothing new about food shortages, and the kulaks had no control of the rail tracks. Lenin needed no reminding that the spark that had exploded the February Revolution had been struck in the lines for bread, which was why the supply of it had been one of the three promises, with peace and land, offered by his agitators.

But Inessa was confident that the revolution she had worked for from her earliest days with Volodya Armand, even if its practical form had always been rather misty, was now on course.

Much of what we know about Inessa at this time was subject later to party control. She presented a difficulty: The fact that Lenin had a warm friendship with a woman that was not entirely appropriate, and subject to rumor, did not fit the desired image of the nation's leader. Yet Lenin's group of exiles, of which she was so prominent a member, was seen in an almost heroic color, which gave her a high ranking in the party mythology. So, as in time Lenin was given iconic status, any written treatment of her acquired a dangerous delicacy.

Within two weeks of the takeover of power, she was back in St. Petersburg with an unusual target: the peasants, who formed so large a proportion of the Russian population. She was there primarily, on behalf of the Moscow soviet, to attend the Congress of Peasant Deputies. The congress was dominated by the SRs, the party of the peasants, as the Bolsheviks were the party of the workers. So Inessa did one of her dramatic walkouts with most of the Bolsheviks, which always caused a stir, even made a point, but had little impact on the voting.[3]

Far more significant was her assignment by the Bolshevik Central Committee to work for two months on peasant matters, using a pass, issued on Lenin's orders, to attend meetings of the Council of People's Commissars, Lenin's inner cabinet.[4]

She was clearly chosen by Lenin, supported probably by those commissars she had known in exile. It underlines his high opinion of her but also indicates how important the peasants were now regarded.

As has been seen, Lenin—like Marx—had expected revolution to break out among the workers in industrially advanced countries. Only Russia had such a huge number of peasants. The fact that Russia had become the starting point of the new social order had not exactly caught the Bolsheviks on the wrong foot, but it did not conform with the party's philosophy nor its long-term planning.

So the SR Party, with which the Bolsheviks had often cooperated, had now become a major rival. They were well entrenched with some 70 percent of the nation. What's more, their romantic if violent background and their inheritance of the aura of the old terrorist martyrs gave them a defining cachet.

This all came to a climax when the Constituent Assembly, an elected all-Russian parliament planned in mid-1917 by Kerensky, met for the first time in January 1918. Thirty-eight percent of the delegates elected were SRs, while only 24 percent were Bolsheviks. So Lenin decided he could manage without such a body and closed it down to cries of alarm, even within his own party, since the assembly could have been a truly democratic base. Lenin shrugged off the protests. The power would now rest within his party, which is where he wanted it.

Meanwhile, the peasants remained a great issue, being crucial to the whole question of land, another of the three Bolshevik rallying cries. And Inessa was a curious choice to help handle it. For what could she know about the intricacies of peasant lives, apart from what she'd learned as the young wife of a rich landlord? Perhaps not that much, though even as a young wife she had been shocked by the conditions in which they lived. More important, she was a person on whom Lenin could rely.

These were crucial days. Lenin was using a broad sword wildly, making laws by a series of decrees—"meaningless decrees," as Maxim Gorky, the people's writer and Lenin's friend, was to accuse, "written with a fork on water."[5] One of the first decrees was to abolish the ownership of land, though just how was rather vague. "The peasantry," wrote Robert Service, "was invoked to take collective action to seize . . . all land not currently owned by peasants." It was a war on the wealthy and the bourgeoisie, whom Lenin had hated ever since the hanging of his brother Alexander had made pariahs of his family in Simbirsk.

What was not vague was the absorption of the Bolsheviks' military force (the MRO), still directed by Podvoisky, into a new secret police, the Cheka, which was to become far more ruthless, indiscriminate, and all-embracing than the Okhrana had ever been.

The nature of the new society soon became horrifyingly plain. The people were urged to destroy and even to kill the wealthy and the middle class, to strip from them their possessions—the "looting of the looters," wealth being seen as theft.[6] This was justified by Lenin as a natural need for revenge. The management of companies, like those owned by the Armands, was to be controlled by workers' committees. The holding of shares and bonds was forbidden. Banks were nationalized, and one thousand rubles was the maximum withdrawal permitted. (Even that amount was soon made worthless by soaring inflation.) Jewelery, foreign currency, and valuables were confiscated by the local state authority.

The local soviets started to impose their own taxes on bourgeois families at levels they could not possibly afford. They would then take a son or a father hostage, under the threat of death or transport to a labor camp. Sometimes they threatened an entire family if the levy was not paid.

The sharing of living space in bourgeois homes was introduced and controlled by vigilant "housing committees," which sometimes urged servants and their friends to take over the best rooms, leaving their onetime employers their old quarters.

Black marketeers were to be shot on the spot. But who exactly did this order cover? The black market was a fact of almost everyone's life. Lynch mobs were encouraged and in time were institutionalized with people's courts and revolutionary tribunals, rich in their echoes of the French Revolution. The judges, usually with no legal background, were elected by local people. So, many old scores were soon settled. Hundreds of thousands, perhaps millions, of innocent people were condemned to labor camps and often to death.

In the army, officers were elected by their soldiers. Suspected tsarist-loyal officers were to be arrested and detained with their wives and families until local authorities were satisfied that each was a "compliant hero." Should any army commissar report adversely, the officer would be sentenced to prison or hard labor.

Armed gangs roamed the country under the pretense of this political cover and fought for their spoils with other armed gangs. It was mayhem, and Lenin delighted in it. He saw it as "cleansing." What emerged would be strong—a kind of Darwinian survival of the fittest.

Maxim Gorky continued to condemn it. "Lenin and Trotsky," he wrote, "are forcing the working class to organize bloody butcheries, pogroms, arrests of people who are not guilty of anything." By destroying press freedom, "they are legalizing their own suppression." Later he was to despair that "we are breeding a new crop of brutal and corrupt bureaucrats and a terrible new generation of youth who are learning to laugh at daily bloody scenes of beatings, shootings, cripplings, lynchings."

Lenin had closed down the opposition press in October, but he allowed *Novaya Zhizn*, Gorky's newspaper, to continue publishing for a while, and the writer did not let up. He described people dropping dead from starvation in the street and even went to the zoo, where the animals were dying from hunger. No one had even thought to shoot them.

By August 1918, Lenin was stepping up the terror. Responding to insurrections in five kulak districts, he demanded: "Hang, in full view of the people, no fewer than one hundred Kulaks, rich men, bloodsuckers. Do it in such a fashion that . . . people might see, tremble, know, shout: They are strangling and will strangle to death the blood-sucking kulaks. . . . Telegraph implementation. Find some truly hard people [to do it]."[7]

"In every grain-growing district," he ruled later, convinced that prosperous peasants were hoarding, "twenty-five to thirty rich hostages should be taken who will answer with their lives for the collection and loading of all surpluses."

It was holy war, waged with terror but little logic beyond the destruction of the bourgeoisie, which had run the country. Engineers were needed to build a bridge. The heads of the civil service had been arrested early, their places being taken by ambitious and often unscrupulous juniors.

Lenin conceded that middle-class "specialists" might be needed until ordinary "workers" could be trained to take their places, but within months he was forced by practicalities to change his mind, to the despair of the visionary left of the party that included Inessa.

Lenin's object, written during one of his breaks at Halila in Finland just after taking power, was clear and admirable: namely, "everyone should have bread, sturdy footwear, decent clothing, a warm dwelling—and should work conscientiously." It was his method that was so chillingly dubious.[8]

• • •

Set against so large and multifaceted a canvas, Lenin's complex relationship with Inessa must be seen in perspective. She was still in love with him, and always would be, as she was to confirm in writing only days before she died. That he still loved her, too, in his way, was also in time to be vividly demonstrated.

The two of them were bound by a visionary faith in a common cause, shared for years, which had now come to its first fruition, though whether Inessa had realized in those exile days quite what barbarity, terror, violence, and injustice Lenin would unleash in a nation with no real rule of law is uncertain.

But when it happened, she seemed to accept without question that everything he ordered was necessary. She wrote with somewhat bated breath to Inna, who was in Astrakhan with the Red Army in September 1918: "The masses understand how dear he is to us and how indispensable he is to the Revolution. More than ever," she emphasized, "we understand how important he is for our cause."[9]

This was written just after the savagely crude murder of the tsar, his wife, daughters, invalid son, servants, and his doctor, as well as six other royal relatives. *Izvestia* announced only the death of the tsar, but the whole truth would have been known in the upper echelons of the party and had probably reached her. Her old friend Georgi Safarov had been one of the three signatories to the order, though it had been initiated at the top level. Still, perhaps she considered that this had been necessary for the greater good. Certainly, any of the Romanovs, left alive, would have been an icon to rally to, and the Czech Legion, thirty-five thousand troops whose loyalties were seen as anti-Bolshevik, *had* actually been at the gates of Ekaterinburg, where the royal family had been held.

Throughout history, of course, women have loved men who did terrible things, though Lenin was operating on a massive scale. Inessa had positioned herself against him, with many others, on one issue that was an immense threat in the months following October 1917: how to deal with the German Army that was breathing down Russia's neck.

For the Germans, their funding of Lenin had worked out quite brilliantly. The collapse of the Russian Army was almost complete, in part because of Bolshevik-provoked mutiny, but also because the Land Decree had sent many soldiers dashing for home to claim their shares.

So nothing stood in the way of the Germans' easy conquest. They could write their own peace terms, and they did, shocking the Russians at the peace conference held in January 1918 at the frontier town of Brest-Litovsk. These called for the handover of a huge amount of territory containing one third of the Russian population, one third of its cultivated land, and one half of its industry. They also demanded payment of 120 million gold rubles, far more than the funds they had contributed to the Bolshevik cause.

Lenin was aghast but urged acceptance, only to be fiercely opposed by Bukharin, one of the most revered of the leaders, who was convinced the revolution would fast spread into Germany, so agreement was unnecessary. Bukharin had a large majority of the Central Committee behind him, believing in what was truly a fantasy.

The Germans, though, with their eyes on the Americans, were in no mood for delay. On February 9, 1918, the Kaiser ordered a new attack, and in five days the Germans gained more territory than they had won in the previous three years. Now their army was advancing on St. Petersburg.

Lenin called a large meeting of party leaders and begged them to agree to the German terms, arguing that if the revolution did travel as they all hoped, they could rewrite the treaty later. Meanwhile, not to sign was like a pet "lying down with a tiger."[10] For him, the danger of military defeat by the Germans was enormous. It would doom his revolution and rob him of the tenuous power he had won. A peace treaty, even as humiliating as this, could save him.

Bukharin was adamant in his opposition. At last, though, Lenin gained a majority of one in the Central Committee, with four members abstaining. The Russians signed the humiliating treaty, but the internal backlash of the horrified soviets throughout the nation was violent, especially by the left wing of the SRs, who had become close on this issue to Inessa and the left-wing Bolsheviks.

Inessa, of course, was on the executive of the Moscow soviet and insisted vehemently that they should *not* ratify the treaty. Like others, she just could not believe that Europe would not grasp their glorious revolution.[11]

A crisis came in July when an SR zealot with much support in the party murdered the German ambassador, Wilhelm von Mirbach, in the hope that this would incite the Germans to attack again. An anxious, angry Lenin ordered the arrest of the SR leaders and apologized to the Germans in person.

The issue was soon to become academic. Germany lost the war in the West, and Lenin annulled the treaty. Nevertheless, the arrested SRs were sent to labor camps, and one was executed.

Since Inessa had placed herself firmly among the left over the signing of the peace treaty, it is tempting to wonder if she'd sailed a bit too close to the wind. But with Lenin, she knew precisely how far she could go, and she took what might seem a careful precaution: She would never, she said, at the time, support a split in the Bolshevik Party. She was, of course, highly familiar with party splits.

In March 1918, Lenin had moved the government to Moscow, mainly because of the German threat to St. Petersburg. The National Hotel was taken over to house government functionaries, and Inessa moved there, too. Quite why she left the apartment in Denezhnyi Lane is not certain. Perhaps, with Lenin now in Moscow, she chose to be closer to the action.

. . .

Meanwhile, the Armands, once liberal employers, did not escape what their children and the people they'd married had helped to bring about. Gangs roamed through the territory. In one of the Armand homes, probably Alyoshino, not far from Eldigino, Alexander was present when looters swept through the property. He saw one man readying to smash a beautiful old mirror and said, "For God's sake if you want it, take it. But don't break it."[12]

An elderly couple—probably Emil, Alexander's uncle, and his wife—went to register the family property, as required, with the Moscow Regional Party Committee. Their city holdings consisted of four houses and a factory. On their return to their home on Trubnikovsky Lane, they found that the locks had been changed. They were not allowed access to even their clothes and personal possessions.

Inessa still saw something of Alexander. In fact, he stayed in Denezhnyi Lane when he was in Moscow. She had persuaded the Bolshevik Party to accept him as a member, which was an honor in itself but would also give him what was now a much-needed protection. He was a dubious choice for them, being both bourgeois and wealthy, but she used her influence to argue that he was a "natural" communist.

But Alexander declined the offer. He believed he would be conspicuous in party circles, which would render him more vulnerable, not less. He was also, possibly again thanks to Inessa's influence, invited to continue running the Armand factories in Pushkino. He turned this down, too, for much the same reason. To him, a low profile seemed highly advisable.[13]

Inessa had a more receptive response from Inna, who was doing political work with the Red Army in Astrakhan. "Your absence weighs heavily on me," Inessa wrote to her in September 1918, "but I rejoice at your enthusiasm for the cause. I have been wanting to tell you this for a long time."[14]

Inessa missed her daughter badly. "I not only think about you every day, my darling, but several times a day. I long for you. For me, you are not only my daughter, but also a very dear friend,"[15] as well as now a fellow revolutionary.

The older Armands continued to live in the main complex at Pushkino for a while. Yury Gautier visited Pushkino a few months later. "God, what horror in Pushkino," he recorded. "In the garden they are cutting down the trees for firewood, and calves are grazing in the flower beds. The old folks are immobilized in anticipation of death, which has already overtaken half of them."[16]

. . .

Inessa, according to family lore, escaped sometimes from Moscow to Eldigino, her bridal home, to work. It was while she was there, so one story has it, that David Armand, Emil's grandson, then age twelve, went to see her with a letter from his mother. Family "hostages" had been taken, probably relatives of his mother, Lidiya Maryanovna. Could Inessa help with their release?

David is said to have reported that she took the letter but dismissed him abruptly, and the hostages were not released. This seems out of character for Inessa, and the story could reflect the resentment of her in some members of this very large family. Certainly the incident is not mentioned in David's own unpublished autobiography, which he wrote when an adult, though cautiously, under a communist government.

Attitudes toward Inessa remained uncertain, even long after her death. One branch of the Armand family, which interestingly still had servants, maintained a rule that she was never to be mentioned except in French. And even before the Revolution, when Inessa was wanted by the Okhrana, the children were told not to talk about her in front of the staff.

Eldigino followed Pushkino into state ownership in due course. But Alyoshino, the family's third home, about ten miles from Pushkino, was to remain in family control throughout the whole period of communist rule and beyond—a result, some of the family have suggested, of Nadya's intervention, meaning Lenin's. At the end of 1918, Inessa reported to Inna, Alexander had given up the Moscow apartment and was working to repair an old mill near Alyoshino. He understood machinery, having run the family factories.

After several years, he became a brilliant odd-job mechanic, working in what had previously been Armand lands, with the necessary agreement of his former workers. Given the hate and revenge that motivated so many laborers in Russia at that time, this said much for the family.

Inevitably, Inessa had become distanced from many of the other Armands. "Grandmama and Grandpapa are well," she wrote to Inna, "but I haven't seen them for a long time. You know why. It saddens me because I am very fond of them, but there is nothing I can do. It's the way things are. I haven't seen Renee or your other grandmother for a long time either."[17]

Those bleak words were written in December 1918, when the civil war was raging. It truly concerned her, it seems, though there was a note of resignation. It is unclear whether this parting was the wish of the older Armands, whose lives had been devastated by Lenin, or by Inessa herself, embarrassed by her bourgeois background in a proletarian revolution. Most of her prominent comrades were also middle class, a fact many of them tried to conceal. Party propagandists tended to represent even Lenin's bourgeois background in more acceptable form.

The extreme distress of the Armands cannot have been eased by Anna, their eldest child, who had also followed Lenin and was still close to Inessa, nor by several of their other children, who had sympathized with the revolution. The question remains: Did they not realize what they were supporting until it was too late? Had they been absorbed by the drama and the hope on the horizon that had so gripped Inessa?

Through the autumn and early winter of 1918, Inessa wrote several letters to Inna in Astrakhan, reflecting on the immense changes in society. Varya had got into an arts and crafts school, where the pupils chose their teachers. Andre, too, was about to go to a new model school—strangely, a boarding school of which his mother disapproved—where the same was done.

Fedor was serving on a war committee, though he was about to join the Red Army as a pilot-observer, presumably having concealed his political views, which were soon to put him in danger of facing a firing squad. Her son Sasha, despite being in the Red Army, was leaving for Mogilev Province to do educational work in schools.[18]

Inessa was still living in the National Hotel. In one letter to Inna that began, "Sweet Inochka, sweet little girl, sweet little sister," she explains that

Varya and I are sharing the same room. . . . It is a bit of a squash, but we are not too bothered. Varya sleeps curled up on the divan. Every day she works [as an artist], favoring landscapes, drawing with chalk, and sculpture. She has done a head I like, but Varya [herself] doesn't.

[In Varya's school] they enjoy the greatest freedom. . . . At present, they only do drawing, but soon they will have "conferences" [in lieu of lessons?]. There is a workshop without staff. In fact, they do not have a teacher at the moment because they cannot choose one. (Varya says that is slander!)

There is another event. I hesitate to admit it, but Varya says: Go on, go on. I confess. I've had my hair cut. It is Varya who, with her own hands, has committed this crime, assuring me she got a sense of achievement in her heroic act. What a cheeky girl, don't you think? Fidya asks if I have gone mad.[19]

At this time, Inessa is under heavy pressure. One of her many assignments is helping to organize an all-Russian Congress of working women. "Oh, make sure *you* get sent here [presumably as a delegate]," she pleads with Inna. "It will allow us to spend a little while together."

She is soon back writing of "internationalist" politics. In Germany, the revolution is "striding along." Mutiny has broken out in the German and Austrian armies. They are killing their officers and declaring themselves Bolsheviks. At Kharkov, forty thousand German troops have entered the town carrying red flags, shouting "Down with Wilhelm and the war."

"You have probably read Lenin's [public] letter of October 3 and the Resolution of the Central Committee. I think these events are extremely important. Soviet Russia will become the cradle of the proletariat of the entire world."[20]

This was true Inessa. Lenin's public letter declared that Germany was in the throes of a political crisis. "It will inevitably lead to the transfer of power to the German people who are struggling for their liberation." He saw it as an opportunity to create the "Proletarian Red Army"—a European or even a global army in a new world where "the worker has no fatherland."

He was wrong. The main German socialist parties, horrified by what was going on in Russia, favored the more democratic, Menshevik-style philosophies. They failed to support the famous "Spartacist" uprising, which was crushed sharply in 1919, when its the leaders, Rosa Luxemburg and Karl Liebkneckt, were brutally killed as they were being led to jail. Uprisings in Austria and Hungary were also put down.

This ended the hazy, romantic ideas about a proletarian army. Indeed, fifteen years later Germany was to swing to fascism and provoke yet another world war. And though the concept was not yet spoken of, "socialism in one country" was what lay ahead for Russia. And in only a few months, Lenin's party was to change its name, becoming the Communist Party.

In another letter, Inessa returns to domestic news. "Papa . . . has moved to Alyoshino once and for all. He is looking for an engine for his mill, and I think he has found it.

"We no longer have the apartment at Denezhnyi Lane. Now Aunt Anna, Abram, Elena, and Katya live there. [So it is still clearly in Armand hands.] The four of them live where all eleven used to live. In fact, Papa has reserved a room there for himself for when he stays in Moscow." Presumably they escaped scrutiny by the Buildings Committee. Andre was also sleeping in the apartment, his model school having not yet opened.

On this letter there is a postscript from Varya in her own hand: "I will also write to you a lot of stupidities, but not in such a pretty style as Mama's."[21]

By December 1918, Inessa was worrying to Inna about Varya's "passion for you know whom. I don't think he is suitable for her. I can always talk about it to Varya, but I must do it calmly and not rush it."[22] What has happened to the independence Inessa urged from exile on Inna when she, too, had been anxious about falling for a man her mother might not like?

By this time, Inessa's relations with Lenin had changed again, this time dramatically and, so far as she was concerned, very much for the better.

CHAPTER 13

MOSCOW 1918

On August 30, 1918, Lenin had addressed a crowd of workers at the Michelson plant on the far side of the Moscow River.[1] That day, news had come that Mikhail Uritsky, head of the St. Petersburg Cheka, had been killed by an SR assassin. Maria, Lenin's sister, and the family had pleaded with him to call off his visit, but he had refused.

Lenin ended his speech by declaring: "For us there is one alternative: victory or death."

He was leaving the building as two SRs approached through the crowd: a man named Novikov and a woman, thirty-one-year-old Fannie Kaplan. Novikov pushed several workers aside to open Kaplan's view of Lenin. She drew a revolver and fired three shots at him. Lenin fell to the ground. Only two bullets hit him, both in the left shoulder, but one had penetrated his chest cavity and damaged his lung, causing hemorrhaging into the pleura.

Lenin was rushed to his car. Stepan Gill, his chauffeur, drove him at a top speed to the Kremlin, guessing this would be safer than a hospital, where other assassins could be waiting. On arrival, Lenin refused help, put on his jacket, and climbed the stairs to the third floor. Maria opened the door, and Lenin said "I've been slightly wounded, just in the arm." His personal physician dressed his wounds. By that night, several specialists had examined him and decided that his heart function had returned to normal.

By then, Fannie Kaplan had been interrogated in the Cheka headquarters in Lubyanka Square. She had a background as an anarchist and had been sentenced under the tsar to "eternal hard labor," spending years in hard-labor prison camps. She insisted that although she was a member of the SR Party, she had been acting on her own behalf. "I regard [Lenin] as a traitor. The longer he lives, the farther he'll push back the idea of socialism. For dozens of years."

There were rumors of a conspiracy, suggestions that Fannie Kaplan herself had not fired the shot, merely agreed to take the blame. Stepan Gill said he had only seen the revolver, not the killer, but in a woman's hand, attracting theories that another woman did the shooting, and suggestions that Kaplan's sight was so bad she was almost blind. Furthermore, the revolver that was eventually handed in did not match the bullet cases on the Kremlin ground, of which there were four, although only three shots had been heard.

In the climate of the times, justice was done in swift secrecy. Kremlin Commandant Pavel Malkov was ordered by Yakov Sverdlov to shoot Kaplan himself in a garage with a car engine running to muffle the noise, the body to be destroyed without trace.

Lenin was confined to bed for a couple of weeks, but according to his doctors he would have been dead if one bullet had traveled a millimeter in either direction—which, perhaps, caused him to contemplate his life.

Among the first people he sent for was Inessa, who visited him at once with Varya. Nadya took the girl off to look at some old family photographs.[2] Both Lenin and Inessa found the visit rewarding. "We have been very shaken by the attempt on Lenin's life," she wrote Inna.

"This event has re-united us and brought us even closer. It has had much influence on the masses. . . . The meetings are better attended . . . especially in Peter, which is always the first [area] to react.

"I await your letter. I am writing to you from my bed in the middle of the night."[3]

For Inessa, the renewed closeness led to advantages, too. A request from Lenin to Pavel Malkov got her an apartment near the Kremlin in Neglinnaya Street (now Manege Street).[4] When a new closed-circuit telephone system was set up in Moscow so that party leaders and officials could communicate directly with the Kremlin without using an operator, Inessa's new apartment was one of those connected to it.[5]

When Inna returned to Moscow from Afghanistan, she called at the Kremlin with some young friends and asked boldly to see Lenin. The guard at the gate turned her away, so she went home and phoned him on her mother's private line. On being asked who was calling she had replied "Inessa Armand" and was quickly connected.

Lenin took the call but knew at once that it was not Inessa. "Who is this?" he asked.

"Inessa Little," she answered, using a nickname he had given her in exile.

He laughed. "Little but shrewd," he said. But he didn't have time to receive her and her friends.

After the attempt on Lenin's life, Nadya began to behave strangely.[6] She had always tolerated Lenin's relationship with Inessa after he had asked Nadya to stay with him as his wife. She appeared to like Inessa, praising her in her *Memories of Lenin* and, after her death, editing a volume of favorable reminiscences by herself and other people.

Inessa liked Nadya, too, as she had spelled out in the long letter she had written to Lenin from Paris in January 1914 after their first big parting. Never in her letters to anyone is there any of the spite that mistresses sometimes exhibit toward wives.

Lenin was urged by his doctors to convalesce, and he chose to do so at a mansion in the village of Gorki, twenty-two miles south of Moscow, from which he continued to run the country. But Nadya did not go with him. When eventually he returned to the Kremlin, she left almost immediately for Sokolniki Park on Moscow's northeast, staying at a school where she was given a small room on the first floor. Still suffering from Graves' disease, Nadya needed regular visits from her doctors, who could have attended her so much more easily in the Kremlin.

Nadya was distanced from her husband at a time when a wife would normally stay at her husband's side. It seemed a silent protest. She had been sidelined ever since she had arrived in Russia. Before the October coup, she had been made to feel uncomfortable in the Kseshinskaya Mansion. After the October Days, she had been appointed deputy commissar of education, which hardly ranked prominently in the new hierarchy.

Until the attempt on Lenin's life, Inessa may not have seemed to be a continuing threat. Her relations with Lenin had appeared to have stabilized on a platonic level, fond but distant, under the pressures of his position. But suddenly, when he had so nearly died, there was Inessa, back at his bedside. Clearly, since no one could get access to him without his orders, she was there at his instigation. Inessa's large new apartment was just outside the Kremlin walls—leading to rumors that she was living in the Kremlin itself—and this could have done nothing to alleviate a wife's fears and resentments.

Lenin, however, seems to have ignored whatever distress Nadya may have harbored. He traveled out to Sokolniki Park often to see her, usually in the evening after he had finished work. Legend has it in certain Armand circles that once again Nadya offered to leave him and once again he refused. It sounds possible but is unlikely and unconfirmed.

By now, even without Lenin's direct assistance, Inessa had made progress within the party. She held the chair of the important Moscow Economic Council, the most prominent of thirty-eight such councils throughout Russia. She coedited a French-language journal published in Russia, *La IIIe internationale,* and was prominent in a feminist group, as well as on the executive of the Moscow soviet, of which she was a voting delegate for the All-Russian Congress. "Truly I am overworked," she told Inna.

Her position in the political hierarchy is clearly demonstrated in the Moscow diary of the academic Yury Gautier. Members of the Gautier family had come under unlikely suspicion of involvement with a railway explosion, and questions were being asked about both Yury and his brother. The university was hostile to the new regime, especially since a new decree allowed anyone of either sex over sixteen to enroll in it, but blowing up rail tracks was not the way its academics normally showed their disagreement.

"Truly," he wrote in his diary,

> you don't know what affair blind fate will entangle you in. . . . In my search for any means [of help] I ran into Fedor Armand yesterday, who proposed that I turn to the famous Comrade Inessa, his mother and my childhood friend. . . . Today I got from her a *billet d'introduction* to the commissar of the Military District, Muralov: "Respected Comrade. I beg of you to receive my acquaintance, Yury Vladimirovich Gautier. I will be grateful to you. Inessa Armand."[7]

Her wish was enough. It was an indication of the power she could deploy. Gautier does not mention the matter again, but he continued writing his diary of life in Moscow for another four years, so the pressure was clearly off.

Shortly after her help for Gautier, Inessa found herself ranged with her comrades of the left once more against Lenin, despite the new dynamic of their relationship. Lenin had realized that worker control in factories was not proving successful. He promoted the idea of labor discipline (i.e., production efficiency), and shocked Inessa and Bukharin's Baugy Group. To the left, the idea that workers would not strive their hardest now that they were working for the people was anathema.

Lenin, though, was facing the facts. The first thing many workers committees had done was to vote themselves huge wage increases. Reluctantly, Lenin did the unthinkable. He ordered the creation of state managers, supported sometimes by managerial boards.

The same was to happen to the army in the civil war that soon engulfed the nation. The election of officers by soldier committees was not working either. Primitive operational plans were drawn up, declared Leon Trotsky as commander of the Red Army, by men who "could not even read a map." The result was inevitable defeat.

So Trotsky called back officers of the regular army under threats to their families if they failed in their duties; reintroduced saluting; dissolved the soldier committees; and brought back pay scales and privileges. The result was anger from the troops and another howl of outrage from the left, though Inessa allowed others to do the howling, in impassioned attacks in *Pravda*. After a tough start, though, when the White forces seemed overwhelming, Trotsky's new policy was to win battles. Lenin backed Trotsky, since winning in the field was more important immediately than socialist theory.

With her opposition, Inessa was flirting with danger, but she knew Lenin was always on her side and granted her freedom of thought that he often denied to others. And she, though staking out her views, always in the end supported him, no matter what he did.

For Lenin, the radical left was a big problem, for their stubborn clinging to utopian theory did not stand up to immediate conditions. Always Lenin was pragmatic. When in 1917 he had learned that the right-wing Kamenev had proposed that the death penalty be abandoned, he had stepped in at once. "How can we run a revolution," he had demanded, "without the firing squad?"

By the latter part of 1918, the Cheka, now a vast organ of terror with tentacles throughout Russia, was committing ever more ghastly atrocities. Torture techniques varied with the district, ranging from burning the skin off a victim's hands; to fixing a cage of rats to his body with an open door so they could escape only by eating their way out; to sliding him into a furnace.[8]

Cheka roundups of "hostages" were often random. But that is what terror meant: control of a people who lived in fear of a knock on the door in the middle of the night. And Lenin, Sverdlov, and even Trotsky always opposed any attempt to weaken this control.

The civil war, which had been developing in small engagements since the October revolution, became serious in the summer of 1918 and continued until April 1920. It was complex, partially because of differences in aims and tactical views among the various forces. In time, however, there developed two main anti-Bolshevik armies under General Anton Denikin and Admiral Alexander Kolchak. Disaffected officers and many Cossacks were in their ranks, and in 1918 the Allies came in on several fronts to support them.

There were other forces, such as the big Czech Legion that had supported a right-wing SR attempt to establish an independent provincial government in Samara. There were peasant armies, which sometimes switched their alliances and could be just as barbarous as the Cheka; and the "Greens," which were bandit groups made up mainly of army deserters who lived in the forests.

At the heart of the chaos was the need for food. Lenin blamed the greed of the rich kulaks for the shortages, though many kulaks were not wealthy and merely commune leaders. In several areas, a village might have only one horse, which was moved around from family to family. They were accustomed to storing food for themselves in the winters and selling the surplus to the cities, but currency was useless now with soaring inflation. With armies on both sides demanding grain as they swept through the country, often flogging or torturing whole villages to force them to reveal their secret storage places, it is not strange that there were nearly three hundred peasant revolts between July and August 1918.

Lenin sent out food brigades with the same purpose as the armies and, closer to the cities, formed new units to police the trains, confiscating from passengers any excess food over the small legal allowance. This was not successful, for the bagmen acted like bandits and confiscated whatever else might take their fancy as well.

In the cities, the situation grew desperate. Half-starved children were seen pulling carts that would normally be drawn by horses. More and more people fled to the country to be nearer the food sources, as depicted decades later in Boris Pasternak's *Doctor Zhivago*.

By early 1919, Lenin's revolution was under serious military threat in four different areas of Russia, including the north, where British and French troops had landed at Murmansk and Archangel to support the anti-Bolshevik forces. The south, including the North Caucasus, was already under White Russian control. In the east, Soviet power had been overthrown in Siberia, the Urals, and the mid-Volga region. In the northwest, yet another general, Nikolai Yudenich, was also planning an attack on St. Petersburg.

And Trotsky, the highly able commander-in-chief of the Red Army, was racing between the fronts in a special armored train, complete, it was said, with a gourmet kitchen. Until mid-1919 it seemed the White armies might succeed. Denikin launched a three-pronged attack, aimed at Moscow, from different directions—Baron Wrangel leading forces from the Caucasus up the Volga; General Sidorin with a Don army from Tsaritsyn; Mai-Maevsky from Kharkov—all on the main rail tracks. But the front was too wide, making backup hard. The cavalry leaders resisted orders. There was disagreement among the generals. So the Reds started winning.

It was in this setting that Inessa, in addition to all her other areas of activity, had returned to the "woman problem," especially crucial now as more and more men were called up from the factories and the farmlands to join the Red Army. Women were needed at the front both for support purposes, like nursing, but also at times for combat. There were, in fact, women's regiments on both sides, the most famous being Maria Bochkareva's Women's Battalion of Death, the members of which shaved their heads and wore trousers. Bochkareva demanded discipline. In the chaos of Kerensky's failed July offensive in 1917, she'd found one of her girls having sex with a soldier in a shell hole and ran her through with her bayonet.[9]

Inessa's feminist group was built around the onetime editorial board of *Rabotnitsa,* although both this and a sister paper in Moscow had been replaced by women's columns in the main dailies. However, Inessa and her friends had an aim outside the needs of war: to drag the old-fashioned family, which with new laws they now saw as a hangover from the past, into the socialist present.

Within the new movement, Inessa, with Lenin behind her, began to take center stage alongside Alexandra Kollontai, with Sverdlov behind her. The two women were natural rivals—not because of their political aims, which were roughly the same, though Kollontai had a more forward position on sexual freedom—but because of their personalities. They could never have been friends.[10]

Kollontai had a fine mind, was an acknowledged theoretician, and was superb on the platform, a skill with which Inessa was competent but not outstanding. Kollontai was flamboyant but passionately impulsive and, by contrast to Inessa, who now dressed down in the mood of the times, wore challenging, colorful clothes. Although she had been appointed as the only woman on the Central Committee after the October coup, Kollontai had resigned in horror at the terms of the Brest-Litovsk Treaty, unlike Inessa who had simply voted against it in the Moscow soviet without making too many waves.

Kollontai had once been the mistress of Alexander Shlyapnikov, who was prominent among the new leaders. And in 1917, she had fallen in love with Pavel Dybenko, a huge, fine-looking sailor whom she'd met after Podvoisky had recruited her as a sort of celebrity agitator to tour the fleet.

Dybenko, who had won fame by throwing the visiting Kerensky overboard, was seventeen years younger than the forty-five-year-old Kollontai. After the October coup, he was made commissar for the Navy, insisted on marrying her, and had opposed the Brest-Litovsk Treaty in a dangerously hot-blooded way: He had refused to stop fighting, taking his sailors on land, and had checked, temporarily at least, the German advance on St. Petersburg.

For this disobedience, he was arrested for treason, which almost caused a naval mutiny. Kollontai was terrified he would be executed and appealed to Lenin. Dybenko was acquitted but expelled from the party for a time. After this, there was no longer a place for Kollontai on the Central Committee. She did not have the political acumen of Inessa, who had been well schooled by a master in tactics.

The feminist agenda had already been addressed to some extent. After the February revolution in 1917, women had been given full political and civil rights—by the new-style civil marriage in particular. Soon after October, all restrictions on divorce were removed, the demand by one partner being enough. Illegitimate children were given the same rights as others, and women began to receive equal pay for equal work, at least in theory.

In 1917, these laws took Russia way beyond those of most western nations, but Russia was still a deeply patriarchal society, and the peasant families resisted the changes. In this population of 160 million, occupying one sixth of the inhabited surface of the world, some 70 percent were peasants. And peasants were conservative.

May 1918 had seen Inessa's All-Russian Congress of Working Women. It did not prove a great attraction, perhaps because Inessa was too pressed to give it full attention. Only 130 delegates arrived in Moscow, owing, Inessa assessed later, to the allegiance of most women in factories to the SRs and Mensheviks. But when some of them asked to see Lenin, she waved her magic wand and there he was on the platform, not saying too much of record but impressing them with his welcome.

In June, she was elected with Kollontai to a commission to organize a national congress of working women. They were given an office, a staff, and a small budget with a brief that included the dispatch of women agitators across the nation to round up delegates. The campaign was embarrassingly successful. Instead of the three hundred delegates expected for the congress, 1,147 red-kerchiefed women arrived in Moscow from all over Russia after long and dangerous journeys across the war zones. This created an acute crisis as to how they, and the children that some had brought with them, were to be accommodated and fed. They had to be satisfied by soup and porridge, and places were presumably found for them to sleep.

The next day, they assembled in the House of Unions, where the Moscow Duma had once sat. As Elwood writes, the two women "must have derived a sense of satisfaction and accomplishment when they sat on the praesidium and looked out over more than a thousand working women."

What they had to say, however, was not welcomed by everyone. Inessa spoke of women returning home from long hours at work to the "household slavery of cooking, cleaning, and child rearing." The problem could be solved, she said, by communal dining, laundries, schools, and nurseries, thus freeing housewives for other activities. This provoked cries of "We won't give up our children."

(Certainly, Inessa did not believe that collectives could solve her own problems. She had, after all, strongly resisted the idea of Andre attending a state boarding school.)

Kollontai followed Inessa with her optimistic visions of a new kind of relationship, which she called "Great Love"—later the title of a novel she wrote. She described a sexual future that would be free of jealousies and selfishness. She conceded it would take generations to reach this happy state. Meanwhile, however, as people strove to achieve more honesty and equality in their relations, these would not necessarily be monogamous or long lasting. This illuminated Kollontai's belief in full sexual freedom for women, with which neither Lenin, Nadya, nor even Inessa agreed.

Lenin, Sverdlov, and Bukharin all addressed the meeting, which gave it authority. Encouragingly, there were more than one hundred peasant women in the hall. Inessa proposed that, back home, they form local feminist groups, to which the delegates would report and thus spread the ideas discussed in Moscow.

The lesson that shadowed all the speeches and discussions about the "woman problem" was that you could change the law but you could not so easily change long-established customs. But it was with this aim that, in December 1918, the Central Committee appointed Inessa to the chair of a new Central Commission for Agitation and Propaganda, aimed at working women, an appointment that cannot have pleased Kollontai too much.

But there was soon little opportunity for conflict between them. In March 1919, Kollontai was dispatched for five months as a propagandist on the southern front. By then, Inessa had already left on a new assignment, as one of a three-person Red Cross mission to France to make arrangements for the transfer back to Russia of forty-five thousand Russian troops who had been fighting on the western front.

This was potentially dangerous. Four members of another Red Cross delegation to Poland had been taken to a field and shot. Members of a second mission, also under the Red Cross banner, had been arrested in Hungary. Relations with France were particularly bad. One hundred French residents in Russia were being held as hostage. French troops were fighting with the White armies. And leaders of all the developed western countries continued to be terrified that the Russian revolutionary fervor might infect their own workers. George V of Britain, who had once offered asylum to the tsar, had been forced to retract his offer for fear of its effect on British labor.

The French government presumably knew of Inessa's background, but they wanted their nationals released, and they were keen to get the Russian troops off their hands.

"I nearly left for France," Inessa reported in December to Inna in Astrakhan, adding that she "could not go through because of the German events. I think we will be able to pass when the revolution in Germany has further developed. Events take place so quickly! How fast, my dear! Here we joke about not being happy unless each day brings us at least one revolution. . . . I suffer without you, my little girl. I send you a thousand kisses."[11]

Germany would not let the delegation through because diplomatic relations with the Soviet government had been severed. So they had to go by sea. The French had guaranteed their personal immunity but warned that they would be expelled if they used the mission as a cover for propaganda. Although propaganda was certainly Inessa's intention, the most urgent task was to lay the ground for formal peace talks with the French. The Allies had all declined to recognize the Soviet government, leaving the issue for discussion at the Versailles Peace Conference.

All three of the mission delegates were Bolsheviks and fluent in French. The group was headed by D. Z. Manuilsky, whom Inessa had worked with in the St. Petersburg underground in 1912, and the third member was Jacques Davtian.[12]

The two men bought formal clothes suitable for a diplomatic mission, recorded Polina Vinogradskaya. Inessa planned to wear her ordinary, rather drab dresses. The purchase of fashionable frocks, she said, would be a waste of the people's money. Her two companions were worried that the French would think Soviet men forced their wives to wear rags, while they preened in well-cut suits.

The three delegates left by ship on February 4, 1919. From St. Petersburg, Inessa wrote to Inna, enclosing letters to Sasha and Fedor and a third one for Lenin.

> Only you are to know of this last one. . . . Keep [it] yourself for the time being. When we get back I'll tear it up. If something happens to me . . . then you must give the letter personally to Vladimir Ilyich. . . . Go to *Pravda,* where Maria Ilyinichna works, give her the letter, and say that it's from me and is personal for V. I. Meanwhile hang on to it. . . . It's sealed in an envelope.

She did not expect "special danger," she said, but "just in case."[13]

They reached Dunkirk on February 21. To their angry astonishment, their luggage was searched. More than one million rubles and forty-nine thousand Swiss francs were seized. They were somewhat alarmed to be placed under house arrest in Malo-les-Bains, with constant surveillance.

They had been forbidden to bring staff such as translators and secretaries. The French would supply any such needs. They were not permitted to communicate with Moscow by code, and the Quai d'Orsay refused to transmit their first messages in plain language. They were not even allowed to visit the Russian troops.

However, news of their arrival had permeated socialist circles, and after a few days a reporter from *Le Populaire* arrived in Malo, though he gained only a few brief words with Inessa.

Their contact with the outside world was Lieutenant-Colonel Wehrlin, whose orders were strict. The trio complained. They tried to wire G. V. Chicherin, the Soviet commissar for foreign affairs, asking him to intervene; the French refused to send the telegram. The surveillance of them was increased.

They faced stalemate. Then a Colonel Langlois replaced Wehrlin with more scope: They could communicate with Moscow on repatriation matters. They would be allowed to visit the Russian camps, accompanied by French officials. Manuilsky and Davtian were prepared to accept this, but "Madame Armand objected." Langlois concluded that she wanted a "rupture of negotiations," which would have been in character. The Russian Red Cross wired that these conditions were acceptable to it, too, but Inessa continued to dissent, and she wasn't alone. Commissar Chicherin threatened to rearrest those French citizens in Russia who had been released. The French countered angrily by demanding unconditional acceptance of their proposals. Otherwise, the mission would be expelled.

Inessa was "growing increasingly irritable," as Richard K. Debo wrote in his account of the venture. Unlike her two associates, she displayed what Langlois called "a hateful state of mind," demanding that they be allowed to get on with the purpose of their visit. She clearly felt that Manuilsky and Davtian were giving their captors far too easy a time.

She was, Langlois concluded, "prodigiously sly." Inessa, experienced as she was with imprisonment, was clearly in her element. She delighted in tormenting the colonel by such escapades as posing for a photographer for *Le Petit Parisien.*

This whetted Inessa's taste for mischief. Her next stunt was to feign an escape plan. A fast car was to be parked beside the beach on which the mission members were allowed to exercise. Two armed men were to overpower the guard and drive Inessa to Paris, where she hoped to make a triumphal appearance on May Day. It was nonsense, of course. The plan got into the hands of the police, as Inessa must have intended. They believed it, though, and feared that another attempt might be made to rescue her. An order was issued for the three communists, as they were now called, to be transported to the *Dumont d'Urville,* the ship that was to repatriate some of the Russian troops. They were to be held aboard until she sailed.

Manuilsky, who had been unnerved by the fate of the Red Cross mission in Poland, was petrified. "Was the French guarantee of their immunity effective on board ship as well as on shore?" he asked Langlois anxiously. He was assured it was. During the journey, he demanded the escort officer's word that they truly were heading for the ship.

Three days later, he could at last breathe easily. The ship sailed, with one thousand Russian soldiers aboard. But the difficulties were not over. The ship put into Hango, Finland, rather than a Russian port, possibly because of lingering Baltic ice. The Finnish authorities, who were also scared of revolution, refused at first to allow either the soldiers or the mission to disembark, but eventually conceded so they could proceed to Russia.

While Inessa was in Hango, Fedor, serving as a pilot in the Thirty-eighth Detachment in Minsk, was arrested on charges of treason. He had come under suspicion of a new commissar, who doubted the authenticity of documents he produced and, since Fedor was an officer of the old regime, suspected his loyalty. He subjected him and his brother officers to heavy harassment, culminating in arrest.

Fedor had always been a bit cavalier as a military cadet and rather free with his opinions in times when it paid to be careful. Perhaps he had been emboldened by the fact that his mother had access to high places where Lenin had greater power than ever. Perhaps, too, his right-wing allegiances in Moscow during the October revolution had been noted.

Fedor now faced great danger, and his mother was out of touch, on the wrong ship in the wrong port. He gained permission to telegraph the Kremlin, and Lenin was quick to respond. He wired the commissar of the armies in the Minsk region on May 3 that F. A. Armand, "who is personally known to me, is trustworthy even if he is a former officer and noncommunist. I ask the Red Army comrades not to treat him with suspicion."

Three days later, the commissar of the armies telegraphed a reply: "Armand, arrested by the commissar of the West Division, has been released. The commissar of the Thirty-eighth Detachment has been dismissed."[14]

This was more proof of the power Inessa now had. But she was a realist for all her head-in-the-sky idealism, and she used her position with a care and discrimination that was deeply resented by people she had known as children.

"One more remark," wrote Yury Gautier in his diary during July 1919, in the midst of "a beautiful summer." "Inessa has refused to vouch for Georges Wilken; such is her memory for hospitality extended to her in her youth. I admit that I didn't expect that even from her."[15]

Inessa must have had a reason for this. Georges Wilken had been an actual player with Inessa and her sisters in the amateur production of *A Tale of Summer* at Pushkino soon after her marriage. Her reluctance to help him could have been due to a need to distance herself from her bourgeois past, but disloyalty was unusual in her. It is more likely that Wilken had done something unwise that had darkened his record.

Despite the bitterness of Gautier's tone, he seems to have forgotten that only months before Inessa had saved him from almost certain

sentence to a prison camp if not death. It didn't take much to be arrested in those days when the Cheka was flexing its muscles. Even to
be suspected of the remotest link to an explosion was enough to be
shot, especially for a classic bourgeois like Yury Gautier. Still, from
his point of view, Inessa was on the other side and appallingly close to
the Devil himself.

Inessa had also resisted a request from her old comrade Ivan
Popov, whom she had met in Mezen and partnered with at the Brussels Conference in 1914. "Dear Ivan," she wrote, "Unfortunately I
cannot do anything for Boris Konstantinovich Viktorov." She suggests a personal visit by a mutual acquaintance to Felix Dzerzhinsky,
the head of the Cheka and just about the most feared man in Russia.
"I would be happy to see you, dear Ivan," she ends. "Come over one
evening. We are all often at home."[16]

A year later, Gautier again visited the old Armand home in
Pushkino. "Such horror and neglect there, where life once bur-
geoned!" he recorded.

> E.E.'s house [that of Alexander's father] has been turned into
> a club; everything has been pilfered, is falling down and leak-
> ing; A.E.'s house [that of one of Alexander's two uncles] is
> serving as a nursery, and not a single object has remained in
> the rooms.
>
> The two old women have been stuffed into an old peo-
> ple's home and are sadly living out their lives among the ruins
> of the past. The garden is overgrown, and there are tall weeds
> everywhere, the gazebos have been wrecked. Horror and
> abomination.

By then, in 1920, Inessa had been working so hard on the new
world she was helping to create that Lenin was worrying about her.

Soon after she had returned from her disastrous mission to
France, she had been given an important new job as head of the
Women's Section of the Central Committee. This, like the other sec-

tions, had the authority of the committee and could issue edicts in its name, surely enough to make some impact on restrictive paternalism. In effect, it could make law. It was known by its shortened version in Russian as Zhenotdel.[17]

This was another, more serious setback for Alexandra Kollontai, who was given a brief that she regarded as demeaning—the organizing of peasant women—while Inessa, now her chief, ruled Zhenotdel from an office on Vozdvizhenka, near the Kremlin. According to Polina Vinogradskaya, who worked with them both, the two women had quarreled from the start. Possibly, Inessa had chosen Kollontai's assignment to get her out of the office as much as possible. And the job had an important practical purpose. There was a huge army of peasant women, almost certainly larger in number than factory workers, who were backward and in need of political education.

Zhenotdel's original brief was to mobilize Russian women for defense in the civil war by taking over men's jobs in factories so that they could join the Red Army or even themselves serve at the front, as Inna had. An estimated seventy thousand women served with the army; nearly two thousand were killed.

Inessa's new position also allowed her to help women, in practice, catch up with the recent liberal laws, such as decreeing that all worker committees in factories, normally limited to men, should include at least one woman. And, since many women lacked the necessary experience, she enforced a system of apprentice delegates who would actually be trained for the role. In short, Inessa, with the force of the Central Committee behind her, had a degree of muscle that many modern feminists would envy.

The new concept of marriage was aided by the war. Nurseries were set up in factories, as were communal cooking facilities, free canteens, and dining facilities. In cities, this system was widespread. By 1921, 93 percent of Moscow residents were eating in public dining halls.

The workload for Inessa through the latter part of 1919 was immense. Staff shortages were made worse by sickness in a city that was suffering from a huge epidemic of Spanish flu. In November 1919,

Kollontai suffered a heart attack from which she did not recover until March 1920. And that February, Inessa herself fell ill.

Polina Vinogradskaya wrote a vivid account of a visit to Inessa on returning from work at the front.

> I had to knock a long time. The bells didn't work. As I started to return down the stairs, I heard a door opening. Inessa appeared in the doorway. She was ill and because no one else was in the apartment she had to get up and answer the door herself.
>
> When I expressed surprise that she'd been left alone by the family, she became indignant and said, "The children are working and shouldn't stop for such a stupid reason as my illness."
>
> It was terribly cold in the apartment because there was no heating. Thick layers of dust covered everything. Only the books were tidy in the shelves.
>
> She had a terrible cold. She was coughing and shivering. She blew on her fingers to warm them. She looked so haggard I hardly recognized her. She was wearing a very old bed jacket.
>
> She didn't complain, though. She asked me eagerly in her hoarse voice about the front and was pleased about our successes.
>
> I wanted to make some tea, but couldn't find a single match in the house, and I left her still shaking.[18]

Lenin soon discovered her situation, probably because of Polina. "Dear Friend," he wrote, "I wanted to telephone you when I heard you were ill, but the phone doesn't work. Give me the number and I'll tell them to repair it."[19]

Two or three days later, he wrote again: "Please say what's wrong with you. These are appalling times: There's typhus, influenza, Spanish 'flu, cholera. I've just gotten up, and I'm not going out. Nadya has a temperature of 39 [102.2°F] and wants to see you. What's your temperature? Don't you need some medicine? I beg you to tell me frankly. You must get well."[20]

He was soon in touch again. He had given orders for a doctor to attend her. "Has the doctor been?" he asked.

> You have to do exactly as he says. The phone's out of order again. I told them to repair it. I want your daughters to call me and tell me how you are. You must do everything the doctor tells you. To go out with a temperature of 38 or 39 is madness. I beg you earnestly not to go out and to tell your daughters from me that I want them to watch you and not to let you out: (1) until your temperature is back to normal, (2) with the doctor's permission. I want an exact reply on this.[21]

Presumably her daughters obeyed the orders of the head of state, though it seems Inessa was to be soon out of the apartment and back at work. "Comrade Inessa," he wrote again, "I rang to find out what size of galoshes you take. I hope to get hold of some. Write and tell me how your health is. What's wrong with you? Has the doctor been?"[22]

Again, he persists.

> The doctor says it is pneumonia. You must be extremely careful. Tell your daughters to ring me daily. Tell me truly what are you missing? More firewood? Who tends your fire? Do you have food? Who cooks for you? Who is tending you with cold compresses? You're avoiding answering. This is not good. Answer me, even on this piece of paper, all my points. . . . Your Lenin. P.S.: Have they mended the telephone?[23]

What is surprising about this string of these and other letters is Lenin's effort and allocation of time, given the immense range of what he had to direct. The civil war was in its last days, but, only weeks before, St. Petersburg had been so threatened, with White possession of the Polkuvo Heights that overlooked the city, that Lenin had urged its evacuation—a suggestion that shocked Trotsky, who could not accept abandonment of the birthplace of the revolution. He rallied the residents of the city, both men and women. Barricades went up in the streets. Machine guns were posted on high buildings. For three days, although most were armed with little more than rifles, the Bolsheviks held off the Whites, who had tanks, until reserves could be rushed up by rail from the south. The battle had been fierce, with Trotsky at one stage on a horse personally stopping desertions; though he never had to set up the machine guns behind the defenders to deter retreat, as Lenin had urged.

Now Moscow was in the midst of another awful winter. In addition to her articles on the women's page of *Pravda,* also released to other Russian papers, Inessa had launched a new monthly, *Kommunistka,* published by Zhenotdel, and was soon involved in planning three conferences, including the First International Conference of Communist Women, for which, according to Vinogradskaya, "she took on herself all the work of preparing, organizing, and conducting." She had been temporarily stripped of two top members of staff, which, with others ill and Kollontai still away, left her working up to sixteen hours a day. Often, she fled to the reading room of the Rumyantsev Museum, where she had worked as a fugitive in 1908, to gain some peace from the office chatter.

The conference was not a great success, despite a fervent rendering by the audience of the "Internationale." The attendance was small, in part because European women had not been invited, probably because of the Soviet government's uneasy relations with those countries. By the end of it, Nadya recorded, "Inessa was on her last legs."[24]

Lenin remained very concerned. A few days earlier, he had written to her.

My dear friend, it was sad to find out that you were overtired and dissatisfied with your work and the colleagues that surround you. Can I help you by arranging a sanatorium for you?

If you go to France, I'm very afraid that you will be arrested, and I doubt they will exchange you for someone else. . . . Would it be better to go to Norway—many people speak English there—or to Poland? Or to Germany, in the capacity either of a French or a Russian?

I had a wonderful holiday [in the woodland near Pushkino, rather strangely], suntanned, didn't see a single line and not a single phone call. Previously, the hunting was good, but now everything is destroyed. Everywhere I heard your surname. "In their time, there was order," etc.

If you don't want to go to a sanatorium, why not go south to Sergo [Ordzhonikidze] in the Caucasus? Sergo will arrange a good holiday—the sun, good work. . . . There, he is the authority. Think about it. I firmly shake your hand. Your Lenin.[25]

This was a strange suggestion, especially since Kislovodsk was the resort selected. The civil war had ended, but fighting by small units still persisted, especially in the Kuban area, where the conflict was to rumble on in the mountains for quite a long time. Kislovodsk was only fifty miles or so from the Kuban River—although this was further than it sounded, being rugged mountain country. Lenin clearly believed that Sergo Ordzhonikidze had proper control over the territory, though there had to be an element of danger.

Inessa knew Sergo quite well. He had been at the Longjumeau School in 1911, and he had also attended the Prague Conference in 1912. Sergo had actually opposed Lenin on some issues then, which had given the rigged conference a tiny shred of authority.

Inessa had enjoyed, too, her stay in Stavropol in the northern Caucasus in 1912, on her long vacation with the children after being released from the St. Petersburg jail.

The idea of a holiday had much appeal for her, especially since Andre was not well and would benefit from the mountains. So she accepted Lenin's offer. It was a momentous decision.

CHAPTER 14

THE CAUCASUS 1920

he Caucasus, which divides Europe from Asia, is one of the greatest mountain chains in the world, with six peaks rising above sixteen thousand feet, twenty that top Mont Blanc, the highest of the European Alps, and 125 square miles of glaciers. Stretching some 650 miles from Novorossisk on the Black Sea to Baku on the Caspian, the grassed and wooded plateau of the North rises south to the mountains in a series of huge terraces, cut by deep fissures.

It is a wild area of fast-flowing rivers and primeval forests, which enabled the Caucasians to hold off the Great Russians during 160 years of continuous fighting.

The mythology is rich. This is where Prometheus was said to have been chained to a rock for stealing fire from the gods; where the Argonauts came in search of the Golden Fleece; where the fearless Amazon virgins lived.

As promised, Lenin issued his orders to Ordzhonikidze, confirming them on August 18.

> Comrade Sergo, Inessa Armand is leaving today. I am asking you not to forget your promise. Send a telegram to Kislovodsk giving the order to make arrangements for her and her son as appropriate and follow up the execution of this order. If you don't, nothing will be done. Answer me please by letter or, if possible, by telegram: "I have received the letter. I will do everything. I will check it correctly."

Clearly, Lenin was starting to worry whether he had chosen the best place for her holiday. "In view of the dangerous situation in the Kuban," he continued, "I ask you to establish contact with Inessa Armand so that you can evacuate her and her son if necessary to Petrovsk and Astrakhan without delay . . . and in general to take all [necessary] measures."[1]

He had already given Inessa a signed letter to the district administrator of resorts and sanatoriums, requesting that everything possible be done "to provide the best accommodation and treatment for the bearer, Comrade Inessa Fedorovna Armand and her sick son."[2]

Still, Lenin wasn't satisfied. On August 20, two days after Inessa left, he wired Ordzhonikidze again: "Don't forget you promised to arrange for treatment for Inessa Armand and her sick son, who left here on August 18."[3]

She arrived with Andre and Polina Vinogradskaya on August 22. Kislovodsk was a pretty spa town that, together with three others in the area, had been financed by the tsar. In those heady times, it had been popular with officers on leave, and there had been a lively social scene. The local springs gushed a sparkling mineral water called Narzan that was prized in Russia; bathing in it was supposed to cure venereal disease. It was a place of green hills, with juniper and buckthorn bushes, and of skylarks and tall poplar trees.

It should have been just what Inessa needed, except, as soon became apparent, for the sound of gunfire at night. The civil war was supposed to have ended in April, but White "bandits" were active, especially a group under General Fostikov that had remained in the hills not far from the spa town.

Her longtime friend Lyudmilla Stal was already there with her husband, G. N. Kotov, but Inessa was in no mood for socializing. "She looked tired, worn out, and emaciated when she arrived," recorded Stal.

The term *sanatorium* was an exaggeration, as the place was simply a large dacha that the local authorities had taken over on the edge of the town. There were no health facilities, and food was short.

In spite of Lenin's intercession, Inessa lacked the vouchers needed for accommodation in the principal building, which was overcrowded anyway. A voucher was somehow produced for her, and a room was found nearby, but it had no electric light or even proper bedding.

Local party workers, who knew Vinogradskaya had arrived with Inessa, approached her in a very agitated state with a telegram, presumably from Sergo. " 'Could you tell us what to do?' they asked. 'We will do everything if Lenin himself is worried.' So we all went to see Inessa, who said she didn't need anything except a pillow. . . . Three pillows arrived."[4]

The situation with the White bandits was disturbing. The guests and those patients who were well enough were issued rifles and divided into detachments to fight off the enemy, reported Polina. "The Whites . . . did not mount serious attacks but created diversions by sudden sorties."

During alerts, the local revolutionary committee would summon the defenders by siren to the party headquarters. Kotov reported that White bandit attacks were fairly distant at first, but the night alerts were alarming. "People were very frightened. Even party members behaved like cowards." Oddly, in her writings, Inessa makes no reference to this drama or to carrying guns, but she was much occupied by dark thoughts and what appears to have been some kind of psychological breakdown.

She was in no state to fight anyone. "At first I slept night and day," she wrote Inna later. "Now on the contrary I sleep badly. . . .

> Andre is brighter, but he has not yet put on weight. . . . He has made a lot of acquaintances and likes playing croquet.
>
> I sunbathe and have showers, but the sun here is not very hot—nothing like the Crimean sun—and the weather is not good. There are often storms, and yesterday was quite cold. I can't say I'm particularly taken with Kislovodsk.[5]

She was slow to write to her beloved Inna, and this was an indication of her state of mind. "She was not the same," wrote Kotov. "She was exhausted from overwork. She wanted to stay by herself. She used to go for walks in the forest and the mountains. I tried many times to persuade her to play croquet and to enjoy the company of the other people there, but she always answered: 'Later. We still have time. Just for now I'll go and rest in the sun.' "

Kotov played croquet with "Andrushka, who was a merry companion," and amused Polina. "I remember with a smile my arguments with Andre," she recorded, "because he broke the rules of the game. Inessa, of course, [when she heard of them] always took his part in the arguments."

Kotov was watching Inessa anxiously. "She was drunk on loneliness," he wrote colorfully. "If we didn't have to eat, or there hadn't been a bell, she would have stayed on her own [instead of venturing to the dining room in the main building]. This went on for about two weeks. Then she started to become herself again. She was looking better and gaining weight."

Vinogradskaya was also worried about her. "I remember her tall, svelte figure in a black cape and white hat, with a book in her hand, slowly climbing higher and higher into the mountains."

On September 1, nine days after their arrival, Inessa began to write a diary.[6]

Now I have time, I'm going to write every day, although my head is heavy, and I feel as if I've turned into a stomach that craves food the whole time. [Up here] you don't know anything and don't hear about anything.

I also feel a wild desire to be alone. I am tired even when other people are talking around me, let alone having to speak myself. I wonder if this feeling of inner death will ever pass.

I have reached a point where I find it strange when other people laugh and have such pleasure in talking. Now, I hardly ever laugh or smile because I feel joy but just because I have to smile sometimes [to be polite].

I am also surprised by my indifference to nature [the spectacular scenery presumably]. I used to be so moved by it. Now I don't like people so much. Previously I approached everyone with a warm feeling. Now I'm indifferent to everyone and bored by them all.

The only warm feelings I have left are for the children and V. I. In all other respects it's as if my heart has died; as if, having given up all my strength, all my passion to V. I. and the work, I have exhausted all sources of love and compassion toward people to whom previously I was so richly open. I have no one apart from V. I. and my children. I have no relations with other people, except in my work. And people feel this deadness in me and they pay me back with the same indifference and antipathy. And now even my attitude toward my work is fading.

I remember the biblical Lazarus who rose from the dead. He knew the sign of death in him remained, and it scared people, made them need to get away from him. . . . I, too, am a living corpse and this is terrible—especially when life around me is so active.[7]

. . .

Kotov reported that "real battles had started near Kislovodsk. All day long we could hear the noise of artillery and feared that Kislovodsk could be cut off by White Guards. The panic started. Inessa was one of the few people who stayed calm. She tried to stop others leaving, wanting the weak and ill and family people to leave first."

Dr. I. S. Ruzheinikov, another guest, wrote that a new threat was "a guerrilla, Colonel Azarov," who was commander, it seems, of a kind of commando unit. "Everything was mobilized against attack by the Azarov detachments."

Then one night, two members of the committee were killed, which concentrated Inessa's mind when she continued her diary.

> Some patients are very worried. They are afraid of attacks. I'm worried only for Andrushka, my little son. In this respect I am weak—not like a Roman matron who could easily sacrifice her children in the interest of the Republic. I could not. I am terribly worried about my children.
>
> I was never a coward for myself, but I'm a big coward when it concerns my children, especially Andrushka. I can't even begin to think about what I could live through if one day he has to go to the front, as I'm afraid one day he will have to. The war [presumably the international revolutionary war] will last a long time when our foreign friends will rise.
>
> We are still very far from the time when the personal interest and that of society will coincide. Now there is no personal life because all our time and effort is devoted to the common cause. Or maybe other people can find a bit of time and a little corner of happiness. I don't know how to do it for myself.

On September 2, Lenin had signaled Ordzhonikidze again: "Please add fullest details about the progress of the fight against banditry and about arrangements you have made in Kislovodsk for Soviet functionaries about whom I spoke to you here personally."[8]

After this had filtered through, two men, the district Red Army commander Davydov and Stepanov-Nazarov from the local party committee, called to see Inessa. They decided she should be evacuated. She refused, saying she wanted no special treatment. She would leave when everyone left.

According to Kotov, Stepanov-Nazarov was under pressure from the regional command, following Lenin's repeated signals. He warned her that if she would not leave with him, he would use the Red Army to move her, which was not the way to handle Inessa. It is apparent that he did not carry out his threat—at least not then and not in that way.

Vinogradskaya had decided to return and urged Inessa to come with her, but she declined. She was there for a holiday and was going to finish it. She even teased Vinogradskaya "in a light-hearted way," which hardly conforms with Inessa's diary gloom, for leaving before the end of her vacation, almost ranking her with the "shkurniks." This was what she called the healthy people who wanted to "save their skins" at the expense of those who were ill. However, it is strange that she did not consider leaving for Andre's sake.

After another day, the military situation had improved. The White bandits had been driven off, but they were still present in the more distant hills. Stepanov-Nazarov decided that since there was still danger of further attacks, he would evacuate the town, though this was to take some days to organize. Already some people had left—the very ill, who had been sent off in ambulance carriages or trains; and others, who had their own horse-drawn transport.

On the eve of Vinogradskaya's departure, Inessa played the sanatorium piano after dinner for the guests. Presumably, Lyudmilla Stal knew she was a pianist, but her talent as a musician was a surprise to Vinogradskaya. Oddly, she was reluctant to play, since usually she found the piano so settling, but at last she consented.

"At first," wrote Vinogradskaya, Inessa was not at ease. "Then she got involved with the playing. Her face became warm. Her scarf slipped from her shoulders. She played a sonata by Beethoven, a Schumann concerto, a Liszt rhapsody. I can still see her at the piano and hear her playing. It was her swan song." She continued at the piano for the rest of the evening, a dramatic scene given the sound of distant gunfire.

Inessa remained untouched by the danger around her and strangely distanced from it. By September 9, she had been resting for the best part of three weeks, yet the gloom still enclosed her. It is hard to see why, though logic, of course, cannot necessarily produce contentment or repair a chronic condition.

She was arguably the most powerful woman in Moscow. Her job was to make conditions better for millions of women but, by contrast to Emily Pankhurst and other women in several other democratic countries still fighting for equality in the vote, she could to some extent enforce it.

Her relations with Lenin, now the unquestioned ruler of Russia, were clearly extremely close. She even had a long, warm friendship with his wife, who, despite her behavior after the assassination attempt, still regarded herself as a favorite aunt to her children.

Finally, as seen in her diary, her faith that their Revolution, to which she had devoted so much of her life, would spread throughout the world was still untarnished by doubt.

Why did the future seem so dark? "It seems to me," she wrote in her diary,

> that I walk among people, trying to hide my secret from them—that I am a dead person among the living. Like an actor who a hundred times has to repeat the same scene which no longer inspires him, I repeat by memory the gestures, smiles, even the words that previously I used when I felt emotional.
>
> But now my heart is dead, my soul is silent, and I cannot manage to hide from people my sad mystery. There is a cold

breeze that people can feel from me. They move away. Now I am no longer tired, but this inner deadness remains within me. And because I have no warmth, as I no longer radiate warmth, I am unable to give happiness to anyone.

Her last diary entry two days later, on September 11, gives a glimmer of a clue. She has devoted herself to a man she loves—and appears to love her—but he has convinced her that the cause has priority over personal feelings, over the individual. It is a stark denial of human emotion and of human nature in a woman for whom love, as she has shown both in her life and in her writings, is a constant theme.

"For romantic people," she confided to her diary,

love takes first place in the life of a person. Love is higher than anything else. And until recently I was nearer to this idea than I am now. It is true that, for me, love was never the only thing. Together with love, there was always the cause, and in the past there were many times when I sacrificed my happiness and my love for it.

Previously, it seemed that love was as important as the cause. Now this is not the case. . . . It is true that in my life even now love has a big place and makes me suffer much and takes up many of my thoughts. But not for a moment do I cease to recognize that, however painful for me, love and personal relationships are nothing compared to the needs of the struggle.

What is she saying? What has changed? She now believes that the cause is more important than love. She says she has given up much for it, but what does she mean by this? The children? Exile and prison had, of course, parted her from them—fairly often and, during the war, for the best part of three years. Volodya's death? Would he have died so soon but for those hard, freezing months in Mezen?

Perhaps she included Lenin among the things she had given up, though their parting in Cracow was his decision. Anyway, Lenin and the cause were inextricably linked. Without the cause, it is doubtful if he would have appealed to her.

Her musings were soon to stop. Five days later, she consented, under pressure up to the last minute, to leave Kislovodsk and, with Andre, board a rail coach linked to an armored military train that would take them to Vladikavkaz. Stal and Kotov were with her, as were Dr. Ruzheinikov and his pregnant wife. There was one other woman present, and she was also pregnant.

Vladikavkaz was some 130 miles to the south. The plan was to move on from there to Nalchik, to the northwest, which was deemed safer. The journey took them across the Kabarda plain, through country that had mountains to the west and plains to the east.

Repeatedly, they came under both machine-gun and artillery fire. "Inessa was very calm," reported Dr. Ruzheinikov, "but she was worried for Andrushka and our two pregnant women."

At last, they passed through Beslan and approached Vladikavkaz, once a Russian fortress since it lies at the foot of Mount Kasbek, a crucial position on the Georgian Military Highway, one of the two main passes through the mountains from the south. The station was very dirty. Which was not encouraging since there had been a few cases of cholera there earlier in the year.

Inessa went into the town to find accommodation, but it was crowded with Cossacks and refugees from Georgia. She concluded that their best option was to continue sleeping on the train.

The next day, Sergo Ordzhonikidze arrived at the station and offered Inessa a car so she could explore the Georgian Military Highway. Inessa thought she was being offered special treatment again since the car was too small to take everyone. However, she was pressed and reluctantly accepted. There was more on her mind than sight-seeing.

"After two days," wrote Dr. Ruzheinikov, "it became clear that it would be better for us to go on to Nalchik," where hopefully they could relax.[9] The next day, the train moved off but was forced to stop at Beslan for a day and a half owing to bandit activity farther up the line. Beslan was "terribly filthy," so the doctor reported, even worse than Vladikavkaz, "with no accommodation, inadequate and disgusting toilets, and nowhere to buy food. We ate what we could find—a lot of raw fruit and melons."

Inessa was worried because Kotov, who had second-degree TB, needed milk and eggs. She went into the village and evidently had some success, for the doctor reported she "came back radiant and immediately started cooking and preparing something for Comrade Kotov," though he omits to say what. It was at Beslan, in the doctor's view, that she contracted cholera.

However, there was no sign she was unwell the next day when the train moved again. At last they reached Nalchik, a place less sophisticated than Kislovodsk, with old men in tall Astrakhan hats called papakhas and Caucasian women with shawls over their heads.

The local party had arranged a dacha for them. Though, after the experience of the journey, almost anything would have satisfied them. Then in the evening they attended a meeting of the local party. Inessa discussed Lenin's brochure, *The Childish Illness of Left-Wing Communism*, of which she and her friends in the Baugy Group, and indeed herself, were presumably the target. Yet she could not speak of Lenin without enthusiasm, even given the sadness expressed in her diary.

That night, she fell ill. She did not want to disturb anyone, so it was not until the next morning that the doctor found her suffering from convulsions, vomiting, and diarrhea. During the convulsions, the doctor and his wife, Rogova, started massaging her feet, but Inessa protested that the pregnant Rogova was putting herself and her child at risk.

The doctor arranged a bed for her in the local hospital. By then, she was so weak she could hardly walk. In the hospital she was diagnosed with cholera and put in a separate ward with a special medical staff. Doctor Ruzheinikov and Andre stayed with her. By the evening, her condition was much worse. The convulsions were increasing.

Again the doctor, a nurse, and Andre took turns massaging her feet, which must have been very distressing for the boy. Later, when Andre left the ward for a moment, Inessa asked the doctor to send him away in case he contracted the disease.

The Nalchik doctors feared she might have a heart attack and gave her an intravenous injection of saline solution, using common salt. After about half an hour, she appeared to improve. The color returned to her face. The vomiting and convulsions stopped. Her voice became clear, and she calmed down, apologizing that she was spoiling Dr. Ruzheinikov's holiday. She persuaded him to return to the dacha and get some rest. Then she fell asleep.

The next morning, when Andre arrived, she spoke to him through the window. She told him to eat something. By noon, she was declining again, and the cholera symptoms returned.

They repeated the saline solution, and as before she became a little calmer. Later, she asked Ruzheinikov to call Andre, and she talked to him for a few minutes and told him not to worry. Despite the early hour, she suggested he try to catch up on his sleep since she was feeling better. She insisted that the doctor rest, as well, and to please her he went into the next room. She instructed the staff that no telegrams were to be sent to Moscow about her condition.

By evening on September 23, her condition had deteriorated, and this time the saline solution had no effect. At midnight she became unconscious. The medical staff stayed by her bed all night, doing everything they could for her. But her system was exhausted, and her heart was weak. She failed to respond to treatment.

"In the morning," the doctor concluded briefly, "she left us." It was September 24.[10]

• • •

Just over two weeks later, early in the darkness of the morning of October 11, Lenin stood on the platform of Moscow's Kazan Station. With him was Nadya, Alexander, and Inessa's four older children, as well as Polina Vinogradskaya, whom Lenin had awoken by phone at

3:00 A.M. to suggest she join them. Also present was the new Kremlin commander, Abram Belenky, and several women from Zhenotdel. A catafalque was waiting with two white horses in traditional decorative bridles, harnesses, and ornamental headdresses that covered their ears.

Seventeen days had passed since Inessa had died. For eight of these her body had been in the Nalchik mortuary waiting for a zinc-lined coffin and a suitable rail car to take her to Moscow.

Suddenly, on October 9, it had dawned on a distraught Lenin (or more probably Nadya) that no one had thought about Andre, who, at sixteen, would have had little more than pocket money. Telegrams were sent at once to the revolutionary committee at Vladikavkaz, the executive committee of Nalchik, and the local Chekas ordering a search for the boy. Reports were to be made to Comrade Klishin at the Hotel Russia in Stavropol, who had been ordered to accompany the boy to Moscow.[11]

Since the train bearing Inessa would already have left, Andre might not be on it, and it is strange that Dr. Ruzheinikov did not mention in his account the boy, who must have been overwhelmingly shocked by his mother's sudden death. Georges Bardawil reports that he was on the train with his mother's body. Certainly, there is no doubt that he arrived safely at some stage. According to his son, Vladimir, he continued to live in Inessa's apartment by the Kremlin.

At last, in the morning darkness, the train from the Caucasus drew into the station. The coffin, with a black drape and red overlay, was moved to the catafalque.

Dawn was breaking as the procession left from the station. "We tried to persuade Lenin to sit in the car," wrote Vinogradskaya, "since it was a long way, but he refused. 'I will walk behind the coffin,' he said." "The long walk through the deserted streets behind her horse-drawn hearse," wrote R. C. Elwood, "was a form of penance for the Bolshevik leader."

"He walked with his head down," Vinogradskaya wrote, "absorbed by his thoughts. From time to time he slightly raised his hand, his eyes narrowed [in grief]." He had much to disturb him. If he had not urged Inessa to go to the Caucasus and made all those elaborate arrangements, she might still be alive. It was a desolate irony that had it not been for his persistent messages she might have stayed in Kislovodsk and finished her holiday in good health—physical if not mental.

The cortege progressed by Kalanchevskaya Square and Myasnitskaya, where the buildings were dilapidated, Vinogradskaya commented, being "unrepaired since the start of the war." Workers were on their way to their factories and offices—more of them than usual because the city trains were not running. Seeing the mourning procession, some of them stopped and joined it. Others queried, "Is it Lenin?"

At last they reached the House of Unions, where Inessa was to rest in state until the next day, with an overnight guard of honor chosen from among women she had been working with at Zhenotdel. There was a wreath of white hyacinths on the coffin, with the words "To Comrade Inessa from Lenin," as well as wreaths from other friends. She lay in a high-ceilinged room next to the big hall where Alexander, and Inessa herself for a short while, once sat as a member of the Moscow Duma; where Inessa, together with Alexandra Kollontai, had addressed an audience of more than a thousand women the previous year.

The next day, in bright autumn sunshine, she was borne from the House of Unions to Red Square in procession, this time a big one, with women from all the organizations in different regions with which Inessa had been involved. There were banners with such slogans as "The leaders die but their deeds live" and, according to *Izvestia,* a military band.

The Bolshoi Theatre Orchestra played Chopin, Beethoven, and Mozart. There were speeches, one rather surprisingly by Kollontai, who spoke of the collaboration Inessa had inspired "among the working women in Russia and in the international arena." But no one gave an address, again surprisingly, from the left-wing Baugy Group nor from any of her companions in exile.

"It was not until the end of the speeches that Lenin appeared, with Nadya, to say good-bye to his friend," reported Vinogradskaya. "He stood with bare head in his autumn coat, buttoned to the neck, at the side of the newly dug grave."

He shocked the women who were present. "He was unrecognizable," reported Kollontai. "He was plunged in despair. At any moment we thought he would collapse." Angelica Balabanov was equally overwhelmed. "Not only his face but his whole body expressed so much sorrow that I dared not greet him, not even with the slightest gesture. . . . He seemed to have shrunk. . . . His eyes seemed drowned in tears held back with effort."

Inessa's body was slowly lowered into the grave beside the high redbrick walls of the Kremlin as the crowd of mourners sang "The Internationale." "So, comrades, come rally, and the last fight let us face."

Vinogradskaya's description was vivid: "N. K. was crying, but Lenin stood straight, intense, immobile, his face contorted with anger." Then Nadya embraced Inessa's children. And the massed voices echoed across Red Square with the stirring final verse of the anthem, written to celebrate the Paris Commune of 1871.

"No saviour from on high delivers; no faith have we in prince or peer; our own right hand the chains must shiver, chains of hatred, greed and fear."

As many in that great square would have noted, with the sound of the singing fading, it was the ideal to which Inessa had devoted most of her adult life.

AND AFTERWARD . . .

By the time of Inessa's funeral in October 1920, the dangers to the Bolshevik regime had declined. The White armies had been fought off. The socialist opposition had been sharply curbed, with five thousand Mensheviks being sent to prison camps in 1919 and show trials of the leading SRs in 1920.

At last, Lenin could concentrate on his new order. But he did not have long to live himself.

At the time of Inessa's death, Inna was twenty-two, Varya was just shy of nineteen, and Andre was sixteen. According to Inna, Lenin and Nadya "became the guardians of my sister, my youngest brother, and me." Presumably the Armands already had passes into the Kremlin, but they now spent much time in the apartment and at the mansion in Gorki, though Inna and Andre moved for several weeks after their mother's death to the Chaika rest home on the Moscow outskirts.

For Andre, the sudden loss of his mother must have been traumatic. Inna, perhaps the closest to Inessa of all her children—and politically in tune with her—must have found it almost as hard. Lenin understood this, may even have found some consolation in sharing the mourning with her children, and took to visiting them.

He set Andre some chess problems. He also urged them to take up skiing, as he had urged their mother. The next year, according to Boris Souverine, who worked with Inna, "she used to live in the Kremlin in Lenin's home, where she was the object of great affection."

In 1922, Lenin learned that Inna had fallen ill during a holiday in the Crimea. He wrote to the doctor in charge of her, asking for details of her diet and condition, ordering him to keep him informed, an almost eerie reflection of her mother's last weeks. The scared doctor kept her in bed for a week longer than was needed.

He sent Varvara with Sasha to Teheran, under the protection of the Soviet ambassador, hoping the change of scene would appeal to them. Sasha was appointed secretary to the Russian Trade Commission there, but Varvara was not very happy, so he recalled her. Later, Sasha worked in the Commission for Heavy Industry, finishing up as its head of research.

Inna married Hugo Eberlein, a prominent German communist, and she joined him in Berlin, where she worked in the Soviet embassy and had a daughter named Inessa. When Hitler took power, Eberlein fled to Russia, only to be arrested in the purges and to die in prison. Inna became an editor of Lenin's collected works.

Varvara became a decorative artist and married Yakov Blomas, an artist and academician of note. She had a daughter, Blona, named after one of Inessa's pseudonyms, "Blonina," inspired by the Polish word for meadows, those of Cracow being where she had often walked with Lenin. After the Second World War, a retrospective exhibition of Varvara's work was held in Moscow.

Fedor, the only child of Inessa who never joined the party, remained in the air force, becoming an instructor. Andre trained to be an engineer and worked in the automobile works in Moscow and Gorki. He joined the party only in 1944 before being killed in the Second World War.

Lenin's health had been poor since early 1921—its closeness to Inessa's death being one reason why Alexandra Kollontai, romantic as ever, suggested it was a cause of his decline. He became steadily worse over the next two years, with several strokes, and he had to accept that, as he himself said, "My song is sung."

Maria and Nadya were at constant war over his care, his sister believing that visits from young people were damaging to him, while Nadya was convinced he enjoyed them. On one occasion, the arrival of Inna and Sasha at Gorki was the cause of so heated a quarrel between the two women that Lenin's personal bodyguard quietly suggested that the Armands should leave.

Nadya did not accept a situation in which the children could not visit. In the summer, she wrote to Inna in Germany, starting "Dear sweet girl" and asking, "Why can't you stay with us? On the contrary, this year we're going to live in a more 'family-like fashion.' . . . since it is impossible to occupy V. I. more than eight hours a day . . . he'll be delighted to have guests."

Lenin died in January 1924, and the next day Nadya wrote to Inna, "My very own dearest Inochka, we buried Vladimir Ilyich yesterday. . . . Lenin's death was the best outcome. Death had already been suffered by him so many times [in strokes] in the previous year." Several months before, she had written that "I wanted so much to have a child" and saying how alone she felt.

Inna replied to the news about his death, "Don't think you are completely alone. You still have us, your little girls as you call us. We love you very much and are grieving with you about Vladimir Ilyich. He was so dear, so loved. I did not believe it. Here everyone cried."

Nadya was disgusted by the plan to preserve the body and place it on public display in the marble mausoleum. "What they should have done," she wrote Inna, "was to bury him with his comrades so that they could be together beneath the red wall." This, again, was remarkable. The meaning is clear.

"Nadya had a generous spirit," wrote Robert Service. "Something made her want to keep the two families together even in death;

she was willing for her husband to lie by his former lover Inessa in the cold Moscow ground."

In April 1921, Lenin had written to Kamenev, chair of the Moscow soviet, about placing a permanent memorial to Inessa in Red Square, but it hadn't happened in the form he planned. In time, Inessa shared a granite memorial stone with John Reed, author of *Ten Days That Shook the World,* and two other comrades of lesser fame.

Nadya did more still for Inessa, writing articles in her memory and, in 1926, editing a collection of essays, *Pamyati Inessy Armand,* with contributions by former colleagues and herself.

After the death of Lenin, Nadya developed a working relationship with Stalin, who approved of her help in building the Lenin cult, but it was not always easy. In 1925, when she was supporting Kamenev and Zinoviev against him, he advised her to take care. "Otherwise," he is reported to have said, "I will tell the world who was really Lenin's wife."

Andre married a feisty young woman named Hienna, who bore him two sons and is reported, in Armand lore, to have made such a scene with "visitors" from the NKVD (which had replaced the Cheka), threatening to call Stalin's secretary, that the heavies retired in disorder.

This is not as strange as it may seem, since the Armands survived relatively untouched, with no arrests, throughout the entire period of communist rule, unlike hardly any of the more notable early Bolsheviks or even those who traveled on the sealed train. As has been seen, the Armands were allowed to keep Alyoshino in the Armand estate, and the family still has it, though the house is smaller now. Inessa's six-room apartment on the fourth floor at 9 Manege Street, procured for her on Lenin's order, stayed in possession of her descendants for fifty years until 1970. Blona and Vladimir, Andre's son, spent their childhoods there.

Alexander, Inessa's husband, married again in 1927. There was a state farm, as well as a family home, at Alyoshino, and Alexander applied in 1930, after collectivization, to be a member. His former peasants were surprised and embarrassed but voted for his admission. He worked there as a blacksmith and was also expert with engines. Alexander did not entirely escape class censure, though. A meadow near Alyoshino was showing muddy signs of overgrazing. When Alexander suggested the cattle should be grazed elsewhere, he was sharply reminded: "You're not in charge here now!" But when he died in 1943, according to Alexei Davidovich Armand, he was mourned by the community. "We've never had such a good black-smith as our old boss" is a reported remark.

It was the old people who suffered most. Alexander's father, Evgenii, and his uncle Emil had died in 1919, as had Inessa's mother, Natalie. Varvara Karlovna, Alexander's mother, lingered on until 1923, reportedly in a makeshift old people's home under a watch-tower next to the church where Inessa and Alexander were married.

In Moscow, Alexandra Kollontai stepped into Inessa's post as head of the Women's Section of the Central Committee, only to be dismissed in 1922. Soon after this, Zhenotdel was disbanded.

After 1926, Inessa's memory faded from public view. This was partly due to her suspect relationship with Lenin, now overshadowed by his godlike image, but also to her background as a rich young wife, which did not fit the picture of a proletarian revolution. The feminist advances that Inessa had worked so hard to promote soon faded under the reaction of what was still a patriarchal society. "She was," wrote R. C. Elwood, "one of those 'herrings with ideas'—an intellectual communist woman—for whom Stalin had no use whatever."

By 1930, the nurseries and communal dining rooms and laundries had gone. Despite the liberal divorce laws, many women were forced back to what was once derided as the dying concept of the bourgeois marriage. "The withering away of the family," as Beatrice Farnsworth, Kollontai's biographer, has commented, "became just another Socialist myth."

So what was there to remember Inessa for? She had devoted her life from 1909 to helping Lenin give flesh to his dream of a new world, being a sounding board, doing his dirty work, feeding his courage, celebrating with him his successes. Once, he told Maxim Gorky that the children of that day would "have happier lives than we had. They will not experience much that we lived through. There will not be so much cruelty in their lives."

There was as much, of course, and indeed far more, for Stalin institutionalized what Lenin had started. It is arguable that, without the bloody years of revolution, social democracy, in its milder modern form, would not have become accepted so widely. But the price was high.

This book records a tragedy. For the millions of people who died or were tortured or suffered in the gulags. For Lenin because he was proved so wrong. For Inessa because, if revolution was for her a religion, the god she worshipped turned out to be false.

She was a woman, though, of great courage, of loyalty, of vision, of enormous effort directed at the improvement of the state of women and, indeed, also of mankind. She deserves to be remembered.

CHAPTER 1: PUSHKINO 1893

Main sources: RTsKhIDNI (Archives); members of the Armand family, R. C. Elwood, *Inessa Armand: Revolutionary and Feminist;* Georges Bardawil, *Ines Armand;* and also notably in this chapter the premarital letters of Inessa gained from Armand family sources; Pavel Podliashuk, *Tovarishch Inessa,* 4th ed., a Russian biography written under Communist control; Lev Krasnopecvtsev, curator of the Museum of the Patrons (including Armands); Inessa F. Armand, *Stat'i, rechi, pis'ma;* Nikolai Lepeshkin, keeper of the Pushkino Museum; Robert Service, *Lenin: A Biography.*

1. I call her Nadya, as close associates did. Others addressed her formally as Nadezhda Konstantinovna, as N. K., or as Krupskaya, her code name and also her maiden name.
2. Bardawil, 47; *Le Figaro* obituary, December 29, 1885, supported by certificates and Theodore Stephane's reviews.
3. Inna Armand in E. D. Stasova, ed., *Slavnye Bol'shevichki* (Moscow, 1958).
4. This and subsequent premarital letters are in Bardawil, from Armand family sources, 95.
5. Ibid., 124.
6. Podliashuk, 16.
7. Photograph of the cast list is in the possession of V. M. Fedoseyev-Yegorov.
8. On the social life and early years of marriage, see Bardawil, 108, and Elwood, 27.
9. Bardawil, from Armand family sources, 82. Vladimir later married the younger sister of Stepanida Karassiova, Alexander's second wife.
10. Ibid., 120.
11. Ibid.

12.   The events of Lenin's life up to his meeting with Inessa have been described in many biographies, but I have leaned on Service in this and subsequent chapters.

13.   Elwood, 40.

14.   Polina Vinogradskaya, *Sobytiia i pamyatnye vstrechi*, 209.

15.   To Inna, autumn 1916, in Armand, *Stat'i, rechi, pis'ma*, 247.

16.   To V. E. Armand (Vladimir), December 20, 1908, in Armand, "Pis'ma Inessy Armand," *Novyi mir* 6 (1970): 218.

17.   For Minna Gorbunova-Kablukova and the societies Inessa was involved with, see Elwood, 26–32; Bardawil, 109–13; and Podliashuk, 19–20.

18.   Elwood, 32.

19.   To A. E. Armand, late April 1899, in "Pis'ma Inessy Armand," *Novyi Mir,* 197–98.

20.   Elwood, 33.

CHAPTER 2: MOSCOW 1902

Main sources: Unpublished biography of David Levovich Armand; Elwood; Bardawil; Podliashuk; Armand family members, especially Alexei Davidovich Armand. Also Inessa's letters to Alexander in "Pis'ma Inessy Armand," *Novyi mir* 6 (1970): 196–218; E. D. Stasova, ed., *Slavnye Bol'shevichki.*

1.   By this date, the term *Cossacks* was used loosely. Historically, most Cossacks came from the Dnieper and Don river areas. They were independent, brave fighters but changeable, usually working for the tsarist state but sometimes opposed to it. By 1900, the word was used to cover almost anyone on a horse who dealt with civil unrest, though the real Cossack regiments remained and were prominent during the civil war of 1918–1920.

2.   Elwood, 34–35.

3.   Unpublished autobiography of David Levovich Armand.

4.   Ibid.

5.   Bardawil, 145.

6.   To A. E. Armand in the Far East for the Russo-Japanese War, October 1904, in Armand, "Pis'ma Inessy Armand," 199–200.

7.   Bardawil, citing police records, 157.

8.   To A. E. Armand in the Far East for the Russo-Japanese War, January 7, 1905, in Armand, "Pis'ma Inessy Armand," 200–203.

9.   Ibid., January 14, 1905, 203. In fact, the Japanese did fund propaganda.

10.   Inna in Stasova, *Slavnye Bol'shevichki.*

11.   Elwood, 46.

12.   Inessa to Inna, September 1914, RTsKhIDNI, fond 127, op. 1, 35.18.

CHAPTER 3: MOSCOW BASMANNAYA JAIL 1905

Main sources: Bardawil; Ilya Ehrenburg, *People and Life;* "Pis'ma Inessy Armand"; Elwood.

1.   Bardawil, citing police records, 173.
2.   Ehrenburg, *People and Life.*
3.   Bardawil, 174.
4.   Ibid., 175.
5.   Elwood, 46.
6.   To Alexander, beginning of summer 1905, in "Pis'ma Inessy Armand," *Novyi Mir,* 203.
7.   Beginning of summer 1905 to Alexander. Ibid., 204. (Not the same as the preceding.)

CHAPTER 4: NICE 1905

Main sources: Abraham Ascher, *The Revolution of 1905: Russia in Disarray.* Ehrenburg; RTsKhIDNI; "Pis'ma Inessy Armand," *Novyi Mir;* Service; Stefan T. Possony, *Lenin: The Compulsive Revolutionary;* Krupskaya, ed., *Pamiati Inessy Armand;* Vladimir Sanov, "Mezenskaya ballada," *Sever;* Elwood; Bardawil.

1.   To A. E. Armand, November 9, 1905, in "Pis'ma Inessy Armand," *Novyi Mir,* 205.
2.   Elwood, 49.
3.   Elena Vlasova in N. K. Krupskaya, ed., *Pamyati Inessy Armand* (Moscow, 1926).
4.   Bardawil, citing police records, 189.
5.   Elwood, 51.
6.   Vlasova in Krupskaya, *Pamyati Inessy Armand.*
7.   Elwood, 50.
8.   To V. E. Armand, May 11, 1907, in "Pis'ma Inessy Armand," 206.
9.   Vlasova in Krupskaya, *Pamyati Inessy Armand.*
10.   Bardawil, 198.
11.   Podliashuk, 56; Elwood, 53.
12.   Bardawil, 199.
13.   To V. E. Armand, July 1907, in "Pis'ma Inessy Armand," *Novyi Mir,* 206.
14.   Bardawil, 199.
15.   The negotiations, police activity, and journey to exile are covered in Vladimir Sanov, "Mezenskaya ballada," *Sever* 12 (1971): 82–96.
16.   Both Elwood and Bardawil have described her departure, and she refers later to her bouquet when writing to Alexander from Mezen. See also

letter to A. E. Armand, mid-December 1907, in "Pis'ma Inessy Armand," 207.

17.   What follows derives from Service, whom I have followed for much of
Lenin in the capital (176) and Finland (185), as well as from N. K.
Krupskaya, *Memories of Lenin,* vol. 1, 179–81.

CHAPTER 5: MEZEN IN ARCTIC EXILE 1907

Main sources: Sanov; RTsKhIDNI; "Pis'ma Inessy Armand"; Krupskaya,
Pamyati Inessy Armand; Elwood; Bardawil; Service.

1.   To A. E. Armand, mid-December 1907, in "Pis'ma Inessy Armand,"
Novyi Mir, 207.
2.   To her children, mid-December 1907, in ibid., 208. This appears to
contain her last mention of Volodya (her ward), who presumably left
the family after completing the sixth form (see note 9, chap. 1).
3.   Sanov. It is doubtful Inessa was the author. *Rech* was the newspaper of
the Kadet Party, with a readership that was bourgeois.
4.   To A. E. Armand, February 16, 1908, in Armand, "Pis'ma Inessy Armand," 211.
5.   To A. E. Armand, August 13, 1908, in ibid., op. 1.36.
6.   To Inna, before July 1908, RTsKhIDNI, fond 127, op. 1.34.
7.   To V. E. Armand, May 8, 1908, in Armand, "Pis'ma Inessy Armand,"
212.
8.   To A. E. Armand, May 1908, RTsKhIDNI, fond 127, op. 1.36.
9.   Sanov.
10.   Ibid., 91.
11.   Service, 190.
12.   To Inna, July 25, 1908, RTsKhIDNI, fond 127, op. 1.35.
13.   To Anna Asknazy, August 1908, in Armand, "Pis'ma Inessy Armand,"
213.
14.   Inna has challenged Zubrovich's account, saying someone else (un-
named) had arranged this, though Zubrovich had helped.
15.   To V. E. Armand, November 1, 1908, in Armand, "Pis'ma Inessy Armand," 214.
16.   Ibid., November 2, 1908, 215.
17.   Ibid., end of November 1908, 216.
18.   To A. E. Armand, mid-December 1908, ibid., 217.
19.   Ibid., December 26–27, 1908, 218.
20.   To V. E. Armand, December 20, 1908, ibid., 217.
21.   Several writers have maintained that Vladimir died in Switzerland, but
Elwood says he died in Nice. This is confirmed by Inessa's daughter and

the fact that Inessa's correspondence was sent to Beaulieu. Elena
Vlasova also quotes her when she meets her in Paris as saying he died in
Switzerland, but I have followed Elwood.

22.   Bardawil, 226. There is a degree of speculation, but this seems likely. As
       Elwood agrees. Alexander was always a base for her; her sons were
       with him; she could not return to Russia without risk of arrest. Evi-
       dence of her movements during this period is either nonexistent or con-
       tradictory.
23.   Vinogradskaya, 212.
24.   Inna, late 1916, in Armand, *Stat'i, rechi, pis'ma*, 251.
25.   Vlasova in Krupskaya, *Pamyati Inessy Armand*. Her quote that
       Volodya died in Switzerland is likely wrong, as discussed earlier, as pos-
       sibly is the reference to TB. Vlasova was writing some fifteen years after
       the event.

CHAPTER 6: PARIS 1909

Main sources: Service; Krupskaya, *Memories of Lenin;* Possony; Bardawil; Elwood; Louis Fischer, *The Life of Lenin;* RTsKhIDNI, in particular fond 127,
op. 1.d.61 (a long letter to Lenin, also in *Svobodnaye mysl'* 3 [1992]: 80–88),
cataloged as December 1913.

1.   Elwood, 73.
2.   Bardawil, 243.
3.   To Lenin [December 1913], RTsKhIDNI, fond 127, op. 1.d.61 (see
      headnote).
4.   Ibid.
5.   Ibid.
6.   Marcel Body, "Alexandra Kollontai," *Preuves* 2.14 (1952): 17.
7.   Lidia Fotieva, *Iz zhizni Lenina* (London, 1967), 10.
8.   Service, 206.
9.   RTsKhIDNI, fond 127, op. 1.36.77; Elwood, 91 (speculation).
10.   Bardawil, 270, citing police records.

CHAPTER 7: ST. PETERSBURG 1912

Main sources: Georgi Safarov and V. I. Malakhovsky in Krupskaya, *Pamyati
Inessy Armand;* RTsKhIDNI; Robert B. McKean, *St. Petersburg Between the
Revolutions;* Podliashuk; Inna Armand in Stasova, *Slavnye Bol'shevichki;* Pos-
sony; Krupskaya, *Memories of Lenin;* Armand, *Stat'i, rechi, pis'ma;* Elwood;
Bardawil; Richard Pipes, *The Unknown Lenin* (which contains previously cen-
sored letters).

1. Bardawil, citing police records, 270.
2. Safarov in Krupskaya, *Pamyati Inessy Armand.*
3. McKean, 92.
4. Elwood, citing V. T. Leninskaia, *Pravda, 1912–14* (1972), 64.
5. Bardawil, citing Okhrana dossier, September 1912, 271.
6. Safarov in Krupskaya, *Pamyati Inessy Armand.*
7. Bardawil, 272.
8. Elwood, citing Stasova, in *Pravda,* May 8, 1964, 4.
9. Podliashuk, 124.
10. To Inna, summer 1915, in Armand, *Stat'i, rechi, pis'ma,* 231. Stavropol is not on the Volga, so presumably they went on to Stavropol.
11. To A. E. Armand, RTsKhIDNI, August 4, 1913, fond 127, op. 1.36.54.
12. Ibid., 1.36.59.
13. Ibid., 1.36.61.
14. Ibid., 1.36.65.
15. Ibid., 1.36.66.
16. Ibid., 1.36.69.
17. Ibid., 1.36.71.
18. Ibid., 1.36.74.
19. To V. I. Lenin, in ibid., 1.d.61. (See headnote to notes to chap. 6.)
20. R. C. Elwood, "New Evidence on an Old Affair," *Canadian Slavonic Papers,* forthcoming.
21. Prior to June 23, 1914; in Pipes.
22. There have been conflicting arguments about how long Lenin stayed in Paris on this visit. There is no doubt he was in Brussels by January 25 (vol. 43 of his collected works). Elwood, quoting three sources, insists that the stay lasted only a week. This is a relevant question because the letters between Lenin and Inessa following this visit were exceptionally warm, especially, as will be seen, from him.

CHAPTER 8: PARIS 1914

Main sources: V. I. Lenin, *Collected Works,* 4th ed. (English), vols. 35, 43 (including letters first published in Russian, 5th ed.); Krupskaya, *Memories of Lenin;* Pipes; Armand, *Stat'i, rechi, pis'ma;* the Neizvestnye Dokumenty (letters previously censored); RTsKhIDNI; Elwood.

1. Lenin, December 18, 1913, vol. 35, 130.
2. Ibid., end of December 1913, 131.
3. Ibid., before January 22, 1914, vol. 43, 377.
4. Ibid., before January 26, 1914, 378.
5. Ibid., January 25, 1914, 377.

6.   Ibid., January 26, 1914, 379.

7.   There are a lot of missing pages. Censors did not, however, tear them out—as is shown by the existence of those previously censored but now released. I believe that, as discussed later, Lenin tore them out himself when he received them back from Inessa. He left in the politics because he believed these statements would be part of his legacy. Elwood has argued (see note 20, chap. 7) that Inna may have done so, since she had possession of Inessa's papers before passing them to the Archive.

8.   Neizvestnye Dokumenty, February 23, 1914.

9.   To Inna, spring 1914, RTsKhIDNI, fond 127, op. 1.35.8/9.

10. Ibid., 1.35.5/7.

11. Lenin, after March 15, 1914, vol. 43, 394.

12. Ibid., April 1, 1914, vol. 35, 136.

13. June 7, 1914, in Pipes, 26.

14. Ibid., before June 23, 1914, 27.

15. Ibid., May 25, 1914, 26.

16. Lenin, May 25, 1914, vol. 43, 402.

17. Inessa to Nadya, March 16 to April 1, 1914, in Armand, *Stat'i, rechi, pis'ma,* 219.

18. Ibid., July 1914, RTsKhIDNI, fond 127, op. 1.

19. Elwood, 132.

20. Lenin, before July 4, 1914, vol. 43, 406.

21. Ibid., before July 6, 1914, 408.

22. Ibid., 410.

23. July 3, 1914, in Pipes, 27.

24. Lenin, July 10–16, 1914, vol. 35, 146.

25. Before June 23, 1914, in Pipes, 27.

26. Lenin, before July 13, 1914, vol. 43, 417.

27. Elwood, 139 (including other aspects of the conference).

28. Lenin, July 19, 1914, vol. 43, 423–25.

29. Elwood, 141.

30. Before July 12, 1914, in Pipes, 27.

CHAPTER 9: BERN 1914

Main sources: Lenin; RTsKhIDNI; Armand, *Stat'i, rechi, pis'ma;* Krupskaya, *Memories of Lenin;* Elwood; Bardawil.

1.   To Inna, August 1914, RTsKhIDNI, fond 127, op. 1.35.

2.   To Inessa from Inna, September 3, 1914. Quoted by kind permission of Blona Yakovlevna Romas (Inessa's granddaughter).

3.   To the children, late 1914, RTsKhIDNI, fond 127, op. 1.35.18/20.

4.   To Inna, 1915, in Armand, *Stat'i, rechi, pis'ma,* 239.
5.   Lenin, January 17, 1915, vol. 35, 180. See also letter to Inna, in Armand, *Stat'i, rechi, pis'ma,* 246 (dated 1916 but clearly from 1914–1915).
6.   To Inna, 1915, RTsKhIDNI, fond 127, op. 1.35.37.
7.   To Inna, after June 1915, RTsKhIDNI, fond 127, op. 1.35.
8.   Ibid.
9.   To Inna, autumn 1915, ibid.
10. Elwood, 167, which also covers other background aspects of the Paris venture and the preceding months.
11. Bardawil, 315, citing records of the Okhrana bureau in Paris.
12. Lenin, January 15, 1916, vol. 43, 505.
13. Ibid., January 19, 1916, vol. 43, 505.
14. Krupskaya, *Pamyati Inessy Armand.*
15. Lenin, vol. 43, 507.
16. *Leninskii Sbornik,* vol. 37, 38.
17. Lenin, January 1916, vol. 43, 603.
18. Ibid., November 20, 1916, vol. 35, 246.
19. November 13, 1916, in Pipes, 33.
20. Lenin, December 17, 1916, vol. 43, 588.
21. December 30, 1916, in Pipes, 33.
22. Ibid., January 6, 1917, 34.
23. Lenin, January 14, 1917, vol. 43, 599.
24. Michael Pearson, *The Sealed Train,* 39.
25. Ibid.
26. January 19, 1917, in Pipes, 34.
27. Lenin, March 13, 1917, vol. 43, 615.
28. Elwood, 194. I have drawn on Elwood for guidance on these arguments.
29. Lenin, January 22, 1917, vol. 43, 606.
30. Ibid.
31. Ibid., vol. 35, 247.
32. Ibid., November 30, 1916, 250.
33. Ibid., December 23, 1916, 264.
34. Ibid., between March 25 and 31, 1917, 306.
35. Elwood, 199, which also covers other background aspects.

CHAPTER 10: ZURICH 1917

Main sources: Pearson; Lenin; Krupskaya, *Memories of Lenin,* and a long article in *Pravda,* April 16, 1924; R. H. McNeal, *Bride of the Revolution,* and *Revolution in Russia;* W. Hahlweg, *Lenin's Journey to Russia 1917;* G. Zinoviev, *V. I. Lenin;* Edmund Wilson, *To the Finland Station;* Z. A. B. Zeman and W. B.

Scharlau, *Merchant of Revolution* (*Helphand*); German and British Foreign Office files; Fritz Platten, *Lenin's Journey Through Germany in the Sealed Car*; N. F. Platten, "From the Spiegelgasse to the Kremlin," *Grani* 77, 79 (1972).

1. After the outbreak of war, *St. Petersburg* was deemed to appear too German, so the name was changed to Petrograd. Later, it became Leningrad for some decades before reverting to its original name, as it is today. I stay with *St. Petersburg*, except in quotations. Many people normally called it *Peter*.
2. Lenin, March 15, 1917, vol. 35, 294.
3. In 1915, Lenin had considered moving to Scandinavia to have easier access to Russia than he had in Switzerland, surrounded as it was by warring nations, and there were possibly other plans.
4. Lenin, March 18, 1917, vol. 43, 616.
5. Ibid., March 19, 1917.
6. Ibid., March 23, 1917, 620.
7. Ibid., March 25, 1917, vol. 35, 306.
8. In 1915, Helphand, after contact with the Germans, had gone to Bern to seek a meeting with Lenin. He approached him in a café when he was dining with Nadya and Inessa. Lenin despised him, but the two men did go off for a private meeting. It is presumed that Helphand wanted Bolshevik help to organize a strike in Russian factories in order to demonstrate to the Germans what he could do for them.

   Almost certainly, he also sought Lenin's cooperation with the "revolutionizing" plan, and almost certainly Lenin rejected him because he was "tainted." It is not known if anything was agreed, but it is probable that Helphand's organization was used after the February revolution to help the Bolsheviks to transfer to Russia money and information.
9. Lenin, March 31, 1917, vol. 43, 623.
10. This was the date in Switzerland, but as mentioned earlier, Russia was still using the Julian calendar, which was thirteen days behind the Gregorian calendar. So what is to the West the March Revolution took place in Russia in February, and the sealed train party, which departed on April 9 (Swiss date), arrived in St. Petersburg on April 3 (Russian date).
11. There is a degree of mystery about the number of travelers. On arrival in Russia, Lenin stated that the party consisted of thirty-two. This conforms with the statement signed on the day of departure in Zurich by twenty-nine travelers, which excluded two children and Fritz Platten. But two people left the party in Stockholm, reducing the number to thirty actually reaching Russia. So Lenin was either speaking loosely or two unidentified others replaced those who left.

12. Accounts of the journey were written by ten of the travelers, either in book form or in articles. See particularly Olga Ravich, "The Journey across Germany," *Pravda,* April 18, 1927; Karl Radek, "In the Sealed Carriage," *Pravda,* April 20, 1924; Krupskaya, *Memories of Lenin,* 209; Lilina (Zinaida Zinovieva), "Comrade Lenin Departs for Russia," *Leningradskaya Pravda,* April 16, 1924.

13. Telegrams of September and December 1917 from the German secretary of state to the Kaiser. For this and further evidence, see George Katkov, *Russia 1917; International Affairs,* April 1956: German Foreign Office documents on financial support of the Bolsheviks; and Pearson, 290.

14. To the children, April 1917, RTsKhIDNI, fond 127, op. 1.35.58.

15. Service, 260, citing G. E. Zinoviev, "Vospominaniya: Malinovsky."

16. Accounts differ as to whether Kollontai was waiting with her bunch of flowers at the Finland Station or at Belo-ostrov, the border town, where Lenin was joined by Kamenev and senior colleagues. The former, reported by Shlyapnikov, seems most likely.

CHAPTER 11: ST. PETERSBURG 1917

Main sources: N. N. Sukhanov, *The Russian Revolution, 1917;* Leon Trotsky, *The History of the Russian Revolution;* Pearson; V. D. Bonch-Bruevich, *Battle Positions in the February and October Revolutions;* N. I. Podvoisky, *The Year 1917;* John Reed, *Ten Days That Shook the World;* Lenin's letters in *Leninskii Sbornik* 38; Elwood; Bardawil.

1. Sukhanov, 286.

2. Vinogradskaya, *Semenovna pamiatnye vstrechi,* 219.

3. Later than May 12, 1917, *Leninskii Sbornik* 37, 58.

4. Ibid., April 20, 1917, 56.

5. Ibid., before May 12, 1917, 57.

6. An unknown witness, in Pearson, 188, supported by Sukhanov, 415–18.

CHAPTER 12: MOSCOW 1917

Main sources: I. V. Gote, *Time of Troubles;* Armand family sources; Service; Inessa's letters to her daughters; Orlando Figes, *A People's Tragedy,* esp. on the Terror, the Cheka, the civil war, and the impact on ordinary people of the mayhem of 1917–1920; Elwood; Bardawil.

1. Gote, 72.

2. This Andrei is not Inessa's son Andre, who is only thirteen.

3.   Elwood, 214.
4.   Ibid.
5.   Bertram D. Wolfe, *The Bridge and the Abyss,* 71.
6.   Figes, 527.
7.   Service, 365.
8.   Ibid., 334.
9.   To Inna, after September 16, 1918, RTsKhIDNI, fond 127, op. 1.35.
10. Service, 343.
11. Elwood, 214.
12. Armand family sources.
13. Ibid.
14. Ibid.
15. To Inna, around September 16, 1918, RTsKhIDNI, fond 127, op. 1.35.
16. Gote, 300.
17. To Inna, around December 16, 1918, RTsKhIDNI, fond 127, op. 1.35.
18. Ibid., after September 16, 1918.
19. Ibid., between October 3 and November 6, 1918.
20. Ibid.
21. Ibid.
22. Ibid., around December 16, 1918.

CHAPTER 13: MOSCOW 1918

Main sources: Figes; Cathy Porter, *Alexandra Kollontai;* Service; Elwood; Dmitri Volkogonov, *Lenin: Life and Legacy;* Gote; Bardawil; *Leninskii sbornik* 37; letters to Inna in Armand, *Stat'i, rechi, pis'ma* and RTsKhIDNI; Vinogradskaya; Carol Eubank Hayden, "Zhenotdel and the Bolshevik Party," *Russian History* 3.2 (1976): 150–73; Richard Stites, "Kolontai, Inessa, and Krupskaya," *Canadian-American Slavic Studies* 9 (spring 1975): 84–92.

1.   There have been descriptions by many historians of this attempted assassination. I have leaned most heavily on Volkogonov.
2.   V. Armand, *Novyi mir* 4 (1967): 198.
3.   To Inna, after September 16, 1918, RTsKhIDNI, fond 127, op. 1.35.
4.   Biog. Khron, vol. 6, 317.
5.   Fischer, 487.
6.   Service, 379.
7.   Gote, 207.
8.   Figes, 646. See also material on the chaos of the civil war and the food shortages that followed.
9.   Figes, 280, citing Bochkareva.
10. Porter, 325ff.

11. To Inna, around December 16, 1918, RTsKhIDNI, fond 127, op. 1.35.
12. Richard K. Debo, "The Manuilskii Mission," *International History Review* 8.2 (1986): 214–35, covers the mission in detail.
13. To Inna, February 1919, previously unpublished. See Bardawil, 361.
14. Bardawil, citing *Aviation and Astronautique* 12 (1968).
15. Gote, 282.
16. To Ivan Popov, RTsKhIDNI, fond 127, op. 1.45.
17. Elwood, 240, which also covers the aftermath of the formation of Zhenotdel.
18. Vinogradskaya; Krupskaya, *Pamyati Inessy Armand,* 61–63.
19. *Leninskii Sbornik,* 35, 108.
20. Ibid.
21. Neizvestnye Dokumenty, not later than February 16, 1920.
22. Ibid.
23. Ibid.
24. Krupskaya, *Pamyati Inessy Armand,* 33.
25. *Leninskii Sbornik,* 37, August 1920, 233.

CHAPTER 14: THE CAUCASUS 1920

Main sources: Vinogradskaya, *Sobytiia i pamiatnye vstrechi;* Lyudmilla Stal, G. N. Kotov, Dr. I. S. Ruzheinikov, and N. Krupskaya, all in Krupskaya, *Pamyati Inessy Armand;* Lenin *Polnoe sobranie sochinenie,* 5th ed., vol. 51; RTsKHIDNI (*Svobodnaye mysl'* 3 [1992]); Negley Farson, *Caucasian Journey;* Michael Pereira, *Across the Caucasus; Pravda,* October 12, 1920; *Izvestia,* October 12–13, 1920; Elwood; Bardawil; Balabanoff, *Impressions of Lenin.*

1. To Sergo Ordzhonikidze, August 18, 1920, *Polnoe sobranie sochinenie* (*PSS*), vol. 51, 261.
2. To the administrator of health resorts and sanatoriums, August 17, 1920, ibid.
3. To Sergo Ordzhonikidze, August 20, 1920, *PSS,* vol. 51, 262.
4. Vinogradskaya has twice described the events in the Caucasus. Here, I have merged her quotes from the two sources.
5. Armand, *Stat'i, rechi, pis'ma,* 257.
6. *Svobodnaye mysl'* 3 (1992).
7. This assumes much. St. John, in the gospel (11), says that some of the Jews who witnessed the Lazarus miracle went to the Pharisees and reported what they had seen. The chief priests and the Pharisees met in council and saw the situation as politically dangerous. It is probable that they did feel uncomfortable in Lazarus's presence, but St. John does not actually say so.

8.   To Sergo Ordzhonikidze, September 2, 1920, *PSS,* vol. 51, 173.

9.   Dr. Ruzheinikov's detailed account of the last days of Inessa's life appears in Krupskaya, *Pamyati Inessy Armand.*

10.   There have been suggestions that, in her state of deep depression, Inessa committed suicide or was even murdered. The detailed evidence of Dr. Ruzheinikov and G. N. Kotov makes it quite clear she died of cholera. Also, it is hard to believe that she would have committed suicide without making proper arrangements for the care of Andre, whom she had always adored—as emphasized in the diary she kept in Kislovodsk.

11.   RTsKhIDNI, fond 127, op. 1.53.3.

BIBLIOGRAPHY AND OTHER SOURCES

Agafanov, V. K. *The Okhrana Abroad*. 1918.

Armand, Inessa A. In *Slavnye Bol'shevichki*. Ed. E. D. Stasova, Moscow, 1958.

Armand, Inessa F. "Pis'ma Inessy Armand." *Novyi mir* 6 (1970): 196–218.

———. *Stat'i, rechi, pis'ma*. Moscow, 1975.

———. *Svobodnaye mysl'*. 1992. Includes a letter to Lenin dated December 1913 (actually January 1914) and a diary written in the days before her death. Also includes Krupskaya letters to Inna and Varvara Armand.

Armand, Varvara A. "Zhivaia nit (Iz vosponianii I perepiski s N. K. Krupskoi)." *Novyi mir* 4, 178.

Ascher, Abraham. *The Revolution of 1905*. Stanford, Calif., 1988.

Balabanoff, Angelica. *Impressions of Lenin*. Ann Arbor, 1964.

Bardawil, Georges. *Inès Armand*. Paris, 1993.

Body, Marcel. "Alexandra Kollontai." *Preuves* 2.14 (1952).

Carr, E. H. *The Bolshevik Revolution*. 3 vols. New York, 1950–1953.

Chernyshevsky, Nikolai. *What Is to Be Done?* Trans. Benjamin Tucker and Cathy Porter. London, 1983.

Clements, Barbara Evans. *The Life of Alexandra Kollontai*. Bloomington, Ind., 1979.

Debo, Richard K. "The Manuilskii Mission." *International History Review* 8 (1986): 214.

Ehrenburg, Ilya. *People and Life, Memoirs of 1891–1917*. Trans. Anna Bostock and Yvonne Kapp. New York, 1961.

Elwood, R. C. *Inessa Armand: Revolutionary and Feminist*. Cambridge, 1992.

Farnsworth, Beatrice. *Aleksandra Kollontai*. Stanford, Calif., 1980.

Farson, Negley. *Caucasian Journey*. London, 1951.

Fischer, Louis. *The Life of Lenin*. London, 1965.

Fofanova, M. "Memories of 1917." *Leningradskaya Pravda* 19 (1928).

Fortnightly Review 108 (July–December 1917).

Fraser, Eugenie. *The House by the Dvina*. New York, 1984.

Fréville, Jean. *Lénine à Paris*. Paris, 1968.

———. *Une grande figure de la Révolution russe: Inessa Armand*. Paris, 1957.

Futrell, Michael. *Northern Underground*. London, 1963.

Gankin, O. H., and H. H. Fisher. *The Bolsheviks and the World War*. Stanford, Calif., 1940.

"German Foreign Office Documents on Financial Support to the Bolsheviks." *International Affairs,* April 1956.

Gorky, Maxim. *Days with Lenin*. New York, 1932.

Gote, I. V. *Time of Troubles*. Trans. Terence Emmons. Princeton, 1988.

Hayden, Carol Eubank. "Zhenotdel and the Bolshevik Party." *Russian History* 3.2 (1976): 150–73.

Izvestia. October 12–13, 1920. Reports of Inessa's funeral.

Katkov, George. *Russia 1917*. New York, 1967.

Kollontai, A. *A Great Love*. Trans. Cathy Porter. New York, 1981.

Krupskaya, N. K. *Memories of Lenin,* vols. 1 and 2, Moscow, 1930 (English edition, 1933).

Krupskaya, N. K., ed. *Pamyati Inessy Armand*. Moscow, 1926. Contributors are Krupskaya, L. B. Kamenev, L. Stal, E. Revlina, P. Vinogradskaya, E. Vlasova, G. Kotov, I. S. Ruzheinikov, V. I. Malakhovsky, and G. Safarov.

Latyshev, A. G. *Rassekrechennyi Lenin*. Moscow, 1996.

Lenin, Vladimir Ilyitch. *Collected Works*. 4th ed. Vols. 35, 43. Vol. 43 contains sixty-one letters to Inessa, first published in 5th edition in Russian (*Polnoe sobranie sochinenie); Vladimir Ilyich Lenin: Biograficheskaya Khronika* (13 vols., 1970–); *Leninskii Sbornik* (40 vols.).

Lenin: Neizvestnye Dokumenty, 1891–1922, Rosspian (Moscow, 1999).

Lilina [Zinaida Zinovieva]. "Comrade Lenin Departs for Russia." *Leningradskaya Pravda* 87, April 16, 1924.

McKean, Robert B. *St. Petersburg Between the Revolutions*. New Haven, 1990.

McNeal, Robert. *Bride of the Revolution*. Ann Arbor, 1972.

Morrisey, Susan K. *Heralds of Revolution*. New York, 1998.

Payne, Robert. *The Fortress*. New York, 1967.

———. *The Life and Death of Lenin*. New York, 1964.

Pearson, Michael. *The Sealed Train*. New York, 1975.

Pereira, Michael. *Across the Caucasus*. London, 1973.

Platten, Fritz. *Lenin's Journey Through Germany in the Sealed Car*. 1924.

Platten, N. F. "From the Spiegelgasse to the Kremlin." *Grani* 77, 79 (1972).

Podliashuk, Pavel. *Tovarishch Inessa*. 4th ed. 1964.

Podvoisky, N. I. *The Year 1917*. Moscow, 1958.

Porter, Cathy. *Alexandra Kollontai*. London, 1980.

Possony, Stefan T. *Lenin: The Compulsive Revolutionary*. Chicago, 1964.

Pravda, October 12, 1920. Includes coverage of Inessa's funeral.

Radek, Karl. "In the Sealed Carriage." *Pravda*, April 20, 1924.

Ravich, Olga. "The Journey across Germany." *Pravda*, April 18, 1927.

Reed, John. *Ten Days That Shook the World*. New York, 1960.

Safarov, Georgi. "Comrade Lenin." *Leningradskaya Pravda*, April 16, 1924.

Sanov, Vladimir. "Mezenskaya ballada." *Sever* 12 (1971): 82–96.

Schapiro, Leonard. *The Origin of the Communist Autocracy*. Cambridge, Mass., 1955.

Senn, A. E. *The Russian Revolution in Switzerland, 1914–1917*. Madison, 1971.

Shukman, Harold. *Lenin and the Russian Revolution*. New York, 1967.

Smith, E. E. *The Okhrana*. Stanford, Calif., 1967.

Sokolnikov, G. "The Return of Lenin from Exile." *Leningradskaya Pravda*, April 18, 1928.

Stasova, E. D., ed. *Slavnye Bol'shevichki*. Moscow, 1958.

Stasova, Elena. *Pages of Life and Fighting*. Moscow, 1957.

Stites, Richard. "Kollontai, Inessa, and Krupskaya." *Canadian-American Slavic Studies* 9 (spring 1975): 84–92.

———. "Zhendotdel: Bolshevism and Russian Women." *Russian History*, 111.2 (1976): 174–93.

Sukhanov, N. N. *The Russian Revolution, 1917*. Trans. Joel Carmichael. London, 1955.

Trotsky, Leon. *The History of the Russian Revolution*. 3 vols. Trans. Max Eastman. New York, 1932.

———. *Lenin*. New York, 1925.

Ulam, Adam B. *Lenin and the Bolsheviks*. London, 1966.

Ulyanova, Maria. *Reminiscences of V. I. Lenin*. 1960.

Valentinov, Nikolay (N. V. Volsky). *Encounters with Lenin*. Oxford, 1968.

Vinogradskaya, Polina. *Sobytiia i pamyatnye vstrechi*. Moscow, 1968.

Volkogonov, Dmitri. *Lenin: Life and Legacy*. Trans. Harold Shukman. London, 1994.

Wilson, Edmund. *To the Finland Station*. New York, 1960.

Wolfe, Bertram D. *The Bridge and the Abyss*. New York, 1967.

———. "Lenin and Inessa Armand." *Slavic Review* 22.1 (March 1963): 96–114.

———. *Three Who Made a Revolution*. New York, 1948.

The Russian Center for the Conservation and Study of Documents of Contemporary History has been noted below as RTsKhIDNI.

Inessa's father, Theodore Stephane. RTsKhIDNI
Inessa, 5, with grandmother. RTsKhIDNI
Inessa, 6, with Aunt Sophie. RTsKhIDNI
Inessa, 10. RTsKhIDNI
Inessa, 15. David King Collection
Inessa, 19. Blona Yakovlevna Romas
Inessa with friends. Blona Yakovlevna Romas
Inessa with her husband, Alexander Evgenevich Armand. RTsKhIDNI
Anna Kostantinovich. RTsKhIDNI
The Armand family in Pushkino.
Armand family home in Pushkino. Renee Pavlovna Armand
Eldigino, Inessa's first marital home. Sergei Yakovlev
Inessa in the mountains. RTsKhIDNI
Inessa in the mountains. RTsKhIDNI
Inessa, 1902. RTsKhIDNI
Inessa with Inna and Varvara. RTsKhIDNI
Inessa with her five children. RTsKhIDNI
Inessa with Andre. RTsKhIDNI
Vladimir Armand.
Nadezhda Krupskaya. David King Collection
Inessa in exile in Mezen. David King Collection
Fannie Kaplan. David King Collection
Alexandra Kollontai. David King Collection
Lenin in 1917. David King Collection
St. Petersburg, 1917. David King Collection
Lenin, 1919. David King Collection
Grigori Zinoviev. David King Collection
Lenin with his sister. David King Collection

Lenin, 1920. David King Collection
Felix Dzerzhinsky with senior officials. David King Collection
Lenin addressing crowd, 1920. David King Collection
Inessa, 1920. David King Collection
Inessa's coffin, lying in state. David King Collection

MICHAEL PEARSON is the author of eleven books, including *The Sealed Train: Lenin's Eight Months from Poverty to Power* and *Those Damned Rebels: The American Revolution as Seen Through British Eyes,* and the novel *The Store,* which was a worldwide bestseller, translated into seven languages. He lives in England.

This book was set in Sabon, a typeface designed by the well-known German typographer Jan Tschichold (1902–1974). Sabon's design is based upon the original letter forms of Claude Garamond and was created specifically to be used for three sources: foundry type for hand composition, Linotype, and Monotype. Tschichold named his typeface for the famous Frankfurt typefounder Jacques Sabon, who died in 1580.